ADAM ARDREY

FINDING MERLIN

THE TRUTH BEHIND THE LEGEND

MAINSTREAM
PUBLISHING

EDINBURGH AND LONDON

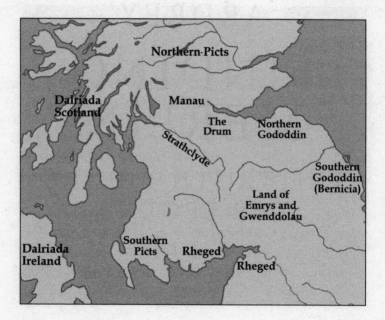

FINDING MERLIN

Adam Ardrey is an advocate and lives in Bothwell, near Glasgow, with his wife and three children. He has previously worked in television and as a solicitor.

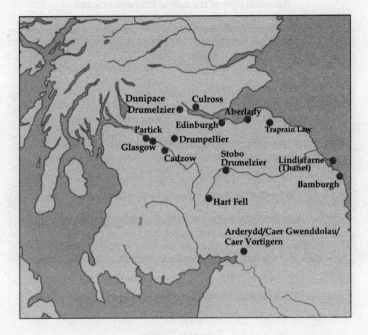

Dunipace
Culross
Drumelzier
Aberlady
Partick
Edinburgh
Traprain Law
Glasgow
Drumpellier
Cadzow
Stobo
Drumelzier
Lindisfarne
(Thanet)
Bamburgh
Hart Fell
Arderydd/Caer Gwenddolau/
Caer Vortigern

First published in Great Britain in 2007 by
MAINSTREAM PUBLISHING COMPANY (EDINBURGH) LTD
7 Albany Street
Edinburgh EH1 3UG

ISBN 9781845967864

A catalogue record for this book is available
from the British Library

Typeset in Goudy

Printed in Great Britain by
CPI Group (UK) LTD, Croydon CR0 4YY

**For Dorothy-Anne,
the most wonderful person known to me**

Acknowledgements

I am grateful to the librarians of Bothwell Library, the British Library, Edinburgh City Library, the National Library of Scotland and the Advocates' Library, for their courteous and efficient reader services. I am particularly grateful to Alistair Johnson and Jane Condie of the Advocates' Library. I thank Bill Campbell, Graeme Blaikie, Neil Graham, Claire Rose and everyone at Mainstream Publishing, especially Kevin O'Brien, my editor, and Lee Fullarton for a truly excellent jacket design; the Reverend Dr Jean Gallagher, Denny and Dunipace, for her advice anent the Hills of Dunipace; Dr Margaret McKay of *Scottish Studies* for help in one copyright connection; Professor John and Mrs Winifred MacQueen for permission to quote from their translation of *Vita Merlini Silvestris*; to Penguin Books for permission to quote from *The History of the Kings of Britain*; to Victoria Nickerson of UWP for doing her best in connection with *Vita Merlini*; special thanks to Cynthia Whiddon Greene of New Mexico, USA, for permission to quote from her stupendous translation of Jocelyn's *Life of Kentigern*. I recommend this work to anyone interested in events in Scotland in the sixth century. It can be easily accessed on the Internet. Thanks to Gavin Parsons of Sabhal Mòr Ostaig for help with Gaelic pronunciations (however, all mistreatment of Gaelic, indeed, all mistakes, misinterpretations, misunderstandings and errors are my responsibility alone); Mark 'Stan' Stanton, literary agent, for his company, kindness and generosity.

I am grateful to the staff and patrons of the Camphill Vaults, Bothwell, who spoke to me and did not speak to me, perfectly, as on occasion I sat in a corner redrafting pages of this book. For keeping my confidences, I thank David and Jayne Ardrey, Taylor R. Brown, David Forbes, Harold Joseph, Euan MacDonald, Hugh S. Neilson, and Alex and Jeanette Palmer. To Michael and Mary Gallagher, for their constant support and encouragement, my heartfelt thanks. I am also grateful to the Reverend Alan J. Hamilton, Bearsden, who, although he did not inspire any part of this book, always inspired me, and to Major Lawrie Hope of the Salvation Army for agreeing and disagreeing with me. Special thanks to Harry and Sheila Paul for their unflinching friendship and support. Above and beyond all, I am grateful that Kay, Claudia and Eliot are my children and grateful to them for their patience with their sometimes distracted but always loving dad.

* * *

In memory of my friends Iain McDougall and Jimmy McGoogan, of Coatbridge.

Adam Ardrey

Contents

Introduction

One of the greatest stories ever told in the Western canon is of Arthur the peerless leader, Merlin the archetypal wise man and Camelot, which could be said to rival Jerusalem as an ideal. I knew the legends from books and films in which the popular version, involving medieval Christian knights, was played out, but I thought that Arthur, Merlin and Camelot were primarily creatures of fiction without real roots in history.

That was until one Friday in 2000. Planning a weekend in the Highlands of Scotland with my then nine-year-old son to visit the place from which our family emigrated to Ireland (probably in the seventeenth century), I went from the Advocates' Library in Edinburgh, where I work, next door to the National Library of Scotland to find out a little more about our family name, Ardrey. In an eighteenth-century book based on sixth- to ninth-century sources, I found evidence that connected our destination and our surname to Arthur the legendary hero and provided proof that Arthur was the Scottish warlord Arthur Mac Aedan (born in 559; died in 596).

I had known about Arthur Mac Aedan since July 1989, when I'd read about him in Richard Barber's *The Figure of Arthur*. Barber considered Arthur Mac Aedan, among other candidates, as a possible 'Arthur', before concluding, 'Short of some . . . discovery . . . Arthur . . . will always elude us.'[1] In that library, I was confident that what I was holding in my hands was that very discovery.

I spent the next three years researching the subject and found that not only did my findings corroborate my original impulse concerning the real-life existence of Arthur and his identity, it also led inevitably to discoveries about Merlin. By this time, I had more material than was manageable for one book. As Merlin is the older figure in history and is, of course, easily compelling enough to warrant a book to himself, I have decided to write about him first. Arthur's side of the story, including that first piece of evidence which started me on my search, will have to wait until later.

Although separate from the Arthur evidence, the Merlin evidence was also connected to my second name. The oldest southern British record of the name Merlin is in the entry in the *Annales Cambriae* (Annals of Wales) for the year 573, which reads, 'The Battle of Arderydd between the sons of Eliffer and Gwenddoleu, son of Ceidio; in which battle Gwenddoleu fell; Merlin went mad.'[2]

Ardrey is a modernised form of Arderydd. It is also almost identical to the name of the place where Merlin lived for the last 20 years of his long life, Ardery. Saying that, though, I am not for a second going to pretend there is some sort of mysterious bloodline connection between my family name and Arthur and Merlin. I know of none. Even if there was, I do not believe in the concept of inherently special families (once you start believing there is, it is but a short step to believing in the monarchy). My grandfather, also called Adam, was the first of my Ardrey ascendants who could read and write, and while it is possible, I suppose, that a secret could be passed down orally in one family for 1,500 years, it is unlikely in the extreme. Certainly, no one told me anything. There is a coincidence of names. My second name has Arthur and Merlin connections, which is what sparked the initial interest that led to me writing this book. That is all.

I have considered the early sources relevant to Arthur and Merlin and found they only present a coherent history if the events they describe occurred in southern Scotland in the late sixth and early seventh centuries. The only contemporary history of the sixth century, *De Excidio et Conquestu Britanniae* (*On the Ruin and Conquest of Britain*), written by a monk called Gildas 'certainly no later than 540, give or take five years', according to the traditional view,[3] was, I was to find, written more than 50 years later than is commonly supposed. It was only then that it made sense.

As each item of evidence fell into place, the part Merlin played, not in legend but in history, became clearer, and I came to understand why he is conventionally held to have flourished in southern Britain. Just before Merlin died, the Angles defeated a British army at Chester (or Carlisle) and divided the Britons of the north from their cousins in the south and west, and, a generation later, in 638, the Angles took Edinburgh. Many northern Britons emigrated south as refugees from what is now southern Scotland, taking with them their stories of a victorious golden age when they had beaten the Angles under Merlin and the martial wonder that was the warlord Arthur. In the south of Britain, it was easy to change names and substitute southern locations for northern originals in the stories told of Merlin. These stories were also worked upon to fit in with the demands of the prevailing religious and political regimes and adapted to fit a southern audience. With the advent of the printed word in the fifteenth century, particularly with the work of Thomas Malory, these stories became fixed in their modern form.

I found that the evidence which placed Merlin in the late

sixth and early seventh centuries and in southern Scotland had unanticipated consequences for other historical figures, primarily for the warlords Ambrosius Aurelianus (Emrys) and his successor Gwenddolau. They are traditionally placed sometimes in Wales, sometimes in south-west England and sometimes in Brittany, usually around the middle of the fifth century. I found that they could be firmly placed in what is now southern Scotland in the mid-sixth century, a century later than is commonly supposed.

If I am right, it would appear that, for 1,500 years, those with the power to do so have presented a history that, literally, suited their book, irrespective of its divergence from the evidence and that the stories of Arthur and Merlin which form the British foundation myth are almost entirely pieces of propaganda based on various biases. If I am right, British history for the period from the late fifth to the early seventh century stands to be rewritten. The conventional view would have us believe in a Camelot canon starring Christian, Anglo-Saxon aristocrats living in southern Britain, when neither Arthur nor Merlin were Christians (on the contrary, they represented the last great hope of the old way of the Celts before the Christians took over); nor were they Anglo-Saxon (indeed, they made their names fighting the Angles). The way of life for which they fought was markedly more egalitarian than anything which would appear in Europe for more than a millennium and anathema to the authorities.

During my research, I identified the supernatural elements that had, almost invariably, been injected into the early historical sources. Magic did not happen in the sixth century any more than it happens today, so the miracles that so many writers had attributed to the saints I read as obvious fiction, although this did not mean that these sources were useless. The River Clyde did not burst its banks and wash Merlin's father's grain upriver to Mungo's storehouses, but by any fair reading of this story it is clear that Mungo stole Merlin's father's grain.

I also treated romantic references with suspicion, because medieval writers, like modern filmmakers, and for the same reason, tended to inject a love-interest into their work. The alterations made over the centuries to promote the prevailing partnership of Church and state and to set the scene in the far south, although extensive, were not carried out with sufficient thoroughness as to entirely obscure the truth. Once romantic passages, along with miracles, were put in perspective and seen for what they were, the Middle Ages equivalent of special effects, much remained to be found in the evidence that rang true.

Again like modern filmmakers, writers of the Middle Ages tended to omit political background, lest it bore their audience, and, in the case of Merlin, because politics could be dangerous for the writer. (Merlin's life was spent fighting the Church that controlled medieval life.) I had to treat the written historical evidence with particular care because it was almost invariably biased in favour of Church and state and so prejudicial to Merlin and the old way he championed. The authorities would have erased all references to Merlin if it had been in their power to do so, but it was not, and so his name, which became synonymous with the old way of the Celts, lived on in the oral tradition, despite efforts by those in power to present him as a Christian.

To appreciate the difficulties involved in finding Merlin, consider how hard it would be to discover how dangerous smoking tobacco is if the tobacco companies had, for 1,500 years, prepared and presented their case without opposition, if the only evidence available was evidence they had produced or left in the record after censoring anything that might serve a potential detractor and if they had complete control of the media for almost all of that time. How hard would it be for the anti-smoking lobby to put up a substantial counter-case with any hope of success, particularly if the interests of the tobacco companies and the interests of those who were to hear and decide upon the matter were the same? It would not be easy, but it would at least be possible.

Even before his death, a campaign of deceit, gauged to warp the people's memory of Merlin, was waged to undermine his place in history and disguise the fact that he was a Druid of the old way. This led, initially, to his being caricatured as a wild wizard of the woods and, later, in late-medieval propaganda, to his being neutered and presented as Arthur's avuncular counsellor, the progenitor of fictional characters such as Gandalf, Obi Wan Kenobi and Professor Dumbledore. I found he was none of these things but a scholar, a politician and a commander-in-chief who lived in central Scotland in the late sixth and early seventh centuries. He was also the twin brother of Languoreth, Queen of the Britons of Strathclyde, a woman who, although almost entirely unknown today, was one of the greatest women in European history.

For centuries after their deaths, both Merlin and Languoreth were prominent in the oral tradition that was then the main means of preserving history. Like the Internet, the oral tradition was easily accessible and difficult to control, so it was well known that Merlin was a Druid who led the people of the old way when they stood in the open against the Christians for the last time and who, together with Arthur as commander, led the Britons and their Scots allies against the Angles. They knew, too, that all of these events were influenced as much by Languoreth as by any man. The Church, of course, found these truths intolerable, and so, as handwritten records became more common, it dictated what was recorded in writing and ensured that every story reflected the prescribed line. By the time the story of Merlin we know today became fixed, Languoreth, as a woman, was 'written out of the picture'.

Almost everything that weighs against early Christianity in these pages is based on Christian sources gauged to show their people in a good light. Christian writers such as Jocelyn, in twelfth-century Glasgow, thought nothing of writing lies to advance the interests of their patrons and Church – indeed, they boasted about it – or of challengers being assassinated. Most patrons were powerful southern British Christians who required that the stories redounded to the credit of the political status quo, were set in the south of Britain and ignored any opposition there might have been to Christian domination of society. Consequently, the part played in events by those of the old way was written out of history. Druids were never mentioned, because this would have been to invite questions concerning their philosophy. The writers self-censored: for example, by using 'code' words such as bard when they meant Druid.

At least Druids were hinted at. Influential, independent, intelligent women and gay men, all of whom had had vital parts to play in the society of the old way, were, to put it mildly, disapproved of by the early Church and, if not deleted from the record entirely, castigated in the vilest way.

I have distinguished between Mungo Christians, who, it seems to me, were a fanatical bunch of religious fundamentalists, akin to the twenty-first-century Taliban, and Telleyr Christians, who were more tolerant, to the extent that they were prepared to live alongside the people of the old way in peace. Both the Telleyr and the Mungo Christians were people of the sixth century, so their actions cannot be held against tolerant Christians of today, although many of the matters that exercised them in the far past remain controversial today: sex, of course, and the distance between faith and reason, between scripture and science. Jocelyn describes sex with reference to 'hog pools of carnal sewage', is illiberal as regards women and vicious in connection with homosexuals. He only obliquely refers to cross-dressers, but it may fairly be supposed that he was averse to them too. Just as an astronomer can deduce something of an unseen planet by the effect it has on its more visible star, I was able to work out something of the old way without direct evidence. Christians have tended to describe those of the old way as licentious libertines, but, given their extreme views concerning sex, one could fairly conclude that those of the old way were simply . . . more relaxed about sex than were Christians.

In Merlin's day, Scotland, England and Wales did not exist as the nations we know them. There were Scots people, but their lands lay in the north of Ireland and in the far west of modern Scotland. The people who were to become the Welsh were descended from the Britons who lived between the line of the rivers Forth and Clyde in modern Scotland and the far south of modern England before Anglo-Saxon pressure pushed them west. The English, the Anglo-Saxons, were relative newcomers in the sixth century. They lived primarily in the east of Britain, from the modern Scotland–England border south to Kent.

I use these labels to describe political groupings active in the sixth century. They do not have the same meaning today. The term Scot today describes the latest descendants of the Neolithic people who were the first to settle in this land, and modern Scots lineage can be traced through a staggering array of prior descendants, including Celtic peoples (Irish-Scots, who gave their name to Scotland, Picts and Britons); Italians (Romans); innumerable non-Roman peoples who came to Scotland with the legions; Jewish people (Isaac, a Jewish doctor, went south with the army of the Gododdin to fight the Angles in the Catterick campaign, c.600); Germans (Angles and Saxons); Danes (Jutes); Scandinavians (Vikings); Flemings

(Belgians); French (Normans); and the people who had become the 'English' (themselves an equally varied genetic mix). In the nineteenth century, more Irish and Italians arrived in Scotland, and in the twentieth century, people from India, Pakistan, China, Malaysia, Malawi, Poland, Iran, Iraq, Greece, Colombia and many more joined in. These people, collectively and individually, make up the modern Scottish community. Being a Scot today is not a matter of blood but of heart.

Merlin played a prominent part in driving back the Angles in the north in the Great Angle War that was fought in the 580s, and so we have a 'Scotland' today and not a 'Greater Angle-land', but he lost his battle against Christianity. Ironically, this led to his becoming one of the most famous names in the world. In what follows, I have tried to tell what I believe is the true story, by restoring Merlin to the land of his birth, life and death and by reviving his forgotten, but perhaps even more influential, sister Languoreth.

CHAPTER ONE

The Legend

Anyone who has read Thomas Malory's *Le Morte d'Arthur* or T.H. White's turgid *Once and Future King* – indeed, almost anyone who has read any book about Arthur, fiction or non-fiction, or who has seen any one of the numerous films or TV programmes set in Camelot – knows the authorised version of Merlin: a perennially old, rather other-worldly wizard involved in Arthur's birth, education and coronation, but who, thereafter, has only a peripheral part to play.

Something of the true story of Merlin's life survived in the oral tradition and in writing for a time, but, as the centuries passed, much was forgotten, pages were lost or destroyed and amended versions were written; eventually, the stories became legends. Despite more than 1,000 years of censorship, these legends still abound with references to the old way that prevailed before the advent of Christianity: Green Men in *Sir Gawain and the Green Knight*, swords in water in almost any story of Arthur, and a sense that, whatever he was, Merlin was not a Christian.

Nowadays, 'Merlin may have been based on a historical figure' is about as much as most historians will concede, and even those who go this far have problems identifying the century in which

23

he lived, because, in the conventional wisdom, expressed here by Phillips and Keatman, 'the Myrddin [Merlin] of history appears to have lived over half a century after the real Arthurian period'[1] (generally accepted as being the early sixth century). However, if the real Arthurian period was the late sixth century, the time of Arthur Mac Aedan, then the historical Merlin and the historical Arthur (Mac Aedan) are contemporaries and there is no disjunction.

Such considerations were far from the mind of Thomas Malory, the man who, more than anyone, gave us the Merlin best known today, in one of the first books to be printed in England, *Le Morte d'Arthur*, published by Thomas Caxton in 1485 (the French name for this English-language book reflecting how many of its stories had come back to England via France). Malory, who was from Warwick, was a soldier and firm partisan of the Lancastrian cause in the Wars of the Roses. He was not shy of displaying his party bias in his writings and was unscrupulous in pursuing his own interests in his private life, to the extent that he was, at one time, imprisoned for armed assault and rape. This was not a man who would hesitate before putting what he wanted to write before what his sources suggested.

Malory sets Arthurian events firmly in the south in his first two lines, when he says, 'It befell in the days of Uther Pendragon, when he was king of all England . . .' Uther is sick with love for Igraine, the wife of the Duke of Cornwall. A courtier says he will 'seek Merlin, and he shall do you remedy'. Merlin's magic changes the king into the shape of Igraine's husband and by this deception Arthur is conceived. Igraine's husband conveniently dies 'through his own issue', enabling Uther to marry Igraine and Arthur to be born in wedlock (even if he was not conceived there). As reward for his services, Merlin is allowed to organise Arthur's upbringing. He fosters him out to the home of the good Sir Ector and his less agreeable son, Kay. During Arthur's childhood, Merlin remains his tutor and his guide. 'So like as Merlin devised, it was done.'[2]

After Uther died, Malory has Merlin go to the Archbishop of Canterbury and suggest to him that he call all the lords and knights to attend a tournament in London in the hope that Jesus Christ would 'show some miracle who should be rightwise king of this realm'. The Archbishop takes Merlin's advice but does not play a large part in the events that follow. Malory introduced him only to bring Jesus into the proceedings and to ensure that the king was seen to be chosen under the aegis of the Church. The selection of a king was far too important to be left to any other body. This would not have been necessary if Merlin was recognised as, or could have been made to appear as, a Christian figure, but this was impossible.

A miracle duly occurred when a large stone with an anvil with a sword stuck in it appeared in a churchyard. About the sword was written, 'Whoso pulleth out this sword of this stone and anvil is rightwise king born of all England.' The young Arthur attended the tournament as squire to his foster brother Kay. When Kay left his sword behind, he sent Arthur back to fetch it, but instead Arthur took the sword from the anvil that was standing on the stone in the churchyard and brought it to Kay. Kay tried to take the credit but Arthur was soon revealed as the true king. Merlin vouches for the fact that Arthur is Uther's son.

The sword-and-the-stone selection process clearly took place under Merlin's control despite Malory's having provided him with a minder in the person of the Archbishop. The same thing happens when Arthur's bodyguard is chosen by the 'Archbishop of Canterbury by Merlin's providence' – on Merlin's recommendation – and when Merlin finds knights for the Round Table, Malory has to have the Archbishop bless their seats. These events do not require two people to be involved. The stories would have worked as well if all had been at the instance of either the Archbishop or Merlin. Clearly, it is the Archbishop who has been added, to dispel any suspicion that the Church was not in charge, there being no reason to add Merlin.

Arthur's sword, presumably the one he took from the stone, was broken in single combat, so Merlin took Arthur to a lake where an arm 'clothed in white Samite mystic wonderful' rose from the water holding the sword Excalibur. The Lady of the Lake emerged and gave this fabulous sword to Arthur.

Malory's Merlin stays by Arthur's side in the early days of his reign but is far from centre stage after Arthur marries Guinevere. There are good dramatic reasons for distancing Merlin from the action at this point. Arthur is about to be cuckolded by Lancelot and Guinevere, and this would be difficult to explain if the wise Merlin was still at his side. Before they were even married, Merlin is made to warn Arthur that his wife will prove unfaithful.[3] If Merlin had been about at the time of the actual adultery, he could not have avoided pointing to evidence of it, but this would have spoiled Malory's story.

Arthur becomes a rather avuncular figure as he presides over a time of peace and plenty in which he rules his realm justly and his knights, particularly Lancelot, carry out heroic deeds. Tragedy sets in when Lancelot takes up with Guinevere, and Mordred, Arthur's nephew, uses this liaison to break the fellowship of the Round Table and later to make an attempt on the throne. In a great battle, Mordred and Arthur are both mortally wounded. The dying Arthur has one of his men throw Excalibur back into a lake before he is taken away on a boat to the Island of Avalon, from which it is hoped he will some day return.

This is the basic story of Merlin and Arthur that I grew up with and broadly the legend most people know; but it did not happen like that. Malory's stories, like those told by Geoffrey of Monmouth in his *Historia Regum Brittaniae* (*History of the Kings of Britain*) (c.1136) and *Vita Merlini* (*Life of Merlin*) (c.1150), are not fixed firmly in history, at least not in history that has anything to do with Arthur and Merlin. Malory, in particular, wrote as if Arthur and Merlin were active in his time. This is why Camelot is often pictured, as in the musical *Camelot*, as having its place in late medieval times. Malory, the Lancastrian, 'even gives Mordred . . . a Yorkist-like army, drawn from south-eastern England'.[4]

When the motives and methods of writers like Thomas Malory and Geoffrey are recognised and the propaganda they were bound to present in the interests of commercial success and to please their patrons are stripped away, it is possible to see Merlin and Arthur as they were, as real men of sixth-century Scotland.

CHAPTER TWO

Morken's Children

It has been said that the name Merlin was derived from *Moridunon*, meaning sea fortress; that Merlin was born in Carmarthen, Wales, and took the name of his place of birth (although the two names do not sound similar); that Merlin means falcon; and that the name Merlin was derived from *Meriage*, said to mean fool, and *Linn*, meaning waterfall, giving a name that means something like the Fool of the Waterfall.

This last alternative cannot be true because the *Lin* ending to Merlin's name was not invented until after the Norman French conquered England in 1066. Before that, as is well known, the man we know as Merlin was known as Myrddin. Myrddin, however, sounded to the ears of French speakers embarrassingly like *merde*, the French word for excrement, so writers such as Geoffrey changed Myrddin to what, for them, was the more euphonic Merlin.

Jocelyn, in his biography of Mungo, patron saint of Glasgow, *The Life of Kentigern*, written in the twelfth century, describes Merlin as 'a certain foolish man' who entertained the king by 'jests and loud laughter [and] by foolish words and gestures'. Jocelyn's Merlin was at best the court jester, and, by implication, a madman (in the tradition of the *Annales Cambriae*, in which

Merlin is said to have gone mad after the Battle of Arderydd).
Jocelyn was unable to maintain this fiction. The Merlin he goes
on to describe is far from foolish. The explanation Jocelyn offers
is that sometimes his God puts wise words in the mouths of fools.
In Geoffrey's *Vita*, Merlin, distressed by the loss of his friends
at the Battle of Arderydd, makes off with 'fast-running tears' on
his cheeks to become a 'Man of the Woods'. Forgetting who he
was, this Merlin lurked like a wild thing, until a messenger, sent
by his sister, the queen, found him hiding among the trees and
with soothing music coaxed 'the madman [Merlin] out by his wild
mood'. Merlin, says Geoffrey, came to himself and thought of his
madness with astonishment. Reason restored, Merlin returned to
court, but before long Geoffrey says he went mad again and had
to be restrained.

Like Jocelyn, Geoffrey is bound to take the prescribed line
concerning Merlin. Merlin had to be portrayed as a madman lest
people asked what it was he stood for and discovered that he offered
an alternative to the regime under which they lived. Like Jocelyn,
Geoffrey found it difficult to present the authorised version while,
at the same time, telling the story contained in his sources. No
sooner has he said that Merlin went mad and the king had him
restrained than he says the king begged Merlin not to go back into
exile in the woods but to stay at court and 'wield a royal sceptre
and rule a nation of warriors'. No one would offer such power to
a madman. Either the offer of power was invented by Geoffrey or
Merlin was not mad. There is no reason why Geoffrey would invent
such an offer when it jarred with his party line, that Merlin was
mad, and so we may suppose that Merlin was not really insane.

In effect, those whom the Church wished to destroy were first
called mad. To make sense of Geoffrey's *Vita*, all that is necessary is
to read it without reference to the madman passages. What is left,

when placed in its true time and place, sixth-century Scotland, and read with the other early sources, is sensible history that reflects the temporal and religious politics of the time. Geoffrey and Jocelyn conceal the struggle between Christianity and the old way by pretending that Merlin was mad.

The *Vita Merlini Silvestris* (*Life of Merlin of the Woods* – not be confused with Geoffrey's *Vita*[1]) says not only that Merlin was a 'madman, naked and hairy', with the unspoken corollary that no one need take him seriously, but, just to be on the safe side, that Merlin was a Christian who begged Mungo to allow him the last rites of his Church.

Even after 1,500 years, during which the media has been almost entirely in the hands of his enemies, no one believes Merlin was a Christian. He was too non-Christian for that. Nor does anyone believe that Merlin was mad. On the contrary, despite a prolonged campaign of vilification, his name is now synonymous with wisdom.

The meaning of the name Merlin – that is, Myrddin – can be explained only when it is considered with reference to the time and place in which it originated: Scotland in the late sixth and early seventh centuries. The Gaelic word *Mear*, according to MacBain's *Etymological Dictionary of Scottish Gaelic*, is derived from the early Irish Gaelic word *Mer*, meaning mad. (The English words 'merry' and 'mirth' have the same root.) The Gaelic for man is *Duine*. In the Gaelic of the early Scots, *Mer-duine* meant madman.

As I have mentioned, refugee Britons of southern Scotland in flight from the Angles took stories of Merlin south, in the seventh century. Before long, these stories were repeated in a language that was strange to them, until, in time, the defamatory element in the name Merlin faded away. The Welsh scribe who wrote the words 'and Merlin went mad' at the end of the Arderydd *Annales*

Cambriae entry cannot have known that he was actually writing 'the madman went mad'.

Much later, Jocelyn, writing in Strathclyde, where Merlin had lived and where many people would have been familiar with Scots Gaelic, did not use the name Merlin. Too many people would have known what it meant and thought it strange that a man should be called, in effect, Madman the Madman. Instead, Jocelyn called Merlin Lailoken.

Lailoken, or Laleocen, or, in Welsh, Llallogan, are all used as alternatives to Merlin in various sources. The *Silvestris* says 'Lailoken, whom some say was Merlin'. This is tentatively phrased, but there is no real doubt over this connection. Lailoken, according to W.F. Skene in *The Four Ancient Books of Wales*, means 'Twin Brother', although there is no evidence to back this up. It has also been held to mean 'friend', for no reason that I know of. Of course, if I am right and the name Lailoken does not originate in Wales, it will not have a sensible Welsh meaning.

The Christians suppressed the old way of the Druids and then rewrote history to obliterate its influence, lest people remember there was an alternative philosophy to that of the Christian Church. The very name Druid was avoided. One dared not speak of the Druids or record the name in writing. The more innocuous word 'bard' came to be used instead of Druid, and references to song came to connote some Druidic connection. The poem *Y Gododdin*, written in about 600 in the Edinburgh area, contains some of the earliest written references to both Arthur and Merlin. Merlin is referred to as 'Merlin of Song'. According to generally accepted history, the Council of Drumceatt, held in 575, was convened to discuss international relations and to destroy the influence of 'bards'. In my view, the bards the Church wished to destroy at Drumceatt were not popular entertainers – this would make no sense – but Druids.

The meaning of the name Lailoken can be explained only if it is broken into two parts. The *Ken* ending is suggestive of the Gaelic *Ceann*, meaning leader or chief (literally head). The name Kenneth has this as a root. Malcolm Canmore, sometimes taken to be Malcolm of the Big Head, was really Malcolm the Great Chief. When I realised the name was made of two parts and that Ken meant 'head of' or chief, all I had to do was find a word that made sense of the first part, 'Lailo'. I found this word in Scots Gaelic. The word *Laoidh* (pronounced Leu-y) means a 'lay'. A lay is, as in Walter Scott's *The Lay of the Last Minstrel*, a narrative poem, especially one that is sung, or simply a song. If the 'Lailo' part of Lailoken is a corrupt form of the Scots Gaelic word *Laoidh*, the name Lailoken makes sense. Lailoken means Chief of Songs, in effect, Chief of Bards, that is, Chief of Druids. *Laoidh*, which ends with a 'y' sound, would euphonically require a vowel when followed by a 'k' sound. *Laoidh Ceann*, phonetically leu-y ken, could easily have been corrupted and become Lai-y-ken, especially given the spelling 'Laoi'. It is not far from this to Lai-o-Ken and Lailoken. It has to considered that when the name lost its meaning, when it was removed from its original linguistic context, it would have been spelt phonetically by innumerable scribes over centuries.

Due to the control of Merlin's enemies over the media for more than a thousand years after his death, the defamatory name Merlin has always been the popular one. I use it throughout this book because it is the most readily recognisable name available, and because his given name, the name by which his family knew him, has been lost.

Geoffrey says in the *Vita* that Merlin had a sister, Ganeida, and that she was the wife of Rodarch, king of Cumbria. This Rodarch was Rhydderch, king of the Strathclyde Britons, who reigned from 580 to 612. Cumbria was, for a time, after 573, part of Strathclyde, but it is disingenuous to say that Rhydderch was king of Cumbria. Geoffrey is simply setting his scene as far south as he can while staying in touch with his source material. The battles fought by Geoffrey's 'Rodarch' are clearly identifiable as battles in which Rhydderch was involved. Geoffrey describes Rodarch as 'the generous'. The sobriquet *Hael*, meaning generous or munificent, is frequently attached to Rhydderch. There is no doubt that Geoffrey's Rodarch and Rhydderch of Strathclyde are the same man. This one item of evidence in Geoffrey's *Vita* clearly connects Merlin with a real historical time and place, late sixth-century Scotland.

From at least the 550s until Mungo's death in 612, Merlin and Mungo were bitter enemies. Although, in the end, Mungo's Christian party won the battle for supremacy, Mungo and his Christians were not always in the ascendant. In the early 570s, Mungo was expelled from Strathclyde. He went south to live in Wales with David, now the patron saint of Wales, but Mungo fell out with David and went off and set up on his own at a place in North Wales that is now called St Asaph, in memory of Mungo's lieutenant, a young monk called Asaph. But Mungo fell out with Asaph too and went off again to set up on his own, this time at Hoddam in the Scottish borders. This left Asaph to take charge of the monastery Mungo had founded – now St Asaph Cathedral in North Wales.

Five hundred years later, about the time he wrote the *Vita*, Geoffrey of Monmouth was appointed Bishop of St Asaph. Geoffrey had written about Merlin in his *Historia Regum Brittaniae* in the 1130s but only insubstantial stuff: stolen stories of Ambrosius Aurelianus (Emrys), fanciful nonsense about Stonehenge and a magical romantic fiction primarily concerning the birth of Arthur. It is likely that Geoffrey's interest in Merlin inspired his connection with St Asaph and led to his finding the material necessary to enable him to write his detailed *Vita Merlini*, a work filled with verifiable detail (all relevant to Scotland). The material contained in Geoffrey's *Vita* includes much that relates to Mungo's life after he left St Asaph, so clearly the connection between St Asaph and its founder, Mungo, continued during his lifetime and indeed after his death. There was even an exchange of myths. A story that related to Mungo, involving a fish, a ring and a queen, was later associated with Asaph.

The wife of Rhydderch, king of the Strathclyde Britons, was 'Ganeida, a beautiful woman with whom he lived most happily: she was Merlin's sister'.[2] Genealogies relevant to the sixth century tend to ignore women, even queens. They are even less likely to identify a woman's father, but Rhydderch's wife, Merlin's sister, is recorded in the genealogy of the House of Strathclyde as Gwenddyydd Ferch Morfryn; Gwynedd daughter of Morken, born 540. Ganeida is simply a clumsy Latinisation of Gwyneth. *Gwyn* means white but is better understood as fair, in the sense of good looking. It is a common prefix in female names. Gwynedd means, in effect, the fair one.

The family tree of Strathclyde also shows Rhydderch with an earlier wife, Languoreth, born 530. This cannot be correct. Jocelyn's *Life of Kentigern* has Rhydderch survived by his queen, Languoreth, when he died in 612. If Languoreth was the first of two wives, she could not have been Rhydderch's widow. Whoever compiled the genealogy did not appreciate that Gwynedd, the name by which Merlin's sister was called as a child, and Languoreth, a sobriquet, were the same person and so gave Rhydderch two wives by mistake. The difference in birth dates, a suspiciously round ten years, was an invention. I have taken the later date of birth, 540, to be correct. By this reckoning, Merlin was nearly eighty when he died and his sister older still at the time of her death. To suppose they lived for ten years further still is, I think, too much. Even eighty was very old in the sixth century.

Men tended to have a name by which they were known in public life. Women tended to be known as the wives of their husbands. Not Merlin's sister. She had a public name. In the genealogies, and in Jocelyn's *Life of Kentigern*, Rhydderch's wife is called Languoreth. As is almost invariably the case with sixth-century names, there are several versions to consider: *Languueth* and *Langueth* are but two alternatives. Languoreth is the most frequently used version.

The only attempt I know of to explain the meaning of the name Languoreth is a rather complicated one: that it 'is a typical dithematic compound', which stands to be split into *Lan* and *guoreth*, which 'may' mean something to do with deliverance or redemption. As Merlin and his sister lived in Scotland, I looked to Q Gaelic. (There are two forms of Gaelic: P and Q. From Q Gaelic, we get Irish and Scottish Gaelic; from P Gaelic, we get Welsh, Cornish and Breton Gaelic.) According to MacBain's *Etymological Dictionary*, *Làn* means full and *òr* means gold. *Lan-òr* is easily transposed to the more euphonic *Lang-or*. The *eth* ending is readily understood as a corrupt form of the common British P Gaelic ending *Edd* or *Ydd* (as in Arderydd). All it would have taken would have been for Jocelyn to make a small mistake (occasioned by the pronunciation peculiarity that has the *edd* ending sound like *eth*) and Merlin's sister, Rhydderch's queen, would have gone from *Lan-or-edd* to Languoreth.

I therefore concluded that Languoreth means, literally, 'Full of Gold', or 'All Gold', but that its sense can best be gained if it is read in context, as the name of a queen, in conjunction with her given name, Gwynedd. Gwyneth Languoreth means Gwyneth the fair, the Golden One.

In the poem 'Dialogue Between Myrddin and His Sister',[3] written some time between 1375 and 1425, but based on much earlier written or oral sources, Merlin meets his sister in the forest where he is hiding after the Battle of Arderydd in the late 570s. It is from this source that we know they are twins, as she addresses him as 'my twin brother Myrddin' and as her 'far-famed twin'. Elis Gruffudd, in the sixteenth century, identifies a man variously called Morfryn or Morvryn (in Scotland, Morken) as Merlin's father before turning to Merlin's sister:

> [T]he writing shows that a man of this name [Morfryn] had a son who was called Myrddin son of Morfryn, and a daughter who was called Gwenddydd as the story shows . . . To him, God had given the gift of prophecy . . . and especially to Gwenddydd his sister, who, as my copy shows, was wise and learned [and] who wrote a great book of his utterances, especially about prophecies as related to this island . . .[4]

Clearly, Gruffudd must have had access to accurate evidence, because it was not common in the sixteenth century for the intellectual ability of a woman to be noticed, far less lauded. It is therefore unlikely that Gruffudd would have simply invented an intelligent sister for Merlin. Merlin's sister was at least as wise and learned as Merlin.

Given Languoreth was born in 540 and given Merlin was her twin brother, we are, of course, bound to conclude that Merlin son of Morken was born in 540. The sources of evidence that place Merlin in the south of Britain were all written with that particular end in view and so are suspect. They also tend to be suspiciously vague. The sources of evidence that place Merlin in Scotland, however, come couched in history: Merlin's sister was Languoreth; Languoreth was married to Rhydderch; Rhydderch reigned in Strathclyde from 580 to 612. They are also convincingly matter of fact.

The Scottish-based sources also include evidence contrary to the interests of the party providing it and, consequently, stand to be given added weight. The *Aberdeen Breviary*, for example, is a Christian work that throws light on the story of Merlin, albeit inadvertently. It was written in the sixteenth century to praise various Scottish saints, including Serf, Mungo's teacher, Taneu, Mungo's mother,[5] Columba, Mungo's junior partner and Mungo himself, all of whom lived in the sixth century and played parts in Merlin's story. The writer of this Christian text does not mention Merlin and has no reason to boost the case for a Scottish Merlin, but he does. In his story of Languoreth's adultery and a missing ring, he says where Languoreth came from: 'It happened that the queen of Cadzow[6] was ill reported of concerning the love of a certain soldier whom the king took out with him to the hunt.'[7]

This is the only time that Languoreth is designated 'of Cadzow'. Languoreth was, of course, queen of Strathclyde at this time, but she was in trouble – she had committed adultery – which perhaps explains why she was identified with reference to the place she came from, just as Marie Antoinette was referred to as The Austrian Woman.

The lands of Cadzow lie on the banks of the River Clyde, 11 miles upriver from Glasgow. There was no reason for the writer of the *Aberdeen Breviary* to invent a place of origin for the queen, Languoreth, nor was there any reason for him to choose Cadzow. He mentions it once, in passing, and then does not refer to it again. It may, therefore, in the absence of contradictory evidence, be taken that Languoreth was from Cadzow. It follows, if Languoreth was from Cadzow, and if Merlin and Languoreth were twins, that Merlin was also from Cadzow. This evidence has particular weight because it comes from a source that would have been hostile to Merlin if it had been concerned with him at all.

I have always known the place called Cadzow, four miles from my home, as a part of the modern town of Hamilton. Cadzow, the modern suburb, lies to the south of the town near the River Avon, where it joins the River Clyde. Near this junction is a hill from which it is possible to look out across Glasgow, Dunbartonshire and Loch Lomond to Ben Arthur, 40 miles away. On this hill today stands the eighteenth-century 'Hunting Lodge' of Chatelherault. The king of France, apparently, gave the duke of Hamilton the French lands of Chatelherault and a title as a reward for some sleekit service rendered at the time of Mary Queen of Scots, hence the name Chatelherault. The ruins of a thirteenth-century castle stand nearby, close to archaeological evidence of a sixth-century fort which, according to Tourist Information, was once the hunting lodge of the 'Ancient kings of Strathclyde'. The site, situated high above a gorge close to where two rivers meet, was not only a natural place for a fortress, which is why a castle was later built there, but strategically placed on what was, in the sixth century, border country. Cadzow was a fortress.

It was here the chiefs of Cadzow, including Merlin's father Morken, lived, and probably where Merlin and Languoreth were born. Morken had other property, downriver, in the Royal Town of Partick, but Languoreth is described as 'the queen of Cadzow', which suggests Cadzow, as opposed to Partick, was the place with which she was most closely associated.

On Sunday, 24 October 2004, with my daughters, I visited Cadzow Castle for the first time. I had expected a small row of stones close to Chatelherault but instead we were directed out of the back door of the visitor centre and along a woodland path with the promise that a five-minute walk would bring us to a bridge and then to the castle. Five minutes later, we were on a bridge high above the fast-flowing River Avon. Although we were less than a mile from the M74 motorway, the main road to England, and in the heart of industrial Lanarkshire, all was quiet except for the noise of the water. There were trees all around us and, across the river, on the edge of the gorge, Cadzow Castle. It was easy to imagine the fortress that had stood there in the time of Merlin. The river was the same river. The trees descendants of the trees he would have seen. There would have been no high bridge in the sixth century (perhaps) but the river ford that lay below would have been there when Merlin and Languoreth were children, playing on the banks of the river.

Cadzow commanded the middle Clyde, across which lay the kingdoms of Manau and the Gododdin, and later the Angles. Cadzow was strategically vital.

The Druids recited the poems, told the tales and sang the songs through which the lore of their people survived. To help them remember what came next, they used triplets of reminders that survived in the oral tradition for which they were created, from the time of Merlin up to the thirteenth century, when they were recorded in writing as the *Welsh Triads*. 'Triad 115' has Merlin numbered among the Three Baptismal Bards of the Isle of Britain. 'Baptismal' was added lest anyone think bards might have something to do with the old way:

> Merddin Emrys,
> And Taliesin, Chief of Bards,
> And Merddin, son of Madoc Morvryn.

Merddin Emrys is listed only because of the confusion between Merlin and Emrys (Ambrosius Aurelianus) that arose when writers such as Geoffrey took stories of Emrys and attributed them to Merlin. Once the figures of Emrys and Merlin became confused, it was but a short step to the creation of the composite character Merlin-Emrys, even though no such person existed. There was a bard called Merlin, but none called Merlin-Emrys. Emrys was a separate person, a warrior chief of the old way.

The second-named bard, Taliesin, was a Druid, the chief counsellor of the hero king, Urien of Rheged, and a friend of Merlin's. Taliesin's stronghold in Galloway, in south-west Scotland, was devastated by Christian armies in the late sixth century because, the Christians said, it was a 'sanctuary of wondrous songs', that is, a place where the old way of the Druids continued to flourish. Taliesin was, like Merlin, a chief of bards. By my account, the real Merlin is the third poet of 'Triad 115': 'Merddin, son of Madoc Morvryn.'

Source material such as this, which suggests there were two Merlins, was used by those who accepted the conventional wisdom that Arthur was a man of the late fifth or early sixth century but who were stuck with the problem that the evidence relevant to Merlin had him a man of the late sixth century, when, as everyone knew, they were contemporaries. They simply said there were two Merlins: one who lived in the early sixth century and one who lived in the late sixth century. Of course, if Arthur and Merlin both lived in the late sixth century, as they did, this problem ceases to exist and only one Merlin is necessary. The 'two Merlin solution' is also used to explain the evidence that places Merlin in both Wales/England and in Scotland. If Merlin was, as he was, a man of Scotland, again, the need for two Merlins ceases to exist.

Once Merlin-Emrys is recognised as a fabrication and any idea of two Merlins is set aside as nonsense, one Merlin remains, the third-named bard, 'Merddin, son of Madoc Morvryn'. Morvryn is mentioned in connection with Merlin in several poems based on the oral tradition and put down in writing in the twelfth and thirteenth centuries. In 'The Dialogue Between Myrddin and His Sister', Merlin is referred to as 'Myrddin, son of Morvryn the skilful'.

In 'A Fugitive Poem of Myrddin in His Grave' (also contained in the *Red Book of Hergest*), Merlin says:

> I have drunk from a bright cup
> with fierce and warlike lords;
> my name is Myrddin, son of Morvryn.

There is, therefore, in more than one early source, corroboration of the evidence in the *Triads* that Merlin's father's name was Morvryn. The 'Fugitive' poem also refers to warriors called Morgenau, Moryal, Moryen and Mordav, although these were not the names by which their families and friends knew them. A name beginning with *Mor* was the name by which a man was known in the warrior circles in which he lived. In Scottish Gaelic, *Mor* means big or great and so, for obvious reasons, it was a common part of many of the names used to describe warriors. Shield walls would have contained many men known to their fellows as 'Big something' or 'Great something'.

Elis Gruffudd reflects the view taken in his time when he says in *The Story of Myrddin Wyllt*, 'According to the narrative of some authors, there was about this time . . . a man who was called Morfryn . . . the writing shows that a man of this name had a son who was called Myrddin.'

Merlin son of Morvryn, or Morfryn, whichever version is chosen, does not exist in the history of the south of Britain. To find him, it is necessary to consider the Scottish sources.

The early part of Jocelyn's *Life of Kentigern* covers the time when Merlin was a child and a youth. It tells of a great chief, a man of the old way, who was foremost among the enemies of the Christians. His name was Morken. We have already seen that *Mor* means great or big and *Ken* means head, in the sense of leader or, colloquially, chief. In modern Scottish Gaelic, both *Ceannabhard* and *Ceannard* mean commander or leader. *Morken, Mor Ken, Mor Ceann* means, almost literally, Great Chief and simply connotes a commander or leader. Again, the names that have come down to us are public names, rather than private ones.

When the history of Scotland is considered, there is to be found a man with the right name, living in the right time and doing exactly what one would expect the father of Merlin to do: fight for the old way against an influx of Christians. Morken also had property in Partick, where Merlin too had a house. Morken was Merlin's father.

To summarise what I hope to have shown so far, Merlin, son of Morken, twin brother of Gwynedd Languoreth, queen of Strathclyde, was born in 540 in Cadzow. This is his story.

CHAPTER THREE

The Angles

All of Britain – modern Scotland, England and Wales – and Ireland were inhabited by Celtic peoples when the Romans first arrived in force in Britain under Julius Caesar in the year 55 BCE. It was not, however, until early in the next century, under the Emperor Claudius, that Roman rule became real – at least, in the south of the main island, the part that is now England and Wales.

Roman society was regimented and authoritarian but tolerant in matters of religion, provided it did not undermine Roman control. The Celts were individualistic and disputatious, but they too were tolerant in matters of religion, and of strangers, provided strangers did not try to control them. It was this, rather than religion, that made war between them inevitable. As the Romans were united and the Celts perpetually at odds with one another, Roman victory too was inevitable, at least in the short term.

The Celts adhered to the old way of the Druids, by which people strove to live in harmony with one another and with nature, but the Romans believed the Druids were the motivating force behind the refusal of the Celts to submit to their rule, so, in the year 60, they attacked the Druids' sacred island of Ynys Mon (modern Anglesey, north-west Wales) and annihilated everyone they found there. The Romans had made a mistake. The Druids were not the source of the Celts' love of freedom but its voice. While Roman backs were turned, crushing the Druids in the west, the Celts rose in the east and under the warrior queen Boudicca sacked the Roman towns of Colchester, London and Verulamium (modern St Albans).

In time, as usual, the discipline of the Romans paid off and Boudicca's army was crushed. The famous individuality of the Celts came back into play, and, riven by rivalry, the Britons who lived in the south were quickly conquered and absorbed into the Empire. For three and a half centuries, southern Britain was forced to accept Roman rule.

The Romans then pushed north into the part of Britain that is now Scotland and in several campaigns, the most successful of which was under Agricola, clashed with the Picts, another Celtic people, under Calgacus, the first person of Scotland to whom we can give a name.[1] Calgacus, taking heart from the fact that for once his people were united in the face of the Romans, says, in words attributed to him by the Roman historian Tacitus:

> We, the choice flower of Britain, were treasured in her most secret places. Out of sight of subject shores, we kept even our eyes free from the defilement of tyranny. We, the last men on earth, the last of the free, have been shielded till today by the very remoteness and the seclusion for which we are famed. . . .
>
> To all of us, slavery is a thing unknown; there are no lands beyond us, and even the sea is not safe, menaced as we are by a Roman fleet. . . . To us who dwell on the uttermost confines of the earth and of freedom, this remote sanctuary of Britain's glory has up to this time been a defence. Now, however, the furthest limits of Britain are thrown open . . .

> But there are no tribes beyond us, nothing indeed but
> waves and rocks, and the yet more terrible Romans, from
> whose oppression escape is vainly sought by obedience
> and submission. Robbers of the world, having by their
> universal plunder exhausted the land, they rifle the deep.
> If the enemy be rich, they are rapacious; if he be poor, they
> lust for dominion; neither the east nor the west has been
> able to satisfy them. . . . To robbery, slaughter, plunder,
> they give the lying name of empire; they make a desert and
> call it peace.[2]

While Tacitus generously allows such noble sentiments to determined enemies in arms, he is less sympathetic towards the Druids, whom he describes as 'Ranged in order, with their hands uplifted, invoking the gods and pouring forth horrible imprecations'.

More than martial battle lines were drawn at Mons Graupius in northern Scotland. Calgacus knew that Roman rule would curb the free nature of his people; he also recognised that a regimented society like that of Rome could not bear men and women of stubbornly independent mind who might act out their dreams and make them reality.

> Valour, too, and high spirit in subjects, are offensive to
> rulers; . . . On the one side, you have a general and an
> army; on the other, tribute, the mines, and all the other
> penalties of an enslaved people. Whether you endure
> these forever, or instantly avenge them, this field is to
> decide. Think, therefore, as you advance to battle, at once
> of your ancestors and of your posterity.'[3]

The superior discipline of the legions allowed Agricola to defeat Calgacus at Mons Graupius, but the devastated Picts refused to accept they had lost the war and stubbornly maintained their resistance to Roman rule. We do not know what prompted them to take this stance, because all we know of the Celts at this time is derived from the writings of their enemies.

Celtic society was what is called 'Heroic', much like that of the Greeks and Trojans at the time of the Trojan War, in that individual champions often acted as surrogates and so minimised casualties. When armies joined in fighting, it tended to be only until one gained the upper hand, although there were many vicious struggles and innumerable deaths. The Roman army was a human mincing machine by comparison. Tacitus's description of the differences between the armies is laconic: '. . . The boldest [Celtic] warriors stepped to the front. As the [Roman] line was forming . . .'[4] Celtic individuals, no matter how bold, were no match for disciplined Roman lines and so went down to a drastic defeat.

Despite defeat in battle, the Celts of the north of Britain were not subdued. In the second century, under the Emperor Hadrian, the furthest point of the Roman Empire was marked by the wall that bears his name and which today still runs roughly along the line of the present Scotland–England border. A generation later, the border was moved north, and the Antonine Wall was built from the estuary of the River Clyde to the Firth of Forth. Thereafter fortunes fluctuated; sometimes the Romans advanced north and sometimes, as in 180, during the reign of the Emperor Commodus, the Caledonian Picts flooded over the walls and invaded the south.

The northern British Celts were less susceptible than their southern cousins to the blandishments and temptations presented by imperial rule and less inclined to ape Roman ways, but even they accepted, by the late fourth century, that the Romans were securely placed in Britain and that there was no immediate prospect of their expulsion.

On the mainland of Europe, the Romans were less secure. Externally, Germanic peoples were pushing south, testing the borders of the Empire along the Rhine. Internally, struggles for power between generals dissipated Roman energy and manpower. When legions were recalled to the mainland of Europe to protect the borders of the Empire and to wage civil war, and later to protect Rome itself, Roman rule in Britain collapsed, and in 410 the last legions left.

The island the Romans left behind was a patchwork of Celtic peoples, Britons who had lived for centuries under the protection of the Romans, and Scots and Picts who had freely bumped about the edges of the Empire. The *Damnonii* (the people of the stag) held the land about the River Clyde (often confused with the *Dumnonii* of south-west England when steps were taken to locate the stories of Merlin and Arthur in the far south). By the end of the fifth century, the *Damnonii* had formed the kingdom of Strathclyde, with its military capital at *Alclyd*, literally Clyde Rock, modern Dumbarton Rock. From there, their king could control the traffic on the river and so exercise power along the Clyde valley. The administrative capital was where the rivers Clyde and Kelvin meet at the Royal Town of Partick.

In the east, the sway of the *Votadini*, who were to evolve into the Gododdin Confederation, extended from Lothian to Northumberland. Their capital fortresses were at Traprain Law, near East Linton in East Lothian, on Edinburgh Castle rock and at *Din Guardyi*, modern Bamburgh, Northumberland.

Argyll was originally the home of a Pictish people the Romans called the *Epidii* (the people of the horse), but its southern tip, Kintyre, literally Head Land, was only 14 miles from Ireland, so there was a substantial admixture of Irish-Scots from Dalriada in the north-east of Ireland. These Scots raided along the west coast of

Britain, but not every contact was hostile; they also formed social, trading and cultural links, and many Irish-Scots stayed and settled among the *Epidii*.

The main lands of the Picts extended from the Antonine Wall to Caithness (the land of the people of the cat) in the far north. They also held lesser lands in the south-west of Scotland, in Dumfriesshire and Galloway. The Romans called them Picts, the painted people, because they decorated their bodies with dyes, but, among themselves, they were the *Cruithne*, that is, simply, the people.

Lying between the kingdom of Strathclyde in the west, the land of the Gododdin in the east and the massive power of the indomitable and unconquered Picts in the north was the relatively small kingdom of Manau, with its capital at Stirling, which R.M. Mitchison called 'the brooch that holds together the . . . parts of the country'.[5]

When the shields of the legions were lifted, raids by Scots and Picts became increasingly numerous and ambitious. The Celtic Britons of Strathclyde and the Gododdin found they were ill prepared to defend themselves against the depredations of the warlike Picts, and, as they came across from Ireland in increasing numbers, the Scots. As Gildas puts it:

> After this [the departure of the Romans], Britain is left
> deprived of all her soldiery and armed bands . . . and
> utterly ignorant as she was of the art of war, groaned
> in amazement for many years under the cruelty of two
> foreign nations – the Scots from the north-west and the
> Picts from the north.[6]

Gildas may have been a small-minded religious fanatic, but he did have a take-no-prisoners writing style and a flair for vicious invective:

No sooner were [the Romans] gone, than the Picts and Scots, like worms which in the heat of mid-day come forth from their holes, hastily land again from their canoes . . . differing one from another in manners, but inspired with the same avidity for blood, and all more eager to shroud their villainous faces in bushy hair than to cover with decent clothing those parts of their body which required it.[7]

The Britons of Strathclyde and the Gododdin had enjoyed the protection of Rome for centuries, and, compared to the northern neighbours who had fought the Romans in Britain to a standstill, they were inexperienced and ill equipped for war. The Scots and Picts took advantage of this, and by the middle of the fifth century they were raiding in force as far south as Hadrian's Wall:

To oppose [the Scots and Picts, the British] placed on the heights a garrison equally slow to fight and ill adapted to run away, a useless and panic-struck company, who clambered away days and nights on their unprofitable watch. Meanwhile the hooked weapons of their enemies were not idle, and our wretched countrymen were dragged from the wall and dashed against the ground.[8]

Those who were dragged from the wall with hooked weapons and dashed against the ground were the lucky ones.

Such premature death, however, painful as it was, saved them from seeing the miserable sufferings of their brothers and children. But why should I say more? They left their cities, abandoned the protection of the wall and dispersed themselves in flight more desperately than before. The enemy, on the other hand, pursued them with more unrelenting cruelty than before, and butchered our countrymen like sheep, so that their habitations were like those of savage beasts; for they turned their arms upon each other, and for the sake of a little sustenance, imbrued

> their hands in the blood of their fellow countrymen. Thus
> foreign calamities were augmented by domestic feuds; so
> that the whole country was entirely destitute of provisions,
> save such as could be procured in the chase.[9]

Increasing raids led to a breakdown of law and order and to famine. Soon, the Britons were refugees in their own land, fighting among themselves for food. Although not yet experienced warriors, they were brave and numerous, and on occasion victorious, but, when they won, according to Gildas, they failed to take advantage of their victories and quickly succumbed to the temptations of the civilised way of life they longed for. 'The boldness of the enemy was for a while checked, but not the wickedness of our countrymen: the enemy left our people, but the people did not leave their sins.'[10]

A period of respite followed some British victories, during which the Britons apparently refused to face reality and, instead, indulged themselves in wild abandon and 'every kind of luxury and licentiousness . . . There arose also every other [vice] to which human nature is liable, and in particular that hatred of truth.'[11]

Everything Gildas wrote was informed by his affinity to the Christian Church. To Gildas, 'good' means good for the Church. When he says the people 'hated the truth', he does not mean they hated the truth; he means the people did not accept his Christianity. The British almost exclusively adhered to the old way at this time.

The Scots and Picts recovered and again prepared to launch themselves upon the Britons of southern Scotland: 'A vague rumour suddenly as if on wings reaches the ears of all: that their inveterate foes were rapidly approaching to destroy the whole country, and to take possession of it, as of old, from one end to the other.'[12]

According to Gildas's account, the Britons panicked. Instead of using the time this intelligence gave them to prepare to defend themselves, they continued to indulge themselves and waste their days until it was too late to arm and train an army to meet the coming onslaught. When they eventually acted, they took a step that would lead to disaster: they hired German mercenaries, the Angles, to protect them.

Before I continue, it needs remarking upon that there is a tendency, in Anglo-Saxon sources, and so in most history books, to bundle the Angles, Saxons and Jutes together, under the umbrella name Saxon. It is from the name Saxon we get, in Scots Gaelic, *Sassenach*, Englishman. The name England is, of course, derived from the name Angle. 'English' people are often referred to as Anglo-Saxon. (No one seems to have been bothered much about the Jutes.) Where the umbrella name Saxon is used and when the name Angle is more accurate, I will use the name Angle.

The Gododdin were particularly vulnerable to attack by the Picts: they had a lengthy coastline to protect at a time when the Picts had a large navy capable of raiding as far south as London.

The Gododdin Britons had traded with the Angles of Germany for centuries. However, normal trading contacts were one thing, relying on commercial competitors for protection quite another. Gildas is unforgiving in his condemnation of those who promulgated this policy:

> Then all the councillors, together with that proud tyrant Vortigern, the British king, were so blinded that, as a protection to their country, they sealed its doom by inviting in among them (like wolves into the sheep-fold), the fierce and impious [Angles],[13] a race hateful both to God and men, to repel the invasions of the northern nations [the Picts and Scots]. Nothing was ever so pernicious to our country, nothing was ever so unlucky. What palpable

> darkness must have enveloped their minds – darkness
> desperate and cruel! Those very people whom, when
> absent, they dreaded more than death itself were invited
> to reside, as one may say, under the selfsame roof.[14]

The impression given in this passage is that the invitation extended to the mercenaries was a unique event, and that one man, Vortigern, was to blame. Vortigern, however, is not a name but a title and means, literally, great or big master. The prefix *Vor* is a corruption of the Gaelic *Mor* – great or big – and *tigern* means master. I favour the loose translation of great chief.

The Vortigern of whom Gildas writes is but the last British king of the southern Gododdin to continue the policy of paying the Angles to fight the Scots and the Picts on behalf of the British. His name was, probably, Morgan Bulc, but given he is the only Vortigern with a significant role to play in the life of Merlin, and given Vortigern is the name by which he is best known, I will use Vortigern from now on as if it were his name.

A fragmentary record from the ninth century, probably written as an example of Latin grammar, says that Ida, an Angle war chief, came to the land of the southern Gododdin, south-east Scotland, north-east England, in 544, and that Ida 'was the son of Eoppa, the son of Eosa . . . It was Eosa who first came to Britain.'[15]

The arrival of the Angles was not in fact a one-off event, so it is difficult to date these events exactly. There were Angles in the land of the southern Gododdin before Eosa, the Angle war chief, arrived c.500, probably since the middle of the fifth century. With the arrival of Eosa, the nature of the relationship between employers and employees changed, and about this time the Angles became a significant political force in the land. The Angles probably recognised there were opportunities for mercenaries in the Gododdin land and brought their fellows across from Germany to fight against the Picts and Scots. The Angle mercenary presence grew gradually, over decades, until the Britons became dependent upon them and they too powerful to expel.

When Ida arrived in 544, the Angles reached critical mass. Gildas could see what was obscure to the Britons in the last half of the fifth century. The raids by the Picts and Scots were not catastrophic, but the presence of a 'fifth column' of hardened Angle fighters living within their walls, able to take their measure and find them wanting, was a great and potentially fatal menace to the Britons. Of what must have been Ida's army, Gildas wrote:

> They first landed on the eastern side of the island, by the invitation of the unlucky king, and there fixed their sharp talons, apparently to fight in favour of the island, but alas, more truly against it. Their mother-land, finding her first brood thus successful, sends forth a larger company of her wolfish offspring, which, sailing over, join themselves to their bastard-born comrades. From that time the germ of iniquity and the root of contention planted their poison amongst us, as we deserved, and shot forth into leaves and branches.[16]

The wonderfully human Nennius, writing in southern Britain, probably Wales, in the ninth century, says he piled up every source of evidence he could find into a large heap in the middle of his room before setting about writing his *Historia Brittonum*. In this, he describes how, win or lose, the power of the first Angle mercenaries only increased: 'The more the [Angles] were vanquished, the more they sought for new supplies of Saxons from Germany; so that kings, commanders and military bands were invited over from almost every province.'[17]

The southern Gododdin were in a parlous state in the first quarter of the sixth century. They had been found wanting in war against the Scots and the Picts and had weakened themselves further by inviting inside their defences people who knew how to fight and, worse, knew that the southern Gododdin did not.

By the end of the fifth century, as the influence of the Angles was increasing in the land of the Gododdin, a Scots army arrived in Argyll under Fergus Mor Mac Erc,[18] who set about establishing his rule from Kintyre to Lorne. Fergus had to fight hard to establish his kingdom; within three years he was dead, as was his son and successor, Domangart, six years later. Domangart left two young sons, Comgall and Gabhran. Comgall succeeded his father and ruled Dalriada for 30 years until his death, c.537. In the late 520s, Gabhran went to Manau, a motley kingdom in the very centre of Scotland, and there married the Pictish princess Lluan. Two years later, they had a son, Aedan Mac Gabhran, who was to be one of the greatest Scottish kings and the father of the hero Arthur. About the time Gabhran moved from Dalriada to Manau, Dumnagual, king of Strathclyde, died. He was succeeded by his son, a Christian sympathiser named Clinoch Mac Dumnagual Hen.

The arrival of the Angles under Ida was the turning point in the affairs of the Britons and their neighbours the Scots. The Picts remained relatively untouched in their far northern fastnesses, but in the south of Scotland everything was about to change.

CHAPTER FOUR

Signs and Portents

The rivalry between Merlin and his arch-enemy Mungo, also known as Kentigern, the patron saint of Glasgow, has been all but lost to history because the Church strove to obliterate references to the old way and its last great champion, Merlin.

The Church in Scotland was originally Celtic-Christian, a hybrid church rooted in both Christianity and the old way. By the end of the sixth century, Roman-Christian influences became more important until, at the Synod of Whitby in 664, the Christian Church in Scotland fell into the thrall of the Roman version, although Celtic-Christian influences were never entirely extinguished. As late as the twelfth century, efforts were still being made to stamp out Celtic-Christian practices such as allowing priests to marry or inherit benefices. It was in this spirit that the bishop of Glasgow decided that the only available biography of Mungo did not accord with current Roman dogma and so had to be rewritten:

> That Life as it seems to many, is tainted throughout as it
> is discoloured by an uneducated language and obscured
> by a poorly written style and before all these faults
> certainly a wise man would more shrink back because in
> the beginning of the narrative itself are stories obviously
> contrary to certain doctrine and catholic faith.[1]

57

Consequently, about 1180, the bishop summoned a monk, Jocelyn of Furness, to his palace at Partick and instructed him to write a new hagiography of Mungo. It is, perhaps, instructive that the monk he chose to create this new biography was from England and not from Scotland, and so less likely to be sympathetic to local traditions.

The old biography, now lost, was written in Gaelic, not 'educated' Latin, the language of churchmen, and made it clear that Mungo's Christianity was not that of Rome in the twelfth century. It is the stories at the start of the old version that seem to be the most deviant. These stories, in keeping with many other biographies, are likely to have related to Mungo's early life. This would make sense because, for most of his life, Mungo was a Celtic Christian. It was only when he was more than 60 years old that he went over to Rome.

Jocelyn of Furness went 'around the nearby city [of Glasgow], through its streets and quarters, searching for a written life of Saint Kentigern'.[2] He 'searched with diligence [to see] if by chance a life of [Mungo] could be discovered which was sustained by greater authority and more visible truth'. Specifically, he sought a life agreeable to and based upon the authority of the Roman Church, as opposed to the Celtic life then in use. All he found was evidence that ran contrary to the story his employer wanted him to write: 'However, I have discovered another codicil, composed in the Scottic style [Gaelic], which is filled with solecisms all the way through and yet contains a more unbroken account of the life and acts of the holy bishop.' An objective biographer would have been pleased to find such extensive material, but not Jocelyn; he was unhappy, because, although he had found a more unbroken account of his subject's life, it again told of Mungo's roots in the Celtic Christian Church.[3] 'Seeing therefore the life of so esteemed a bishop [Mungo/Kentigern], who was glorious with signs and portents and most famous in virtue and doctrine, perversely recited and turned away from the pure faith . . . I confess I suffered greatly.'

But not for long. Jocelyn knew what he had to do. As the evidence did not say what he wanted it to say, he ignored some of it and put a Roman Christian spin on the rest. He is quite unashamed about this:

> On that account [because the evidence did not suit his book], I therefore accepted to mend this life by restoring the material collected from the heart of both small books and, by bending my method to your command, to season with Roman salt what had been ploughed by barbarians.[4]

The reference to 'Roman salt' echoes the actions of the Romans after the fall of Carthage, when they razed the city and sowed the surrounding fields with salt to prevent anything growing there again. Jocelyn had the same aim in view when he took the work of other scholars and destroyed it to protect the 'pure faith' as laid down by Rome.

Despite the fact that Jocelyn deliberately obscured the truth, enough has survived in his *Life of Kentigern* to enable us to see what was going on during Mungo's lifetime and, consequently, given they were contemporaries, the circumstances in which Merlin became famous. According to Jocelyn, Mungo was descended from 'a royal tree . . . his mother was a daughter of a certain king, of a most pagan family, in the North land of the Britons'.[5] The *Aberdeen Breviary* says that Mungo's mother was 'Thennew, daughter of Loth, King of Lothian'. The more common alternative to Loth is Lot. (The name Lothian commemorates him.) Lot's daughter, Taneu, was sympathetic to the teachings of the Christian missionaries who came to her father's court to spread their gospel, although she was not yet a convert when her son was born. Jocelyn continues:

> Her thirsty soul came to the knowledge of the truth and
> she received the . . . word that was able to preserve her
> soul from death. And although she was not yet washed in
> the health-giving water of baptism, nevertheless she was
> running with a wide-open and cheerful heart in the way of
> the commands of God . . . [she] pursued continually . . .
> with frequent and devout prayers . . . as much as she was
> able to on account of her fear of her pagan father.[6]

Despite her father's disapproval, Taneu formed a special devotion
to Mary, the mother of Jesus, and aimed to imitate her by becoming
pregnant while remaining a virgin: 'With the unfolding of some
time, she discovered herself to be with child . . . trusting purely that
her desire had been fulfilled.'

Her desire had not been fulfilled; even Jocelyn accepted that
'that which was born in her womb she received from a human
embrace'. Taneu swore an oath that she did not know who the
father of her child was or 'in what manner she conceived'. The
following passage appears at first to be obscure, but it is, as we will
see, revealing:

> Nevertheless the truth of the matter by no means ought
> to be lost from the soul of anyone who is discerning . . .
> So that for the present we may bury in silence those things
> we found inserted in poetic songs or in histories non-
> canonical . . .

'Discerning' people were expected to know what had happened
without Jocelyn having to spell out what he had found in non-
Christian sources. The reference to poetic songs is, of course, a
coded reference to the old way. Although Jocelyn says he has put
these aside 'for the present', he does not return to them.

The people of Glasgow put it about that Mungo was born of

a virgin, but Jocelyn was not prepared to take this controversial tack and looked for an officially approved way to explain Taneu's impregnation. He found a precedent in the story of another Lot, the Lot of Sodom and Gomorrah. This Old Testament Lot had sexual intercourse when he was too drunk to know what he was doing. Jocelyn supposes this might have happened to Taneu. The 'too much to drink' theory was something of a double-edged sword, because the implication was that it involved a measure of culpability on Taneu's part. Realising this, Jocelyn suggested that someone may have put something in her drink:

> It is possible that something of this kind took place with this girl by the secret judgment of God that she might not feel the mingling of the sexes, so that now she perceived herself to be unblemished although impregnated.

If Jocelyn had not suppressed the evidence, we would know what was in the 'poetic songs and histories non-canonical': who Mungo's father was and the circumstances in which he was conceived. All we know is that the truth was not what Jocelyn wanted to hear and that he went to great lengths to hide it. Jocelyn was bound to broach the identity of Mungo's father, but, when he did, he immediately turned away again:

> But why do we linger over these things? . . . Truly we think the matter absurd to inquire further as to who the sower was and in what manner he ploughed or even planted the earth . . .

Enquire further? He does not enquire at all.

> Meanwhile the woman [Taneu] went out and her womb swelled up as a distinctive sign of her seduction displayed to all the prophets. And now with her face pale, with her heart lodged in her throat, and with milk erupting in her breasts, her pregnancy denounced her.

When Lot, her father, heard of Taneu's pregnancy, he 'earnestly questioned her, now urging her with dread, now soothing her with fawning' as to whom the father was. 'But she, introducing an oath in the name of Christ, proclaimed that she was innocent of all virile consorting', which only made Lot angrier.

According to Jocelyn, the law of Lot's kingdom was that a woman who became pregnant outside marriage should be thrown headlong from a high hill, but this is nonsense. Many, if not most, women in the sixth century became pregnant before they were married; they would not have got married if they had not. Jocelyn, eager to be associated with the zero-tolerance approach to sexual activity, says, if the pagans take the view that sex outside marriage should be severely punished, how much more does it behove a good Christian to take at least as stern a line:

> If such zeal for chastity inflamed pagans, who were ignorant of divine laws, because of their honour and the observance of their fathers' traditions, what should a Christian do, who is bound fast to the custody of chasteness by the divine law, which promises for this good work the joy of divine inspiration, but on the other hand repays its transgression with Tartarus [Hell].[7]

Jocelyn says that Lot sentenced Taneu to death:

> Therefore, the above-mentioned girl was led on the command of the king to the brow of the highest mountain, which is named Dumpelder, so that she could be cast headlong downward from there and be broken bit by bit into pieces and torn limb from limb.[8]

Jocelyn could not have known that with this reference to *Dumpelder* (Dunpelder) he provided evidence that was to prove vital in understanding what happened to Merlin 80 years later and in identifying the place where Merlin died and was buried.

Taneu prayed to Mary, extolling the virtues of chastity before being thrown from *Dumpelder* hill, and then:

> [A] wonderful thing happened and unheard of in former days! When she had fallen, she was not crushed because the Lord put his hand under her; and for that reason she experienced no injury. As it seemed to her, she descended in the fashion of a winged bird falling gently to earth lest by chance she would strike her foot against a rock.[9]

The Christians were very pleased at this turn of events, which is a bit confusing given that a few paragraphs before Jocelyn has them calling pagans the twelfth-century equivalent of bleeding-heart liberals because they only wanted her torn limb from limb. It was decided that Taneu was not at fault and that she should not be punished further. The 'idolaters and adversaries of the Christian faith' – that is, the people of the old way – did not agree, of course (because this is Jocelyn's version of the story), and demanded the sentence of death be carried out:

> So the crowd with a storm of words to one another confused itself, but the sacrilegious multitude gathered strength and they incited their king, who was inwardly delivered up to idolatry, to order a new judgment against his daughter.

Lot sentenced Taneu to be 'set forth on the sea alone in a little boat'.

> Therefore, in order that she should be delivered up to the resulting sanctioned judgment, the servants of the king went up into a ship and led her away to the deepest part of the sea. And there she was placed alone in a very small boat made of hide, according to the custom of the Scots, and after committing her without any oars to fate, they returned to shore by rowing. They related that the

sentence was accomplished to the King and people who had waited for the result of the matter.

In truth, the girl, having been left without any human aid, entrusted herself to him alone who had made the sea and the dry land and faithfully prayed that he would deliver her from the imminent danger, as formerly he had saved her from the precipice. It is a wonder to relate, but for God no act is impossible. That little boat, in which the pregnant girl was held, rode the eddies whirling up and down, and being turned towards the opposite shore, ploughed with a much quicker passage than if it had been borne along by blown sails, or was propelled by the hardest effort of many rowers. . . . [Taneu] came to shore upon the sand near the place called Culenros.[10]

Culenros, now called Culross, on the north side of the Firth of Forth, across the narrows formed by Longannet Point, was where a monk called Serf trained boys 'who were to be delivered up to divine service'.[11] Serf took in Taneu and cared for her.

Soon after she landed, Taneu gave birth to Mungo, later to be called Kentigern (meaning approximately First Master or Head Lord) and the patron saint of Glasgow.

The writer of what is called the *Fragmentary Life* of Mungo, written a generation before Jocelyn's *Life*, says Mungo's father was Ewen, son of Erwegende. The *Fragmentary Life* says Ewen paid court to Taneu, that his suit was unwelcome and that he tricked Taneu by dressing as a woman and 'deflowering' her.[12]

The *Aberdeen Breviary* has Mungo's father as 'Eugenius, king of Cumbria'.[13] It too has Taneu refusing Ewen, but this time Taneu's father threatens her with 'perpetual prostitution with swineherds' if she does not give way and accept Ewen. Taneu remained stubbornly against the match and her father carried out his threat and sent her to live with swineherds. There, a 'young man in virgin's apparel', that is, dressed like a young woman, raped her.

Ewen was neither a king, although he may have been a sub-king, a prince, nor was he of Cumbria, unless Cumbria is a corruption of *Cymry* (the people), although Cumbria was part of Strathclyde late in the sixth century, after Ewen's death. It was common for ranks to be enhanced in stories. Arthur, who was not a king, was later called a king. Ewen was almost certainly a high lord of Strathclyde.

Although both the *Aberdeen Breviary* and the *Fragmentary Life* contain the Ewen-dressing-as-a-woman episode, and Jocelyn's *Life* does not, when all three are read together it is possible to obtain a coherent view of the events that occurred immediately before Mungo was born. To do this, it is necessary to consider the evidence rationally and to rigorously exclude supernatural elements in the narrative as the fictions they always are.

In the 520s, the Strathclyde Britons and the Gododdin Britons of Lothian were aware of the threat presented by the growing power of the Angles who lived among the southern Gododdin in southeast Scotland and concluded that it was in their interests to work together for their mutual security. A marriage between members of their respective royal houses was one way to seal a bond between them.

Lot, king of the northern Gododdin, was born c.470 and so Taneu, born c.512, was probably one of his younger daughters. He and his people adhered to the old way, although Christian missionaries were allowed in his kingdom. Clinoch Mac Dumnagual Hen of Strathclyde was one of the first Christian kings in Scotland. He was born c.490. His reign started some time between 508 and 540 – the exact date is not known. One source says he became king about 530. Mungo was born about 528 – that is, perhaps, about the time Clinoch became king. If Clinoch came to the throne in the mid to late 520s, this may have prompted a match between Ewen of

Strathclyde and Taneu of the Gododdin. A new king would be naturally anxious to gain allies and secure his borders. What better way than by a marriage alliance?

Whatever the reason for the marriage, it was agreed that Taneu, daughter of the Gododdin king, should marry Ewen, a prince of the Strathclyde Britons. Christians were probably already active at Lot's court, but it may be that Clinoch insisted his priests have access to Taneu to prepare her for her future role as a Christian princess of Strathclyde. In any event, Taneu became convinced of the Christian cause, and only her father's opposition prevented her converting openly. Why would Jocelyn say Taneu had not yet converted if it were not true? This small detail lends weight to the other evidence in Jocelyn's *Life* and suggests there is truth in the story he tells, albeit a twisted truth.

While the religious practices of others would have meant little to Lot, he would have had to be wary of the political influence that came with Christianity. Christian missionaries commonly applied to the women of a community, ideally the wives and daughters of the chiefs, and worked to win them over with a view to having them influence their menfolk. If this exercise was successful and the chief was converted, this chief would be expected to impose Christianity upon his followers. This tactic worked with Taneu, but Lot remained unaffected. It makes sense to conclude that Taneu was a genuine convert, even if she had not yet gone public. With the zeal of a convert, she tried her father's patience with constant Christian references.

In his seminal work *A Century of the Scottish People*, Professor T.C. Smout says that, until at least the nineteenth century, the practice in parts of the south of Scotland was to ensure fertility by bedding and impregnating before marrying. He quotes a nineteenth-century Lanarkshire minister who said, 'I really do not remember when I last married a young woman who was not in the family way.'[14] Such a custom is unlikely to have had its roots in Christianity, because Christianity had no truck with sex before marriage. It is more likely that it originated when the old way held sway and that the view was taken there would be little point in getting married if having children was impossible. The sources begin to make sense if this is taken to be true.

Taneu and Ewen were, consequently, expected to have sexual intercourse and, if this resulted in pregnancy, to marry. Taneu was reluctant in the extreme, and at first refused to have any connection with Ewen. It is impossible to say whether Taneu's new-found beliefs, in particular her devotion to Mary, the mother of Jesus, and her hope to emulate the 'virgin birth', led her to reject Ewen, or if she rejected him simply because she did not like him.

The real problem was not that Taneu refused to marry Ewen, as the sources coyly say, but that she initially refused to have sex with him. Ewen had come to Lot's court to get Taneu pregnant with a view to marriage (and a political alliance), and so, when Taneu refused to cooperate, her father was angry. No sex, no pregnancy. No pregnancy, no marriage. No marriage, no alliance.

Taneu's resistance to having sex with Ewen explains the passage in the *Fragmentary Life* that has Ewen pursue Taneu and, when his suit fails, has Taneu's father step in and threaten to send her to live with the swineherds. In effect, Lot said to his daughter that if she would not have sex with Ewen, he would send her to live with 'swillers', who most certainly would have sex with her. This also explains the reference to 'perpetual prostitution' in the *Aberdeen Breviary*: living with the swineherds meant constant sex with swineherds – obviously not an option of choice. Lot is almost certain to have concluded with the P Gaelic equivalent of 'and we will see how you like that, young lady!'

Lot did not intend to carry out his threat; it would have been self-defeating if he had, but Taneu could not be sure that he would not. She had to submit. By all accounts, Taneu becomes pregnant at this point. Ewen was duly accepted as Mungo's father because, when Mungo grew up, he went to Glasgow where his father's family lived and not to Taneu's people in the east.

The conventional wisdom would have us believe that, after Lot threatened Taneu, Ewen dressed as a woman and tricked her into having sex with him.[15] What trick would work in these circumstances? A literal reading makes no sense. The evidence suggests that Ewen did not dress as a woman *to* have sex with Taneu; Ewen dressed as a woman *and* had sex with Taneu. That is, Ewan dressing as a woman was not a ruse; it was simply something he did.

Of course, time and bias have garbled the story, and it would be too much to suggest, based on one reported occasion, without corroborating circumstances, that Ewen dressed as a woman as a matter of course. There is, however, reason to believe that this practice was recognised and accepted among those of the old way before the incursion of Christianity and so to hypothesise that Ewen dressed in women's clothes regularly. I believe that the whole circumstances, considered together, corroborate this.

Men have dressed as women since, literally, time immemorial, and this has always been a frequent feature of myths, stories, history and life. Examples include Hercules, Achilles, Pentheus, countless Romans (particularly in the Rome of Caligula and Nero), the Duke of Anjou (later Henry III of France, who sought the hand of Queen Elizabeth), J. Edgar Hoover and innumerable others. The oldest stories are couched in what purport to be sensible reasons for the man dressing up as a woman. Pentheus, the least well known of the above, was said to have dressed as a woman to enable him to spy on women who worshipped Dionysus. Human nature in the past was the same as human nature today – the only difference being the attitude of people towards it.

Before the advent of religions that sought to control cultures with rigid codes, people were more likely to accept one another for what they were and find everyone a place about the campfire. In time, certain ways of being were frowned upon and ways to explain them in an acceptable form were created. Cultural anthropologists have suggested that cross-dressing was a significant ritualistic practice designed to express the ambiguity of the individual when betwixt childhood and manhood, or between life and death in societies that were close to nature. I prefer a more simple explanation. Transvestites exist – always have, always will – but not because of ritual demands. For some men, dressing like women is natural. They do it because they like it. (Who knows why?) It is easy to forget that there would have been the same mix of gender and sexual orientation in the sixth century as in the twenty-first century. There were gay men and men who liked to dress in women's clothes in the sixth century, just as there are today. We just do not know much about them because of centuries of censorship. If I am correct in this, then a community rooted in nature would naturally find a place for such men, and rituals particular to them would develop.

This, at least, is evident in other very old cultures. There is an enormously complicated cultural phenomenon among Native Americans called *Berdache* (I apologise to those who find this anthrolopological term offensive). The best brief explanation of *Berdache* I have found is in a lecture given by the Native American leader Russell Means at the Navajo Community College in 1995, when he said, 'In my culture, we have people who dress half-man, half-woman. *Winkte*, we call them in our language . . . If you are *Winkte*, that is an honourable term, and you are a special human being. And among my nation and all Plains people, we consider you a teacher of our children and are proud of what and who you are.'

Native American culture is founded in nature, as was the old way. If non-Christian Native Americans are tolerant of natural ways of being, the people of the old way in the sixth century may have been so too. For my present purposes, I need posit only the following: Ewen dressed as a woman, and he was no more minded to marry Taneu than she was to marry him. It was an arranged marriage, and, whether Ewen was also gay or not, it is unlikely that when he got Taneu pregnant, he was doing anything more than his duty. The *Fragmentary Life* and the *Aberdeen Breviary* leave the matter of Ewen's sexuality unclear, and Jocelyn does not mention it at all because the Church vilified any sexual conduct that did not fit with its mores.

It may be that the story of Ewen dressing up as a woman is fiction. If so, it is a strange fiction, and not one a storyteller was likely to invent. The way the evidence reads suggests the original story has been obscured and that what has come down to us is a garbled cover-up. I cannot see that Ewen dressing up as a woman would have been his cunning method of having sex with Taneu. Women were not kept in harems in the sixth century; there was no need to dress as a woman to obtain access to her.

Ewen and Taneu were political pawns. The social pressure upon them is more than enough to explain the sex in which they eventually engaged. Ewen was a transvestite and possibly gay. Taneu's recent conversion to Christianity was said to have left her with a virginity fixation that made her averse to sex. Alternatively, it may be that her aversion to Ewen was based on his cross-dressing predilection and that this led her to seek to escape marriage to him by professing Christian chastity. Whatever her reasons may have been, Taneu did not want to marry Ewen, and he probably did not want to marry her, but they were both bound to do their duty, so the necessary sexual intercourse took place.

Taneu became pregnant. They did not live happily ever after. Taneu came out as Christian, and Ewen was recognised as what the Plains Indians would call *Winkte*. The parties to the negotiations recognised they had a problem. When Taneu refused to go ahead with the marriage, people could see her point, so a compromise was reached. It was agreed that she be put out of the way into exile under the care of Serf in Culross.

In the hands of Christian scribes, a story grew of pagan brutality, in which a pregnant Taneu was thrown from a hill, and of a Christian miracle by which the Virgin Mary caught Taneu in mid-air. This was followed by pagan cruelty when they then insisted Taneu be left alone at sea to die, and another Christian miracle, which saw her wafted to safety at Culross. How likely is that?

Jocelyn's *Life*, the *Fragmentary Life* and the *Aberdeen Breviary* only make sense if it is recognised that Jocelyn turned the truth on its head when he made the Christians sympathetic to Taneu and those of the old way her enemies. With this end in view, Jocelyn, or someone with the same agenda, invented a 'pagan' law that required Taneu's death. There is no authority for a Gododdin law requiring a potential single mother to be thrown from a high hill or, indeed, sentenced to death in any way. People of the old way were not exercised by such matters. For them, pregnancy was natural and pregnancy outside marriage was common, if not the norm. All we know of the old ways points to a reverence for nature and all it had to offer, including sex. It is ironic that some of the best evidence for this comes from Christian sources excoriating what they call licentiousness among what they call pagans.

According to Jocelyn, however, the pagans were baying for

Taneu's blood because she was unmarried and pregnant, while the Christians were relaxed about her sexual impropriety. This version is entirely at variance with the rest of Jocelyn's *Life*, which refers to sex in connection with hog pools of carnal sewage and all kinds of contagion and which promises 'hell as the punishment for the hammerer of the entire earth, namely the breath of fornication'. The scenario presented by Jocelyn also runs counter to the next 1,500 years and more of Church history, in which any sexual conduct outside an extraordinarily limited range was officially abominated.

Given these facts, and the fact that 'pagans' were more tolerant than Christians of individual sexual proclivities, we may reasonably suppose there was no law that required Taneu to be sentenced to death because she was about to be an unmarried mother.

I have turned the story told by the Christians on its head because it makes more sense that way and concluded that the people of the old way, not the Christians, were sympathetic toward Taneu. Jocelyn, of course, had to have the Christians on Taneu's side because she is the mother of his subject saint. This meant that, in Jocelyn's book, the people of the old way had to be the villains who wanted Taneu punished.

It is curious that Jocelyn, who is so unabashed about the censorship he uses to deceive his readers for propaganda purposes, is coy when considering the identity of Mungo's father, particularly when parentage was of such intense interest to people in the sixth century. What was Jocelyn's motive? His most obvious motive, indeed his permanent and prime motivation, was his desire to please his patron.

The question then arises: why should his bishop care who Mungo's father was after 600 years? The answer had to be to protect the interests of something that existed in the sixth century and had survived into the twelfth. If Mungo's father were a churchman, that would have been sufficient. The Church would not have wanted it known that one of their own had had sex before marriage, indeed, had sex instead of marriage, nor that he was homosexual and worse, in the eyes of the Church, a cross-dresser. There is, however, no evidence that Ewen was a churchman, and, in the circumstances, this must be unlikely. The only other body that has the necessary continuous link over six centuries is the ruling house of Strathclyde. Although Strathclyde ceased to exist as a separate political entity in the tenth century, the erstwhile royal family would still have been about to take umbrage in the twelfth. In any event, Jocelyn would not have wanted it to be widely known that Mungo's father was a cross-dresser and a homosexual.

Strathclyde and the Gododdin arranged a political marriage that did not work out, despite the fact that the bride-to-be was pregnant. This was no one's fault, and a compromise was agreed. The marriage was called off, and the pregnant Taneu was bundled into the care of the monk Serf in Culross, where her child could be born and brought up a Christian.

CHAPTER FIVE

The Old Way of the Druids

The writings of the Druids and the people of the old way have been destroyed; all we have left is their echo in works prompted by Greek curiosity and Roman and Christian propaganda. In the words of Dr Samuel Johnson, 'All that is really known of the ancient state of Britain is contained in a few pages. We can know no more than what old writers have told us.'[1]

Aristotle talked respectfully of the philosophy of the Druids in the fourth century BCE, a view echoed by Greek philosophers in Alexandria and Rome in the first century CE. Diogenes Laertius, a historian of philosophy in the third century CE, saw the Druids as high intellectuals steeped in ancient wisdom, whose creed was honour the gods, do no evil and be brave.[2] He even considered the possibility that the study of philosophy originated not in Greece but in the east, and, with reference to the writings of Aristotle and Solon, that it came to Greece through Indian Gymnosophists, Persian Magis and Celtic Druids.

At the same time, Hippolytus of Alexandria taught that the Druids used Pythagorean methods in calculating their prophecies. Even the early Christian, Clement of Alexandria, believed that the Druids learnt from Pythagoras. The whole tenor of these early records is of Druids who were respectable philosophers. It is only later, for reasons of political propaganda, and later still for the purposes of promoting Christianity, that the Druids are presented in a derogatory way.

Strabo and Pliny the Elder say the name Druid is derived from the same root as the Greek word *Drus*, oak.[3] It has also been supposed to have Indo-European origins and to mean strong. The last part of the word Druid, *uid/wid/vid*, it has been supposed, is derived from the Sanskrit *Vid*, to know or to see, and is also found in the Hindu *Vedas* (meaning, roughly, knowledge). The historian Peter Berresford Ellis concludes that 'Druid means "those whose knowledge is great"'.[4]

In modern Gaelic, Druid is *draoi, draoidh, Druidh*; in early Irish *drui, drai*; and in old Celtic *drúi-s, Druid-os*. In these Celtic languages, Druid means wise person or learned person. For these present purposes, whatever the derivation of the word may be, I take a Druid to be one of the intellectual class of the Celts. Although classical and Christian sources tend to concentrate on the men, the Celtic sources refer to women too. There were male and female Druids.

I do not suppose that the Celts were or are inherently any better or worse than any other people, and I write what follows only to counterbalance the tendency to portray them as woad-painted, barbarian pagans. In the fourth century, the historian Ammianus Marcellinus noted that the Gauls (Celts) were a remarkably clean and well-presented people. According to Pliny, the Celts invented soap and had taken to bathing before the Romans:

> The women used perfumes and cosmetics, checking their appearance in delicately decorated bronze mirrors. The men were generally clean-shaven, except for their characteristic long, drooping moustaches. The Celts had a great reverence for natural beauty, including that of the

human body. Obese men, unsightly and unfit for war, could be fined.[5]

Strabo added that:

> To the frankness and high-spiritedness of their temperament must be added the traits of childish boastfulness and love of decoration. They wear ornaments of gold, torques on their necks and bracelets on their arms and wrists, while people of high rank wear dyed garments besprinkled with gold. It is this vanity which makes them unbearable in victory and so completely downcast in defeat.[6]

Although, among other things, the Celts taught the Romans how to build roads, the Romans were less sympathetic towards the Druids and the old way than the Greeks. This was not because the Celts had invaded Italy and sacked Rome (in 390 BCE) – the Celts had also invaded Greece and sacked Delphi – but because the Romans were intent upon attacking the Celts and needed to rationalise their actions. Those whom the Romans wished to destroy, they first maligned.

The sack of Rome had inspired a fear of the Celts in the Roman people that lasted until Caesar invaded Gaul in the middle of the first century BCE. Writing of the late second century BCE, Tom Holland says:

> Within living memory [in Caesar's time] a nation of giants [Celts], three hundred thousand of them, it was reckoned, had appeared suddenly from the wastelands of the north, destroying everything in their way, subhuman monsters from the icy rim of the world. Their men had eaten raw flesh; their women had attacked legionaries with their bare hands. Had Marius . . . not managed to annihilate the invaders, then Rome and the world with her would have come to an end.[7]

Even as Julius Caesar's legions marched against the Celts of Gaul, stories abounded of Celtic barbarity: 'Travellers whispered of strange rites of sacrifice, performed in the dead of oaken glades, or by the side of black-watered bottomless lakes.'[8] Some whispered of a giant wicker man filled with prisoners and set alight. Such rumours demonised the enemy and readied men to fight fiercely.

Some of the rumours bandied about had a basis in reality. Two generations before Caesar, Posidonius reported that the Celts duelled for the best cut of meat. This is explicable. The Celts, who were famous for feasting, awarded the best cut of meat to the hero of the hour as a mark of honour. The modern Scottish equivalent would be a place at the top table. The Celts did not duel over the best cut of meat. They strove to excel in combat. If they did, they earned the best cut of meat at the feast that would invariably follow a fight. It was said that the Celts took the heads of their enemies; but then so too did the Parthians, who took the head of the Roman general Crassus after the Battle of Carrhae, and Caesar, who, on one famous occasion, used the bodies of his enemies as building material and had their heads stuck on poles.[9]

Aside from the wild excesses of imagination indulged in by Romans inspired by ignorance and fear, Julius Caesar himself provides a reasonably fair and informative account of the Druids as he saw them:

> The Druids officiate at the worship of the gods, regulate public and private sacrifices, and give rulings on all religious questions. Large numbers of young men flock to them for instruction, and they are held in great honour by the people. They act as judges in practically all disputes, whether between tribes or between individuals; when any crime is committed or a murder takes place, or a dispute arises about an inheritance or a boundary, it is they who

adjudicate the matter and appoint the compensation to be
paid and received by the parties concerned. Any individual
or tribe failing to accept their award is banned from taking
part in sacrifice – the heaviest punishment that can be
inflicted upon a Gaul [Celt].[10]

The evidence that large numbers of young men flocked to the
Druids for instruction suggests that the status of Druid was not
hereditary. The Druids were a class of intellectuals whose range
of activities extended beyond religious rituals and superstition.
According to Strabo:

[The Druids] in addition to the science of nature, study
also moral philosophy. They are believed to be the most
just of men, and are therefore entrusted with the decision
of cases affecting either individuals or the public; indeed
in former times they arbitrated in war and brought to a
standstill the opponents when about to draw up in line
of battle; and murder cases have been mostly entrusted to
their decision . . .[11]

Druids were scientists, philosophers, doctors, teachers, judges,
lawyers, astronomers and counsellors. It would have been too
much to expect that any one person could be expert in all these
fields, even 1,500 years ago. Common sense dictates that different
Druids specialised in different areas, depending upon their natural
aptitudes. Julius Caesar described how Celtic society was divided
into distinct classes of people, including Druids and warriors:

Druids are not accustomed to take part in war, nor do
they pay taxes like the rest of the people. They are exempt
from military service and from all obligations. Such great
rewards encourage many to begin training, either of their
own accord or sent by parents and relatives. They are told
to memorize a large number of lines of poetry, and so
spend twenty years in training.[12]

Just as a man who proved to be a good warrior might be able to make a full-time career of it, so too might a man or woman who displayed sufficient expertise be accepted as a Druid, probably after some form of initiation ceremony. People have always liked rituals, and a ritual would have served to demark those who were entitled to the privileges of the Druidic station.

Pliny the Elder provided the liveliest account of a Druidic ceremony when he described a grove of oaks where white-robed Druids with gold pruning hooks cut mistletoe from the trees on the sixth day of the moon. This was followed by feasting and the sacrifice of two white bulls. The traditional view is that this account is entirely without substance, but I do not see why it should be. The ritual seems to me to be tame, as these things go.

The Romans defamed the Celts when the occasion demanded it, but their intellectual curiosity led them to record something of the Druids' place in society, unlike their successors. The Christians simply obliterated almost every source of evidence relevant to the Druids, even to the extent of fixing diplomatic records. It is only on rare occasions, when a villain is needed, that Druids appear, and even then their identity tends to be disguised. In a propaganda battle for hearts and minds, it did not make sense to the Christians to allow an alternative view to be aired if this could be avoided. Where the Christian writ ran, scholars were bound to disguise any material that might allow their audience to understand the old way.

As a philosophy and theology, the old ways developed over thousands of years, so what Merlin believed was not necessarily the same as the beliefs of Druids in preceding and succeeding generations. Indeed, what Merlin believed probably did not accord with the beliefs of the Druid he met the day before, such was the nature of Celtic culture.[13]

The old way, according to Caesar's evidence, originated in the British Isles (and, it follows, Ireland), although this probably means that by the first century BCE the purest forms of the old ways survived only in the places furthest from the influence of Rome and Greece and the powerful Germanic peoples of northern Europe: 'The Druidic doctrine is believed to have been found existing in Britain and thence imported into Gaul; even today those who want to make a profound study of it generally go to Britain for that purpose.'[14]

After the first century CE, the Druids of Gaul all but disappear from history, and their beliefs with them. They were, almost, lost in the shadow of Rome.

The learning of the Druids was most efficiently saved in individual memories, but it was also set down in writing.[15] Caesar describes the Gallic Druids using Greek letters:

> Nor do they think it proper to commit this teaching to writing, although for almost all other purposes, including public and private accounts, they use Greek characters. They seem to me to have adopted this practice for two reasons: first, they do not want their teaching spread abroad, and secondly, if those in training rely on written texts they concentrate less on memory.[16]

For the next 1,000 years in Western Europe, almost the only people who could read and write were Christian priests and monks. They were determined to show the old way in a bad light, or, better still, not to refer to it at all. None of the writing left by the people of the old way has survived; everything has been obliterated.

As I have mentioned, the Druidic community was firmly founded in nature and consequently allowed both males and females into its ranks. Many early religious systems reflected this natural foundation by favouring male and female couples, most famously, Isis and

Osiris in Egypt. The only other early contender for prime deity was the female figure alone, the mother goddess. The Sumerians and the people of the Indus Valley Civilisation, two of the world's oldest civilisations, both worshipped mother goddesses.[17] Women occupied the central place in many ancient religious systems, or, at the very least, they held an equal place next to a male god. This was natural: women produce life directly; men produce life indirectly. Male gods standing alone were unnatural.

With the arrival of the three main patriarchal religions, Judaism, Christianity and Islam, everything changed. Over the last 2,500 years, most people have come to think of a male main deity.

A difference in attitudes to sex is only one of the many differences in attitude between the old ways and Christianity, but it is the most evident one. Throughout history, the Church has vilified the old ways as licentious and claimed its people were wanton. We may infer from this that there was a significant difference in sexual attitudes between Christians and the people they saw as pagan. In the old way, sex was one of many complexities that made life worth living. Sex was natural and so, to that extent, unremarkable. For Christianity, sex complicated lives and made them difficult to control. The distance between the humanity of Christian people and their Church's teaching in the sixth century was unnatural.[18] Put simply, sex went from being a good thing to being a necessary evil. Certainly, homosexual practices, which had been accepted as the part of life they were, were excoriated[19] (at least in public). In the late fourth century, the wife of the Christian Sulpicius Severus (the writer, historian, biographer of Martin of Tours) accused Celtic women of licentiousness and was told, 'We fulfil the demands of Nature in a much better way than do you Roman women. We consort openly with the best men, whereas you let yourselves be debauched in secret by the most vile.'[20]

82

Another major difference between the two ways of thinking was the attitude to learning. The relatively rudimentary science of the day was directly accessible only to a few, so most people in the sixth century, like many people today, found comfort in their imaginations. They imagined that, as there was life in things such as animals and trees, they could relate to these things, and more, that they could communicate with them. Streams and lochs were lively, or at least changeable things, so they too were thought of, not as alive themselves, but as inhabited by some spirit. Today, we might say that someone who is lively is spirited.

Many beliefs that originated in the old ways still play a part in modern life. People still touch wood, and, to a lesser extent, iron, for luck and have done so long before wood was associated with the Christian cross. The iron connection survives in the practice of nailing up a horseshoe for luck. It was believed that the malign were unable to cross the pure and lively water of a flowing stream for millennia before Tam O'Shanter, in Robert Burns's immortal poem, made a run for the River Doon on his good horse Meg, with all the fiends of hell behind them.

On family holidays on the Black Isle with my wife and young children, we passed what we called the 'Sock Tree'. This was a wooded glade where the trees were covered with pieces of cloth. This was, no doubt, an ancient sacred site. Even today, the superstitious believe that if you leave a piece of cloth there, you will leave a trouble behind you, but if you touch a cloth put there by another person, you will take their trouble home with you.

Whether it is making contact with nature by touching wood, distancing danger with benign running water, leaving trouble behind in the form of a cloth or, in a time when metal was expensive, nailing it up on display in the hope that foregoing its use might prompt some reciprocal return, these things enabled people to relate to life. The above are but slight, and doubtless warped-with-time, glimmerings of old practices.

Behind these superstitions was a fundamental respect for nature that can still be seen today in what is left of the culture of Native Americans. Alongside this was an inherent culture of enquiry and love of learning that became manifest in art, science and technology. To return to Caesar's descriptions:

> Besides this [reincarnation] they debate many subjects and teach them to their young men – for example, the stars and their movements, the size of the universe and the earth, the nature of things and the strength and power of the immortal gods.[21]

Throughout his life, when not occupied with politics and war, Merlin is almost invariably described as engaged in what we would recognise as science. This spirit of enquiry and predilection for asking awkward questions is naturally human and will out unless some other stifling force overpowers it.

CHAPTER SIX

Merlin and Languoreth

In the account given in Jocelyn's *Life of Kentigern*, 'When the age of discernment approached him' Mungo was taught 'the discipline of letters and, not less . . . the practice of the holy virtues'[1] as part of an education that was entirely gauged to fit him for the work of the Church. These holy virtues were narrowly couched to preclude valuing women and homosexual men as the equals of heterosexual men and to discourage any rational enquiry that might inspire dissent.

When Serf enjoined his students 'to consider the work of the bees', it was not to learn about their ways, '[but] so that in their little bodies they might learn the beautiful discipline of ministry'.[2] Science and rational enquiry were firmly subjected to dogma and the politics of the Church.

The rod was a 'most severe instrument of torture for boys'[3] who found themselves subject to Serf's tutelage, but Mungo was ambitious and so was probably an assiduous student and less likely than most of his fellows to be his teacher's victim. His peers, however, 'hated him, and . . . were not able to speak anything peacefully to him either privately or publicly'.[4]

Some insight into Mungo's character may be gained by reference to his most famous miracle. When he was still a student at Culross, according to Jocelyn, Mungo restored a dead robin to life. Despite 1,500 years during which Mungo's supporters have promulgated a version of history favourable to him and determinedly eradicated all contrary views, evidence remains that throws a different light on this event. The thirteenth-century *Sprouston Breviary* is a Christian source, and so may be allowed added weight as evidence contrary to the interest of the party providing it. The *Breviary* says that Mungo tore off the robin's head and then, frightened to face Serf's anger, put it on again and brought the bird back to life. The bringing back to life element can be dismissed as fiction, but Mungo's killing of the bird provides some insight into the way things might have happened. Torturing animals when young is a sign of a psychopathic nature, and, as Mungo's later life shows, there is ample evidence to corroborate the conclusion that Mungo was a psychopath.

According to Jocelyn, the 'fragrance of [Mungo's] virtues'[5] was lost on the other student monks, who 'derived an odour of death from this life-giving aroma'. That is, Mungo's holiness caused lesser men to envy him. Jocelyn continues:

> And his holy reputation . . . was an incentive for them to sow great hatred against the saint of God. The boy, being wise in the Lord, understood that their malice against him had filled them, and thus it was not possible to cease the long-standing, embedded, and incurable envy in their restless hearts. And he did not think it was safe to be lulled to sleep surrounded by a venomous crowd of serpents, lest perhaps he should feel the loss of inner sweetness.

It does not make sense to suppose that Jocelyn invented a story in which Mungo was unpopular and then went on to offer a clumsy explanation all in order to show Mungo in a favourable light. It is more likely that Mungo was truly unpopular and had to get out and get out fast. He did not wait for good weather and avoided the ferry at Kincardine. Serf came with him to offer his protection:

> . . . And so [Mungo] secretly left that place . . . Heading eagerly on this journey, he reached the Friscan shore, where the river called Mallena, exceeding its channel because of the inflowing tides of the sea, took away all hope of crossing over.

Jocelyn says that Mungo's God divided the river waters to allow him to cross on dry land, but this may safely be disregarded as fiction.

> Then crossing over a little arm of the sea by means of a bridge, which is called by the inhabitants the Pons Servani, he looked back to the bank and saw the waters, which earlier had stood in a heap, flowing back with force and filling the channel of the Mallena – even overflowing the above-mentioned bridge and totally denying passage to anyone trying to cross the river.

Serf left Mungo at the river and went back to Culross, where he died shortly afterwards.

In the late 540s, while Mungo was running away from Culross, Merlin and Languoreth were children living by the banks of the Clyde. The river was the kingdom's main thoroughfare, so they would have had many opportunities to meet travellers who stopped at Cadzow. Tutgual the king was bound to progress about his kingdom maintaining contacts, dispensing justice, obtaining tribute, extending largesse, inspecting the men who were fit to fight and determining their state of readiness, and so must have been a regular visitor to Cadzow, which lay on the border of his kingdom. Perhaps it was Cadzow's strategic location that inspired the idea of a marriage between Languoreth and the king's then second son, Rhydderch. Rhydderch was an almost exact contemporary of Mungo's, and so some dozen years older than Languoreth.

Merlin was the opposite of Mungo, an open-minded, wayward and ill-disciplined scholar whose life displayed a distinct lack of judgement in practical matters; a failing often found in those who are said to be too 'wrapped up in books'. In his later life, he is frequently described as enthralled by innumerable intellectual disciplines: astronomy, botany, meteorology. It is impossible to believe that Merlin and Languoreth were not grounded in these subjects when they were children, and, if this is so, only the Druids could have provided them with such an education. The Romans said that it took 20 years to become a Druid, but this was simply their imposing Roman rigidity upon a fluid process. To a Druid, the idea that one 'qualified' after a fixed period of study lasting 20 years would have been absurd. Anyone who loves learning for its own sake knows it is a lifetime pursuit. Merlin and Languoreth, like all who love knowledge for its own sake, spent the whole of their long lives, more than 70 years, learning about the world.

Despite some rather half-hearted attempts to pretend that Merlin was a Christian, no one believes that he was. The *Vita*, for example, says that, just before he died, Merlin asked Mungo to allow him to confess as a Christian (despite the fact that Mungo had died some six years before Merlin). Nor was Merlin a warrior, although he went to war like all young men at that time – indeed, he chose to fight as part of the resistance to the Angles, even before his home was threatened. Although he may have been an adequate, or even an able, warrior, it was not war that primarily engaged his interest but scholarship and the struggle to preserve a way of life that would allow freedom of thought to survive. Merlin has consequently been remembered not as a warrior, like Arthur, but as a bard. He is described as 'Merlin of Song' in the poem Y *Gododdin*, *c*.600, and later as a wizard and magician, all of which was meant to disguise the fact that Merlin was a Druid.

A love of learning cannot be beaten into a child, because it comes from within; it can, however, be beaten out, or left to wither, if it is not encouraged. Merlin and Languoreth learnt from the multifarious Druids with whom they unavoidably came into contact when they were young. Even the Christian apologist John Macleod, no friend of Druidism – indeed, he refers to it as a cult – says the 'Druids are best remembered for their intellectualism. They were experts in the arts, in mathematics, in astronomy and philosophy. They were authorities in matters of law. Of their occult and religious practices we know virtually nothing.'[6]

As Merlin and Languoreth grew up, they were well placed to learn from these many Druids who, although they all shared a fundamental corpus of knowledge, were all skilled to various degrees in different subjects. They would all have had something to teach interested and intellectually able children such as Merlin and Languoreth. The innate intelligence and energy evident in Merlin's and Languoreth's later lives suggests that, when they were children, they were quick and avid to learn all that the various visitors to Cadzow had to teach them. They would have been excited when a visiting warlord arrived with fighting men behind him, more excited when the men of Cadzow went off to raid or to war and most excited of all when Cadzow was raided or war waged at its gates.

Merlin and Languoreth were scholars. During what were literally his wilderness years, when he was in exile, hiding in the woods, Merlin is described as involved in scientific research. Towards the end of his life, with all hope of personal power gone, he stepped back from public life to carry on with his academic work. The gender-politics of record keepers in the 1,500 years after her death have concentrated on Languoreth's sex life and obliterated all direct evidence to her intellectual interests, although, when Merlin died, she became the leader of the people of the old way, so it may be taken as given that she was a highly educated woman.

Most of the people of Cadzow would have had few, if any, occasions to travel far from home. The most far-travelled men would have been those who went with Morken, as part of his retinue, when he visited the king, or who accompanied him on raids or to war. They would all have had wonderful stories to tell when they returned. Boatmen, traders, peddlers, quack-doctors, itinerant farm hands, landless men of war and the wandering poor would all have had news to impart as they passed through Cadzow, but it was the Druids, who were free to travel from land to land, hall to hall, and who were treated with respect wherever they went, who provided the main medium for the exchange of information and knowledge.

Given the way that Merlin and Languoreth lived their lives, there can be no doubt they were brought up in the old way. In the middle sixth century, Christianity was only taking its first tentative steps in Scotland. Most of the people were content to continue with the beliefs that had been passed down to them over thousands of years. Almost certainly, a wandering priest of the Christian Church would have visited Cadzow and been accepted there. The old way took the same pragmatic view of religion as the Romans and allowed each individual to believe what he or she wanted to believe, provided that belief did not detract from the welfare of the community.

Morken's men were only occasional warriors; most of the time, they were farmers, artisans, merchants and tradesmen working with their wives to bring up their families. There were very few full-time fighting men; they were too expensive. Although Merlin and Languoreth were the children of the chief, their rank was not so high as to exclude them from the whole life of their small community. They would have played in the woods and fields and on river banks with the other children of Cadzow, sat around firesides listening to stories told by adults and pushed to the front of the throng in the hall when the bards performed. They would have watched and listened and asked questions when the Druids effected their cures and gave advice concerning the people's daily activities.

Merlin would have been recognised by the Druids at an early age as someone with potential and so taken and trained. Languoreth's choices were more restricted. Taking up the sword was not a viable option for a woman. A life devoted to learning and teaching was closed to her too, not because of her gender but because she was the daughter of a chief and so a useful pawn to be given in marriage for political advantage. Her father's fiefdom lay on the border of Manau (the Celtic Sparta, where the man who would be Arthur's grandfather ruled). Cadzow also lay between the heartlands of the Strathclyde Britons and the south-east, where the Angles were a gathering danger. Morken's lands and people were strategically vital, so Morken was a man of importance and his daughter a valuable asset.

Tutgual the king had a young son, Rhydderch. Languoreth and Rhydderch were married probably when Languoreth was in her mid-teens, about 556. They had four children: two daughters, Gladys and Angharad, and two sons. Their elder son, whose name is not known, was killed at the Battle of Arderydd when he was 15 years old, the age when Celts, like warriors of the Sioux nation, first went into battle. The younger son, Constantine, was to prove to be a Celtic Caligula. His date of birth is variously given. One source says he was born c.550, with Gladys born c.552 and Angharad c.554. Another says he was born c.570. If Languoreth was betrothed or married when she was 16 (girls were married young in the sixth century) and her first son was born, say, c.558, with Constantine following about 560, Gladys about 562 and Angharad about 564, the various children would be the right age to play the parts attributed to them in the events that occurred later in their lives.

Merlin and Mungo were opposites. Merlin was always trying to understand something. Mungo never evinced doubt about anything. Merlin learnt how to think and enjoyed questions he could not answer. Mungo learnt what to think and specialised in answers that could not be questioned. Merlin and Mungo were to fight for 50 years.

CHAPTER SEVEN

The Magi and the Bards

The Merlin presented for popular consumption is a safe, familiar, fictional wizard. The historical Merlin, a Druid who represented a way of life different to that proffered by those in power, was too dangerous to be allowed to survive either in life or in history. Once this is recognised, what passes for the history concerning him in the Western world in the last 1,500 years makes more sense.

The Druids were not the illiterates of common supposition. The Romans found them able to read Greek when they invaded Ynys Mon, the sacred isle of the Druids, and they were to go on, even after they were suppressed, to be a vital part of a tradition that inspired scientific and social inquiry in the next thousand years, despite the anti-intellectual shadow that hung over Western Europe between the end of the Roman Empire and the Renaissance.

Of hundreds of god and goddess figures that have been found at Celtic sites, most appear to be local deities, which is what one would expect in a decentralised, individualistic religion.[1] Some were family deities, because there was an active element of ancestor veneration in the ways of some of the oldest Celts. There were, of course, also the more powerful gods, such as Cernunnos, who was thought of in the form of a man with a stag's horns. On the first-century BCE Gundestrup cauldron, found in Denmark, there is a wonderful image of a godlike figure, perhaps Cernunnos, holding men by the ankles, dipping them into a cauldron of life and restoring them to our world. The horned one remained a powerful positive symbol for centuries until given negative characteristics and presented as the Devil in the Christian belief system. We cannot be sure of the place, if any, that Cernunnos had in central Scotland in the late sixth century, although he has been equated with the Dagda, the Good God of the ancient Irish.[2]

The Celts' Dagda, Morrigan, his consort, and their daughter, Bridgit, are the triptych equivalent of the Egyptians' Osiris, Isis and Horus, and the Christians' Jehovah, Mary and Jesus of Nazareth.

The people of the old way believed that the soul was immortal and that when a person died, his or her soul travelled to an Otherworld, which was either underground or an island in the sea and, apparently, a pleasant place. It was called, among other names, Tir-na-nog, Land of the Young. One refinement of this theory contained an element of continuity and had a soul come back to this world at the same time as a soul from this world travelled to the Otherworld. We learn the following from Julius Caesar:

> A lesson which they take particular pains to inculcate is that the soul does not perish, but after death passes from one body to another; they think this is the best incentive to bravery, because it teaches men to disregard the terrors of death.[3]

The Celts believed that once a year on the feast of *Samhain*, when 31 October becomes 1 November, this world and the Otherworld overlap and the inhabitants of each can visit the other. Christians, unable to eradicate such beliefs, and in accordance with their policy of adopting ideas of the old way, adopted *Samhain*. The first of

November became All Hallows Day and the night before Hallowe'en, when, as in Burns's poem 'Tam O'Shanter', the dead rise up.

The Celts had no single, fixed belief system. Like the ancient Egyptians, they brought together a number of creation stories and religious systems to make one big mishmash of a religion. Existing parallel to the idea of gods such as Cernunnos were fundamental objects of worship, the most important of which was, of course, the sun. Sun wheels and swastikas are common Celtic symbols that hark back to the Indian roots of their philosophy.

Affection for the nurturing power of the environment and a deep love of truth that echoes the ideas of Zoroaster permeates early Celtic literature.[4] Respect for truth (which can be conflated with worthiness and honour) infuses the oldest Celtic texts, even though they have been under the censorious eye of the Church for a millennium and more. The *Vedas* of ancient India, which hold that it is by means of truth that the Earth endures, have been connected to ancient Irish writings such as the *Will of the Brehon* in *Leabhar Laignech* (*Book of Leinster*).

Once gods, rituals and 'spiritual authorities' are stripped away, a love of life and truth is predominant in what remains: that is, in human nature. Even today, in Ireland, a bastion of the Christian Church, people say when a person dies that he or she is in the place of truth.[5]

The staunch individualism of the Druids threatened the authority of Rome. The first emperor, Augustus, forbade Romans from taking part in ceremonies under the aegis of Druids. His successors, Tiberius and Claudius, passed measures to suppress them. Steps were taken to annihilate them entirely in 60 CE when the sacred isle of Ynys Mon, modern Anglesey, was razed and the resident Druids exterminated. By the end of the first century CE, the Druids were a broken force on the continental mainland and in the south of Britain. It was only in Ireland and Scotland, lands the Romans did not subjugate, that the old way remained strong enough to play a prominent part in affairs.

When the Romans' race was run in the West and they laid down the baton they had used to beat the Druids, the Roman Christians picked it up. The predominantly Celtic, Pelagian and Arian Christians in the western lands of Ireland and Scotland rubbed along relatively well with the people of the old way.

I have called the Christians who favoured Mungo the Mungo Christians to distinguish them from the other Christian sects that were active at the time. After Mungo went to Rome for the last time and came back a Roman Christian, I use the term Roman Christian.

From the sixth century, the old way was increasingly suppressed by the temporal powers at the behest of the Christians and submerged by the propaganda promulgated by the Christians after they took control of the media.

In Nennius's *Historia Brittonum*, he tells of the excommunication of Vortigern the king by the Christian Germanus and of how Vortigern called 12 Druids to help him. In the story of 'Darthool and the Sons of Usna',[6] told in the *Ulster Cycle*, we hear of Cathbad, who is identified as a Druid, being accompanied by a large number of students. However, Jocelyn barely mentions people of the old way. When he does, they are not identified as such but as 'certain men'. This is further testimony to how the old way was steadily 'airbrushed' out of history with a dedication and efficiency that would have left Stalin open-mouthed in amazement.

After the Druids were crushed as an overt political force in Scotland *c.*600 CE, they ceased to exist as a widely based intellectual class of learned men and women. Their public roles as judges, arbiters, and counsellors to kings and chiefs were taken by the

Christian clergy and their ceremonies driven underground, as they were necessarily conducted away from the eyes of the authorities. All they were left with was the part of poet and singer, a part later played by the troubadours.[7] Apparently, the clergy did not see themselves as entertainers.

As oppression became more prevalent, some Druids turned to whatever had been their special skill to enable them to find a place in ordinary life, and some would have ended up as the seventh-century equivalents of veterinary consultants, agricultural advisers, doctors, midwives, accountants, lawyers and teachers, although they would have had to watch how they conducted themselves lest they were accused of black magic or heresy. In succeeding centuries, most practitioners of the above professions managed to bring themselves under the wing of the Church. The exception, of course, was midwifery, because this tended to be the preserve of women, and there was no place for women in the prevailing professional or academic scheme that developed under the Church's wing. T.C. Smout tells us that in Scotland between 1560 and 1707, 'considerably more than 3,000 people, and perhaps as many as 4,500, perished horribly because their contemporaries thought they were witches'.[8] The great majority of these were poor women who were simply helping other women.

In 575, leaders of Dalriada in Ireland met the leaders of their offshoot kingdom of Dalriada in Scotland[9] at Drumceatt, near Newtonlimavady, in the north-west of Ireland. Also present at this Council of Drumceatt were abbots and other clergy from both sides of the sea, including Columba, who came in the train of Aedan, king of the Scots of Scotland. According to the historian W.F. Skene in *Celtic Scotland*, written in the late nineteenth century, they met in council for fourteen months and decided two important matters:

> The first related to the bards of Ireland. They were a
> powerful order, and presuming on their high office, they
> had been guilty of some arrogant acts which had kindled
> the popular wrath against them; and at this moment a
> decree of expulsion hung over their heads.[10]

The second was the relationship between Irish Dalriada and Scottish Dalriada. The independence of the Scottish-Scots was recognised by their Irish-Scots cousins, and the two branches became allies.

It is impossible to believe that this great gathering, concerned as it was with the status of kingdoms, gave priority to the subjugation of singers and poets, no matter how arrogant they may have been. If read in context while bearing in mind how these events were reported, it can be seen that the council dealt with the internal affairs of the kingdoms when they circumscribed the power of the Druids, and the external affairs of the kingdoms when they agreed to the independence of the Scots of Scotland.

The conventional wisdom has the bards causing the community to turn against them by their overweening arrogance, leading to the threat of their expulsion from the kingdom. In reality, although the once-great power of the Druids was waning, they were still popular among the people. It was the aristocracy who had turned against the Druids. They wanted to limit the power of the leaders of the old way to curry favour with the Church.

Propaganda purposes dictated that, over the centuries, reports of proceedings were censored to dilute any connection with the Druids, with the result that the records read as if the Council of Drumceatt was concerned with the excesses of entertainers. The decision at Drumceatt makes sense only if for bards we read Druids. The bards had remained important – it could hardly be otherwise in a 'heroic' society that loved music and stories, poems and songs – but when they were shorn of political influence they were all but neutered.

Some Druids doubtless 'sold out' and became Christians (such is human nature), but others who believed what the Druids believed and who found these beliefs naturally congenial continued as before, although bound to act as if they were Christians. Eventually, the position of Druid ceased to exist for all practical purposes, and all that was left was a vague communal memory and a few superstitions that were allowed to subsist because they were adopted into the Christian milieu. Mistletoe at Christmas is but one example.

By the late seventh century, Roman Christians felt sufficiently secure to turn on the Celtic Church. As Bede of Jarrow tells us in his *Ecclesiastical History of the English People*, a great council was held at Whitby, in the north-east of England: 'And when discussion arose on the questions of Easter, the tonsure, and various other church matters, it was decided to hold a synod to put an end to this dispute at the monastery of Streanaeshalch [Whitby] . . .'[11]

The date of Easter was a problem because the Celtic Church calculated it differently from the Roman Christians. Bede continues, quoting the Roman case:

> The only people who stupidly contend against the whole world are those Irish-men [Scots] and their partners in obstinacy the Picts and Britons, who inhabit only a portion of the uttermost islands of the ocean . . . But you . . . are most certainly guilty of sin if you reject the decrees of the Apostolic See . . . for, although your fathers were holy men, do you imagine that they, a few men in a corner of a remote island, are to be preferred before the universal Church of Christ throughout the world?"[12]

The Roman way was chosen.

The Druids would have been puzzled by any interest in any date that did not relate to some event in nature, such as the summer equinox. For them, if a date did not have some practical point, it had no point. The date of Easter had no practical point. On the contrary, it was calculated by a convoluted formula that meant it bobbed about the calendar.

The other big issue, we are asked to believe, concerned hairstyles. The form of tonsure favoured by the Celtic Church differed from that of the Roman Church. This was an issue partly because uniformity in the Church was seen to be vital. The very fact that the synod was held in Anglo-Saxon England suggests the Christians there were more politically powerful than their fellow Celtic Christians of Scotland. Again, there was no prospect but that the Roman form would be chosen; individuality was not favoured by the Church.

I believe there was another, more important, issue bound up in the tonsure question. The Celtic Christians preferred to shave the front half of the head in the style of the Druids. Columba and his people adopted the Druids' form of tonsure to mark them out as wise men. The Romans preferred to shave the crown of the head – the style made famous by Friar Tuck in Robin Hood films. When the Druids were forced out of mainstream life, it must have become dangerous for them to be readily identified as such. It is reasonable to suppose they stopped signalling that they were Druids and left the Celtic form of tonsure to the Celtic Christians. No one in the sixth and seventh centuries would have been unaware of its provenance. It was therefore even more important to eradicate it.

Even the *Catholic Encyclopaedia* recognises the origins of the Celtic tonsure in the history of the Druids, although it cannot bring itself to say so directly and couches the matter cagily when it says there is no real evidence for this (while, at the same time, providing ample evidence to the contrary):

> The Britons were accustomed to shave the whole head in front of a line drawn from ear to ear, instead of using the coronal tonsure of the Romans. This, though there is no real evidence that it was the practice of the Druids, was nicknamed tonsura magorum. (Magus was accepted as equivalent to Druid, and to this day the Magoi[13] of Matthew 2 are Druidhean in the Scottish Gaelic Bible.) Later, the Roman party jeered at it as the tonsura Simonis Magi,[14] in contradistinction to their 'tonsure of St Peter'.[15]

While enforcing uniformity was important for the purposes of the Church, enforcing a common hairstyle was not what primarily exercised the parties at Whitby; obliterating vestiges of the old way was the vital matter. I cannot believe that of all the things discussed on this grand occasion, the date of Easter and the shape of a bald patch were the most important. I suspect that many matters relevant to the old way and the extent to which the Celtic Church had absorbed its philosophy were discussed, and that these were bundled together under the catch-all heading of the tonsure question.

The Celtic cross is a standard Christian cross with a circle centred at the point where the vertical and horizontal axes meet, the vertical beam of the cross carrying on down below it. There is no universally accepted history of the Celtic-cross symbol. There are, however, many theories to explain its origin. Modern Roman Catholic Christians might say that the circle symbolises a halo or the endless love of God, which does not explain why this cross is found only in Celtic lands and not in, say, Lorraine, France (where they have their own non-standard cross).

It has been suggested that the Celtic cross was created when a standard cross was carved over standing stones that had phallic shapes on them. This idea is hardly likely to be correct. I cannot see that Christians would have adopted as their logo an amalgam of a standard cross and a penis.

The simplest solution is also the one that most closely fits the evidence. The Christians usurped time-honoured places, practices and symbols to wean people away from the old way; indeed, they were enjoined to do so by no less a figure than Pope Gregory the Great. Glasgow's sacred hill became a graveyard. The winter equinox became Christmas. Mistletoe, famously connected with the Druids by Pliny the Elder, became part of the symbolism of the Christian Christmas, although, it seems to me, it never quite fits in – it has no inherent part in the Christmas story, and people are allowed to kiss under it. Mistletoe, the old way, sex: how much clearer can it be that mistletoe is a remnant of the old way and not a true part of the Christian Christmas ritual? It is possible then, and in my opinion probable, that the early Celtic Christians adopted a symbol of the old way and made it their own when they added it to their standard cross. One legend has the British Christian Patrick, later canonised, shown a stone marked with a circle representing the moon and overlaying it with his Christian cross, the inference being that he wished to absorb old-way symbols into his new religion. This, I believe, is the most likely explanation: that the Celtic cross was adapted from an earlier old-way moon or sun symbol.

The Druids revered nature. The most obvious and most fundamental power in nature is the sun. The year was broken up into four parts: *Samhain*, the first of November; *Imbolc*, the first of February; *Beltane*, the first of May, and *Lugnasadh*, the first of August. All four involved reverence of the sun, but *Lugnasadh* was a particular sun festival sacred to the solar god Lugh. The circle is an obvious solar symbol and has been in use as such since time immemorial in many places – perhaps most famously by the Pharaoh Akhenaten when he broke away from the polytheistic, priest-ridden religious centres of Luxor and Memphis and set up a relatively simple religion in which the Aten, the solar disc of the sun, was given precedence. It is thought that as far back as the building of Stonehenge, people in Britain revered the sun. The modern Celtic cross is, in my view at least, an amalgam of an old-way sun symbol and the standard Christian Cross. It may be, given that the moon was often represented by a circle and the sun by a circle with a cross through it, that the whole symbol belongs to the old way and was adopted in its entirety by the Christians.

Symbols, old-way suns and Christian deities are but accretions. The real matter is how people see themselves and how they relate to other people. It has been said that it is impossible, without access to the writings of the Druids, to piece together the old way. However, if the old way was based on nature, in particular, on human nature, we have the same raw materials available to us as the people of the old way. By deleting, or treating as optional extras, distracting symbols, rituals and divisive personality cults, we come back to what we have in common. The answer to the fundamental question of why are we here is simply this: we are here for each other.

CHAPTER EIGHT

Angle Land

As I have argued, a mercenary army under the Angle war chief Ida landed on the east coast of Scotland, near the present border with England, when Merlin and Languoreth were four years old. In the words of Gildas: 'A multitude of whelps came forth . . . in three cyuls, as they call them, that is, in three ships of war, with their sails wafted by the wind and with omens and prophecies favourable . . .'[1] The Angles had been in contact with the Gododdin since the departure of the Romans more than a century before and had fought on their behalf for most of that time, so they knew how militarily feeble the British leaders were. Ostensibly, Ida came to reinforce the Angles whom the Gododdin had employed to protect them from the depredations of the Scots and Picts, but his secret intention was to stage a coup and usurp the power of the Gododdin king.

Ida was the son of Eopa son of Eosa and the latest in a family of Angle warriors who had been coming to Britain since, at least, the turn of the century. They were allowed the island of Thanet, Lindisfarne, as their base. (Nennius's reference to the Isle of Thanet is not to the one-time island in Kent but to Lindisfarne.[2]) Ida had no doubt been brought up on disparaging stories of the faint martial capacity of the Britons, and, as Angle strength increased, he became more ambitious and less cautious than his father and grandfather.

Vortigern had not foreseen the dangers inherent in using substantial numbers of able and well-armed mercenaries for protection, or, if he had, he had not taken steps to prevent his supposed protectors turning on him. It is testament to the disdain in which Ida held the Gododdin leaders that, with a relatively few men, he thought he could stage a successful coup. All he needed was a pretext to unite the various Angle bands. We can see from Gildas that this appeared in 547, when a dispute arose over pay:

> The barbarians being thus introduced as soldiers into the island, to encounter, as they falsely said, any dangers in defence of their hospitable entertainers, obtain an allowance of provisions, which, for some time being plentifully bestowed, stopped their doggish mouths. Yet, they complain that their monthly supplies are not furnished in sufficient abundance, and they industriously aggravate each occasion of quarrel, saying that unless more liberality is shown them, they will break the treaty and plunder the whole island. In a short time, they follow up their threats with deeds.[3]

Ida fostered discontent and, when this erupted into an open dispute, set himself up as the Angle leader. By the time negotiations broke down (probably because Ida had no intention of reaching an amicable solution), Ida was firmly in charge and able to rise against the ineffectual Vortigern. The king made no more than a gesture in his own defence, and the power of the traditional lords quickly collapsed, although, according to Nennius, Vortimer (another nickname, roughly meaning Big Strong One), one of Vortigern's sons, fought back bravely and was killed.[4] Resistance was quickly and comprehensively put down and Vortigern brought to collaborate with the usurpers. Nennius continues:

> After this, the barbarians became firmly incorporated, and were assisted by foreign pagans; for Vortigern was their friend, on account of the daughter of Hengist [an Angle chief], whom he so much loved . . . in the meantime they [the Angles] soothed the imprudent king, and whilst practising every appearance of fondness, were plotting with his enemies. And let him that reads understand, that the [Angles] were victorious, and ruled Britain, not from their superior prowess, but on account of the great sins of the Britons: God so permitting it.[5]

It is unlikely that the king was truly taken with one individual woman. In the sixth century, just like today, 'romance sold' and accounts written or told of famous people strained to introduce some 'love interest'. Given all we know of this Vortigern, we may take it that he was addicted to pleasure and that 'wine, women and song' were among the 'great sins' Gildas attributes to him.

Vortigern's position deteriorated rapidly as Ida became more confident of his hold on the kingdom. Vortigern knew that he would soon become an embarrassment and expendable, so he gathered his advisers about him and asked them what he should do. The advice they gave sprang from their craven natures and was just what Vortigern wanted to hear:

> 'Retire to the remote boundaries of your kingdom; there build and fortify a city to defend yourself, for the people you have received are treacherous; they are seeking to subdue you by stratagem, and, even during your life, to seize upon all the countries subject to your power, how much more will they attempt, after your death!' The king, pleased with this advice, departed with his wise men, and travelled through many parts of his territories, in search of a place

> convenient for the purpose of building a citadel . . . [until]
> they discovered, on the summit of one of them, a situation,
> adapted to the construction of a citadel.[6]

Vortigern and the traditional British leaders took to the hills, built a fortress and hid behind its walls. Ida's ruthless deceit coupled with Vortigern's selfish gullibility had one inevitable conclusion, as described here by Bede: 'In the year 547, Ida began to reign; he was the founder of the royal family of the Northumbrians, and he reigned twelve years.'[7]

Ida renamed the Gododdin capital of Dun Guardyi (the Joyous or Dolorous Guard of the medieval stories) Bebbanburgh (Bamburgh) after his wife Bebba and built a capital fortress there. The *Anglo-Saxon Chronicle*, under the year 547, says this 'was first surrounded with a hedge, and afterwards with a wall'. Ida then turned to deal with what little British resistance there was in the hinterland. His army burst from its base on the coast and rampaged along the line of the modern Scotland–England border. As Gildas so eloquently put it:

> For the fire of vengeance, justly kindled by former crimes,
> spread from sea to sea, fed by the hands of our foes in the
> east, and did not cease, until, destroying the neighbouring
> towns and lands, it reached the other side of the island,
> and dipped its red and savage tongue in the western
> ocean.[8]

This expedition was meant to be no more than a raid in force, but when the British opposition the Angles had anticipated failed to appear, their momentum carried them on to the sea. They did not have enough men to hold the land they had taken, so they soon withdrew.

Gildas was born in 544, the year Ida landed. (The conventional wisdom has him born at least a generation earlier.) He was a young child, living in Cambuslang, south-east of Glasgow, when the Angle threat first became real. The vehemence with which he wrote about this terrible time can be explained by the frightening reports he must have heard of Angle incursions:

> So that all the columns were levelled with the ground by the frequent strokes of the battering-ram, all the husbandmen routed, together with their bishops, priests, and people, whilst the sword gleamed, and the flames crackled around them on every side. Lamentable to behold, in the midst of the streets lay the tops of lofty towers, tumbled to the ground, stones of high walls, holy altars, fragments of human bodies, covered with livid clots of coagulated blood, looking as if they had been squeezed together in a press; and with no chance of being buried, save in the ruins of the houses, or in the ravening bellies of wild beasts and birds . . .[9]

In these events, the beginning of the break-up of the power of the British establishment in the south can be seen. In the next two decades, the authority of the traditional leaders of the Britons dissolved and with it the influence of the Christian Church in the south of Scotland. These changes gave rise to the conditions that spawned the Arderydd campaign in the 570s, in which Merlin was all but destroyed, and laid the foundation for the massive Angle War in which Arthur made his name in the 580s.

Gildas describes how the Britons who could not find shelter in Vortigern's fortresses were hunted down and killed. Others saw no alternative but to surrender, while still others became refugees in foreign lands:

> Some, therefore, of the miserable remnant, being taken in the mountains, were murdered in great numbers; others, constrained by famine, came and yielded themselves to be slaves for ever to their foes, running the risk of being

> instantly slain, which truly was the greatest favour that
> could be offered them: some others passed beyond the
> seas with loud lamentations . . .[10]

Some of these refugees doubtless brought their tales of woe to Cadzow, where they would have fascinated the young Merlin and Languoreth, and to Cambuslang, where they would have had a telling effect on a Gildas who was not yet ten years old. It would have been in the interests of these escapees to exaggerate the power and violence of the Angles and to suggest they would attack the Britons of Strathclyde next, unless, of course, an army from Strathclyde came to their aid and fought to re-establish them in their old lands.

Gildas says that not every Briton of the southern Gododdin hid or surrendered or fled. Some took to the hills and waged guerrilla war: '. . . committing the safeguard of their lives, which were in continual jeopardy, to the mountains, precipices, thickly wooded forests, and to the rocks of the seas (albeit with trembling hearts), remained still in their country'.[11]

There they languished in wild places and waited and hoped for someone to lead them as they deserved. The traditional leaders remained behind their fortress walls, so we can only suppose that captains arose from among the people and that it was they who fought a guerrilla rearguard action until the Angles reached the western sea.

When the Angle tide ebbed, the poor remnants of the British emerged from their hiding places. In Scotland in the 1290s, when the king and the nobles failed their people, William Wallace, a man of no great social standing, 'raised his head' and led the resistance to English rule. In the 550s, another man of lowly rank but real nobility, by the name of Emrys, became his people's captain of captains. Emrys had made his name resisting the Angle advance.

He was to become the first of the Pen Dragons.

Gildas used the name Ambrosius Aurelianus for Emrys. Nennius uses the name Ambrose, but then goes on to say that, originally, in British, he was called Embresguletic (Emrys Guletic), that is, Emrys the War Lord.

> [They] took arms under the conduct of Ambrosius Aurelianus, a modest man, who of the entire Roman nation was then alone in the confusion of this troubled period by chance left alive. His parents, who for their merit were adorned with the purple, had been slain in these same broils, and now his progeny in these our days, although shamefully degenerated from the worthiness of their ancestors, provoke to battle their cruel conquerors, and by the goodness of our Lord obtain the victory.[12]

When Gildas says that Emrys was a 'modest man', he does not mean he was a humble, unassuming chap. Modest, in this context, means Emrys gave the appearance of an ordinary man of humble origins (which is exactly what he was). Emrys was a simple captain, at best a sub-chief, not one of the 'nobility'. The establishment was stuck with a popular hero who was not of their number.

When the monarchy was restored after Emrys's death, it would not have done to have had it put about that the hero who defeated the Angles was not a man of rank. The stories told about Emrys could not be obliterated, so men such as Gildas tried to disguise the fact that Emrys was a man of relatively humble birth who had risen to high command on merit. For a time, 1,500 years, this worked. Now, when he is considered in his true historical context, it is possible to see who Emrys really was and what happened when he raised his head.

Gildas could have simply said that Emrys was a man of high rank, but genealogy was important to sixth-century Celts; every one of them would have been able to recite a list of his or her ascendants going back many generations, and certainly as far back as grandparents. If Gildas had tried to slip Emrys into some real-life family tree, especially a royal family tree, his attempted deceit would have been noticed immediately. Thinking outside the box, Gildas made Emrys a man of noble Roman stock, the son of an imperial family, no less, and gave him a fancy Latin name. No one could argue with such a rootless story.

The idea that Emrys was the son of a Roman emperor or consul, though, is an obviously anachronistic fiction. The empire had disappeared as a force in Britain generations before Emrys was born, but Gildas's tactic nevertheless proved successful, aided by the fact that Emrys's true descendants were not in the high ranks of society and so their voices could be ignored. Gildas explained the absence of contemporary family members by claiming that 'of all the Roman nation . . . [Emrys was] by chance left alive'.[13] Emrys's descendants' lack of social standing also had to be explained. Gildas said that they had gone downhill since Emrys died. How likely is that? If Emrys was of some special Roman blood, and if this explained his rise to fame and glory, how likely is it that one or two generations later his descendants were so obviously not 'top drawer'? It is much more likely, going by modern experience, that his descendants would have battened on Emrys's celebrity and gained some social advantage from his success.

Emrys, then, was a man of relatively humble origins who rose on merit to the rank of warlord. The Latin name attributed to him, Ambrosius Aurelianus, is an invention used to provide an aristocratic façade behind which his 'lowly' rank could be hidden.

In the historical part of De Excidio, Gildas mentions three Roman emperors, three Christian saints, two kings, one Roman general and one world-famous theologian. With the exception of Vortigern the king, Emrys was the only contemporary that Gildas wrote about. Indeed, immediately after the above passage, Gildas writes of Arthur's most famous battle, the Battle of Badon, without ever mentioning Arthur, although he must have known his name and the part he played. Why, then, of all the figures he could have mentioned, does Gildas make Emrys his hero? I suspect it was because this is what Emrys was: Gildas's hero (this is one of the few likeable things about Gildas).

If I am right, Gildas was born in 544 and lived in Cambuslang. He would therefore have grown up in fear of the Angles who were waging war not far south of his home in the 550s. He would have been alarmed and humiliated when his fellow Britons were defeated by the Angles and relieved and proud when Emrys obtained his victory. If I am right, the battles in which Emrys's descendants won the victory that Gildas describes above were those fought in Arthur's war against the Angles in the 580s, a war which culminated with the Battle of Badon in 588.

The name, or rather title, Pen Dragon and the man or men to whom it was attached have puzzled scholars for centuries. The general consensus is that it means not a dragon's head but head dragon, in the sense of chief dragon. (*Pen* is the P Gaelic equivalent of the Q Gaelic *Ceann*, meaning head in the sense of leader.) As for those who were called Pen Dragon, the theories range from him being just one man, Uther Pendragon (who is often supposed to have been Arthur's father) to the name applying to a line of Pendragons running from the first century to the seventh century CE.[14]

It is my belief that Emrys was the first Pen Dragon. He was not a king or even a member of the royal family, so, because he had no significant rank, he took a title that reflected his status as a leader and which sounded loud in the stories of the people he led.

Many of these people were descended from Sarmatian auxiliaries who were stationed on Hadrian's Wall in the last centuries of the Roman Empire, and they were proud of this association. The Sarmatians famously rode into battle under dragon standards, long, wind-tunnel-like constructions that in a charge made a frightening noise. These Sarmatians were the dragon soldiers of the stories that every Gododdin child would have grown up with. When they needed a title for a leader who was not a king or a man of high social rank, then, they chose a title that was significant to them, a title that meant, almost literally, leader of the dragon soldiers: Pen Dragon.

Nennius tells of Emrys in a story that Geoffrey later stole and used with Merlin as the hero. (Geoffrey claimed that Merlin was also called Ambrosius.) According to Nennius, Vortigern tried to build a citadel in which to hide but its construction was thwarted because tools and materials disappeared every night. When Vortigern asked his wise men what he should do, they told him to find a child born without a father, put him to death and sprinkle his blood on the foundations of the citadel.[15] The king's men found a likely boy playing ball. When they questioned his mother about her son's paternity, she replied, 'In what manner he was conceived, I know not, for I have never had intercourse with any man.' The officers believed this and took the boy back to the king. When the boy heard that he was to be put to death and his blood sprinkled on the foundations of the king's fortress to stop tools and materials disappearing, he was understandably displeased. He had the king bring forward the wise men who had suggested this solution and, in their presence, identified the real problem. He said that below the site of the fortress there was a pool in which were two vases in which were two tents in which were two serpents, one red and one white:

> The pool is the emblem of this world, and the tent that
> of your kingdom: the two serpents are two dragons; the
> red serpent is your dragon, but the white serpent is the
> dragon of the [Angles] . . . however, our people shall rise
> and drive [them] away . . .[16]

When the king asked, 'What is your origin?' the boy answered,
'A Roman consul was my father.' Of course, if Emrys was the son
of an emperor – indeed, the son of anyone – he could not, by
definition, be a boy without a father, unless this was not meant
to be read literally, at least by the more educated in society. When
Nennius says this, he does not mean that Emrys was an orphan, a
posthumous birth or a birth out of wedlock. It is also unlikely that
he meant a child born of a virgin (an option considered by Jocelyn
when writing about *Kentigern* but dismissed as too dangerous)
or any other supernatural propagation. Far less does it suggest
some conception involving some oversight or forgetfulness on
his mother's part. The phrase 'a boy without a father' connotes a
boy without an aristocratic father, a boy who did not come from a
family of note, a boy who was, in effect, the son of a 'nobody'.

There is no academic consensus concerning Ambrosius
Aurelianus's place in history. It has even been suggested that
there were two Emryses, just as it has been suggested there were
two Merlins, and for the same reason: the written evidence does
not fit with the historical context. Almost invariably, Emrys is
placed in the south of Britain, in the fifth century, and presented
as an aristocratic Christian. He has even been confused with and
supposed to be Arthur.[17] He was none of these things.

Gildas and Nennius both describe a catastrophic time for
the Britons that produced the hero Emrys. Gildas deals with
Vortigern, then Ambrosius Aurelianus (Emrys), then the Battle
of Badon (Arthur). Nennius deals with Vortigern, then Ambrose,
which, Nennius says, is in British Emrys, then Arthur. Clearly,

Emrys flourished after Vortigern and before Arthur. Vortigern was deposed in 547. Arthur's first prominent part in history was in 573. By my reckoning, Emrys was active between the late 540s and the late 550s or early 560s, when he was assassinated. He was not a man of the fifth but of the mid-sixth century.

The building that would not stand and which required blood to save it symbolises an organisational structure or establishment, not a literal building. Today, we would call it the state. (The same story is told in relation to Columba on Iona, except on that occasion it was a church that kept falling down.) When looked at in context, again, this story makes sense. The established order was rotten. It wavered and toppled when the Angles pushed Vortigern from his throne. Vortigern fled and unsuccessfully tried to rebuild his power, but he was a weak coward and instead the people rose under Emrys's leadership. It was the blood of the people, symbolised by Emrys's blood in the story, that provided the base upon which British power was re-established.

For political and commercial reasons, writers such as Gildas were unable to say what happened in reality, even if they had been minded to, so they couched history in a fanciful fable. Later writers such as Nennius followed their sources without realising the truth behind what they were writing.

As it is, the story contains many inaccuracies, inserted by later propagandists, and much of it is nonsense, but lying between the lines is evidence that makes clear what happened in reality. Emrys did not tell the king how to build a citadel; he told him how to rebuild his kingdom, and when the king proved unwilling to take the necessary steps, Emrys replaced him at the head of a people's army. Also, Emrys was no boy at this time; he was one of a number of hardened British guerrilla leaders.

Several locations for the fortress in which Vortigern hid have been suggested, including Gwent, Carmarthen and Snowdon in Wales, and Radnorshire in England. None of these suggestions has any substantial evidential foundation. Nennius has Vortigern's fortress to the west of the present Scotland–England border:

> Then the king [Vortigern] assigned him [Emrys] that city, with all the western Provinces of Britain; and departing with his wise men to the sinistral district, he arrived in the region named Gueneri, where he built a city which, according to his name, was called Cair Guorthegirn [Caer Vortigern].[18]

That is, Vortigern left Emrys to fight the Angles west of the Angle bridgehead on the east coast (somewhere along the present Scottish–English border) and fled further west (to the 'sinistral' district), where he built a fortress. A footnote to the above passage says, 'An ancient scholiast adds, "He [Vortigern] then built [his fortress] near Lugubalia . . ." Some difference of opinion exists among antiquaries respecting the site of Vortigern's castle or city . . .'

According to the conventional wisdom, *Lugubalia*, the city of light, is Carlisle.[19] This would explain the Angle crossing of Britain from Bernicia, their kingdom on the east coast, to the Solway in the west (c.550–2). This also makes sense when read with Geoffrey, who says that Vortigern 'fled in his search for a safe refuge' to 'Kambria' – Cumbria? Nennius is more specific. He says that the fortress was called Cair Guorthegirn. Vortigern's fortress was taken by Gwenddolau, Emrys's successor, and subsequently called Caer Gwenddolau. Vortigern's fortress was about nine miles north of Carlisle. The famous Battle of Arderydd, in which Gwenddolau died and after which Merlin was said to have gone mad, was fought in the shadow of its walls in 573. In my opinion, the king hid out not in Carlisle itself, the city of light, but at a nearby fortress, later called Caer Gwenddolau.

When Vortigern became a puppet king and then a fugitive hiding in the hills, his people were left without effective leadership. The king had failed the people and forfeited his right to rule. When the Angles marched west to the sea, there was no organised opposition, only various guerrilla bands of resistance fighters who subsequently coalesced about Emrys. When the Angle tide ebbed, Emrys turned on Vortigern but was no more successful than the Angles in breaking down the king's fortress walls, and so he burned them down. As Geoffrey describes it in his *Historia Regum Brittaniae*, 'When everything else had failed, they tried fire; and this, once it took hold, went on blazing until it burned up the tower and Vortigern with it.'[20]

The Angles saw the British fighting among themselves, and when Emrys killed Vortigern they thought the British had rendered themselves leaderless. The opposite was true. With a view to seizing what they saw as an opportunity, the Angles marshalled to meet Emrys and his Britons under the warlord Hengist. Hengist failed to appreciate that he was no longer up against a king but a man of the people: 'What is more, he expressed the lowest possible opinion of the island Britons, seeing that he had defeated them so often in battle.'[21] This was a mistake.

The Angles laid a trap for Emrys, but he discovered it and by a bold advance escaped. He then turned on the Angles, and 'the two lines of battle joined combat, matching each other's blows and shedding a great amount of blood.'[22] The Angles were driven back to their fortresses with Emrys in pursuit. Realising they could not win on the defensive, the Angles came out to face him: 'Wherever one looked, there was blood flowing, and the screams of the dying roused to fury those who were still alive.'[23]

The battle was about to turn in favour of the Angles when Emrys threw in his cavalry reserve. The enemy broke, and when Emrys pressed them they were unable to reform. Hengist, the Angle general, was captured and his men routed. In the aftermath of this battle, Emrys became, by right of arms, not just war leader but, according to Nennius, 'a great king among the kings of Britain'.[24] This is standard-issue hyperbole. Emrys was simply, as was Wallace 750 years later, guardian of the people.

According to Geoffrey's *Historia*, Emrys used his power to re-establish order and the rule of law. With this end in view, he restored some of the deserter lords to their erstwhile lands. His alternative was to fight at the head of one part of a divided people while always looking over his shoulder to see if the other part would stab him in the back:

> Emrys reformed the constitution, restored civil law, brought back the families of the exiles and gave them back their family lands; where heirs had been lost in the recent war, he gave the lands they left to his soldiers and so restored the nation.[25]

Emrys restored to Pascent, son of Vortigern, the lands of Builth and Guorthegirnaim. Geoffrey says these lands were 'near Scotland'. In the sixth century, there was no Scotland, only the land of the Scots, Irish Dalriada and Scottish Dalriada (Argyll). In Geoffrey's day, Scotland approximated to modern Scotland, although the border area about the Liddel was disputed ground, part of what were called 'The Debatable Lands'. The modern border is the Liddel Water that runs along the northern side of Gwenddolau's fort. It would be impossible for any place to be nearer Scotland.

According to Nennius, the almost legendary Firbolg were driven from Ireland by the Tuatha De Danaan. Irish tradition says that the Firbolg fled to Manann, the Isle of Man. This was, says Nennius, one of the four settlements of the Scots – that is, the Irish – in Britain and called Builc. Taken in context, given that so much of the action at this time happened on the Isle of Man, Builc can be read as synonymous with the Builth given to Pascent by Emrys. Guorthegirnaim was, by my account, the fortress and lands on and about the River Liddel, north of Longtown, Caer Vortigern, the place where Vortigern was incinerated by Emrys. It was inherited by Emrys's successor, Gwenddolau, and became known as Caer Gwenddolau (modern Carwinley).

Geoffrey's words '[Emrys] distributed [land] among his fellow soldiers' suggest that these men were not lordly soldiers and that there was a significant change in the social order. The actual lords, whom Emrys had restored, were not grateful to him; indeed, they resented him because they were beholden to him, a man they thought low born, for the lands and power on which their self-esteem was founded. Seeing the Angle threat neutralised, the traditional lords became determined to reassert their position. They hated and feared Emrys because they knew that if one man was seen to rise on merit alone, others might be encouraged to try the same thing and there would be no place for those whose entitlement to power relied upon birthright.

Pascent, Vortigern's son, was to prove as useless as his father and duplicitous too. Despite Emrys's generosity, Pascent went over to the Angles and offered to set himself at the head of an Angle army and lead an attack on Emrys.

> At the same time, Pascent, the son of Vortigern, who had fled to Germany [the Angle lands], was stirring up every armed soldier in that kingdom [the Gododdin lands that lay in the Angle thrall] against Aurelius Ambrosius. His great desire was to avenge his father. He promised the Germans limitless gold and silver, if only he could subdue Britain with their help.[26]

Pascent won the Angles over to his side and, bolstered by Angle power, led an army against Emrys and the forces of the free Britons. Emrys assembled his army, marched to meet Pascent and his Angle allies and 'challenged the raging enemy to combat'.[27] Emrys was again victorious. 'Once he had been compelled to run away, Pascent did not dare to return to Germany.' Instead, Pascent sought refuge among the Irish-Scots and entered into an alliance with Gillomanius, one of the great chiefs of the Scots.

Gillomanius was only too willing to help, because he had suffered a defeat at the hands of Gwenddolau. This time, Pascent and his allies attacked from the sea, landing, according to Geoffrey, at a town called Minevia, in Kambria (Cumbria[28]). The name of the Scottish war chief Gillomanius suggests that the Isle of Man had a part to play in this contest. *Gille*, in Gaelic, means servant. *Manius* is obviously connected with man.

Identifying Minevia was more of a problem. I found the clues I was looking for in Skene's *The Four Ancient Books of Wales*.[29] Skene was historiographer royal for Scotland from 1881. In *The Four Ancient Books*, according to his entry in the *Dictionary of National Biography*, he 'attempt[ed] to discriminate what was truly historical from what was imaginative or artificial in Welsh-Celtic historic poetry'. Paulus Orosius, historian and Christian apologist, born c.380–390, says, with reference to the Isle of Man, '*Mevania insula a Scotorum gentibus habitatur.*'[30] (Mevania – the Isle of Man – is an island where Scots people live.) It is easy to see how this could have been misunderstood or confused with the name of the goddess Minerva and ended up as Minevia.[31]

If Minevia is the Isle of Man, then Pascent and Gillomanius did not land there, they set sail from there and landed in Kambria (Cumbria). The subsequent fighting took place, once again, around what was Caer Vortigern, which became Caer Gwenddolau, and which is now Carwinley (the site of the Battle of Arderydd).

Emrys was unwell, so his lieutenant Gwenddolau took command. The baton had been passed to the next generation. That generation included Gwenddolau's distant cousin from Strathclyde, Merlin.

CHAPTER NINE

The Hill of Death

I did not know when I set out to find Dumpelder, the place where Taneu was tried and sentenced, that it would be vital in understanding what happened to Merlin in the last few years of his life. The traditional wisdom says that Taneu was tried at Traprain Law, where her father had a fortress, but when the evidence in this connection is read with reference to a map and a little common sense, this can be seen to be impossible. The clues are all in Jocelyn:

> It was decreed that she . . . would be set forth on the sea alone in a little boat. . . . the servants of the King went up into a ship and led her away to the deepest part of the sea. And there she was placed alone in a very small boat made of hide . . . and after committing her without any oars to fate, they returned to shore by rowing. They related that the sentence was accomplished to the King and people who had waited for the result of the matter . . . It is a wonder to relate, but for God no act is impossible. That little boat, in which the pregnant girl was held, rode the eddies whirling up and down, and being turned towards the opposite shore, ploughed with a much quicker passage than if it had been borne along by blown sails, or was

propelled by the hardest effort of many rowers. . . . guided
the woman safe to the harbour of deliverance . . . The
afore-mentioned woman came to shore upon the sand
near the place called Culross. At this time, Saint Servanus
was living in this place . . .[1]

The *Aberdeen Breviary* says Taneu's launch point was Aberlady.
Aberlady, on the Firth of Forth, is readily accessible from Traprain,
so this would seem to make sense. If, however, Taneu was taken
from Traprain Law to Aberlady and from there taken out to sea
(used loosely in the sources to mean water) and set adrift at the
'deepest part of the sea', that is, halfway between the shores of the
Firth, the king's retainers would have had to row back to shore from
there, thus completing a 12-mile boat trip, before trekking back
across country for 10 miles to where the king and his companions
waited. This round trip by land and sea and land again would have
been an impossibly impractical journey for the king's retainers to
make in one day. I accept that no specific time is stated by Jocelyn
and the king and people could have waited for their return for more
than one day, but the tenor of the passage suggests a relatively short
time. Either way, it seems a roundabout way to execute someone. It
would have been easier to throw her off the hill a few more times.

Jocelyn says that Taneu's little craft turned towards the 'opposite
shore' and was borne along faster than if it had sails or many rowers
rowing as hard as they could. If miracles happened, it would not
matter that there was no opposite shore readily accessible from
Aberlady, nor would it matter that Culross was about 25 miles
upstream, because, as Jocelyn says (dispensing with reality), '[Taneu's
voyage was] a wonder to relate but for God no act is impossible.'

Even if we assume that Taneu's boat was not literally set adrift
in the deepest part of the sea – that is, the North Sea – but in the
Firth of Forth a little way north of Aberlady, it would still have
been impossible for it to have gone all the way up the Firth to

Culross against the flow of the River Forth. The river flows into the Firth west to east, which makes the ebb tide stronger than the flood tide, so anything floating in the Firth will head out to sea as the tides change, not upriver towards Culross. A coastguard officer in Edinburgh told me that even a strong high tide of two knots over six hours would not have taken Taneu anywhere near Culross: 'She would have needed a sail and a good wind to get upstream to Culross from anywhere north of Aberlady.'

It is arguable that we should not read *The Life of Kentigern* literally, although it was written to be read that way and held out as the literal truth for as long as its promoters could get away with it. By disregarding the supernatural aspects, we can get a reasonable idea of what really happened and where. The one certain point available is Taneu's destination. We know that she ended up in Culross. I therefore started in Culross and worked backwards.

Jocelyn has Taneu turning towards 'the opposite shore'. As Culross is on the north bank, this means that Taneu crossed the Firth from south to north. She did not sail along it, against the water's flow (which, as we have seen, would have been impossible). Crossing the Firth at Culross makes sense. Today, the two main crossing places on the Firth are the Forth rail and road bridges at Queensferry to the east of Culross and Kincardine Bridge to the west. They are built at what must be two of the most obvious and advantageous crossing points on the river. Queensferry and Kincardine would have been sensible places for ferries in the sixth century. Kincardine is nearer Culross, so it was more probably there that Taneu crossed the Firth. Taneu was on trial. The parties were the kingdoms of Strathclyde and the Gododdin. The ideal place to deal with matters involving people from more than one kingdom would have been some accepted neutral location. Queensferry, in the land of the Gododdin, was not neutral ground. Kincardine, in Manau, was neutral ground, and the crossing there is short. It would have been an obvious place for a ferry in the sixth century. If I am right and Taneu's story was not simply a 'boy meets girl' affair but a matter of state between Strathclyde and the Gododdin, then it is sensible to suppose that the parties might have met there.

On the south side of the Firth, seven miles from the crossing at Kincardine, halfway between the two great powers of Strathclyde and the Gododdin, in the kingdom of Manau, is the ancient town of Dunipace. Dunipace is situated near Stirling, the very heart of Scotland, on both the north–south and the east–west axes. Its location is too far from the shore of the River Forth for everyone to have gone there to see Taneu's sentence being carried out but close enough for the king's servants to go there and back while the 'king and people . . . waited'.

Politically and geographically, Dunipace was ideally situated for diplomatic purposes in the sixth century. Manau was populated by a motley bundle of Picts, Scots and Britons, but, more importantly, it was centrally located between the main political confederations of the time: Celtic Picts and Scots, and Strathclyde and Gododdin Britons.

Dunipace had been a place of tryst and treaty since, literally, time immemorial. Several peace treaties were concluded there between the Romans and the Picts in the third century, including treaties entered into by Severus, c.210, and by Carausius, c.286. Buchanan says the hills of Dunipace were a place of trial and negotiation in the time of Donald I in the ninth century.[2] Some 700 years after Merlin's time, in 1301, Edward I of England, the Hammer of the Scots, entered into a truce at Dunipace (Dunypas, as the English records have it). This history, spread out over more than 1,000 years, makes it reasonable to conclude that there were other important meetings at Dunipace of which all trace has been lost.

On the occasion of Taneu's trial, Dunipace was not only a convenient neutral place, it was a recognised neutral place where a person accused of a crime in another's land or against a member of another community might be brought to justice and where differences between kingdoms and peoples were debated and agreement reached.

Buchanan says that the name Dunipace is derived, at least in part, from the Latin *Pax*, meaning peace. Hill of Peace is unlikely, as this translation would involve two languages, Gaelic and Latin. It is easy to see how this confusion came about, given the similarity of sound between *Pax* and *Pace* or *Pas*.[3] Dunipace was a place of parley, trial and execution. The most memorable of these must surely have been the executions. It was the executions that gave Dunipace its name.

The meaning of the first part of the name Dunipace is obvious: *Dun-na* (hill of). In the etymological dictionaries of MacBain and Macfarlane, I found the meaning *Bàs* (Old Irish): death. As I have said, Welsh is derived from P Gaelic, and Scottish Gaelic is derived from Q Gaelic. The Welsh 'P' sound passes on occasion into the sound 'B' in Scottish Gaelic and vice versa. In Welsh, for example, the word for a summit or a hill is *Penn*; in Scottish Gaelic, it is *Beann* (Ben). In the mid-sixth century, a significant minority in Manau, many of whom came to the area with Arthur's grandfather, spoke Q Gaelic, and so we would have *Dun-na-bas*. P Gaelic speakers, who controlled Dunipace after Arthur's death in 596, would have said Dun-na-pas. No matter how it was pronounced and later spelt, it means the Hill of Death. Dunipace was the Celts' Tarpeian Rock.

The above evidence suggests that it was to Dunipace that Taneu was taken for trial and from Dunipace that she was taken north to the banks of the Forth and sent across the river into the care of Serf and his monks.

The king's servants took Taneu out and cast her adrift in a very small boat without oars or sails only because Serf's monks were there to pick her up, in accordance with arrangements that had been made previously. While Serf's people took Taneu north to Culross, the king's retainers rowed back to the southern shore to tell the king and the people that all had worked out according to plan. The 'deepest part of the sea' almost certainly means the deepest part of the water between two areas of land. This is usually the middle of a river or loch or sea, and so, if the 'deepest part of the sea' means midstream, Serf's monks, literally, met her halfway. Taneu would have been in no danger if she were collected in good time by Serf's monks. It was never intended that Taneu be killed. Not only was there was no need for a magical rescue because she was never thrown from a hill, there was no need for her to be miraculously wafted upstream, because a deal had been done to send Taneu into exile. Jocelyn, of course, changed everything for the purposes of propaganda.

If I am right, and Taneu was tried at Dunipace, where does that leave the name Dumpelder? The answer to this question enabled me to discover what happened to Merlin 90 years after Taneu was tried, in the last few years of his long life.

CHAPTER TEN

The Murder of Telleyr

Mungo probably fled from Culross to Glasgow when he was between fifteen and twenty years old, 443–8, when Merlin and Languoreth were between three and eight years old. They lived only a few hours by boat from Glasgow, so it is very possible that they saw Mungo soon after he arrived, even if he was only pointed out to them from a distance.

On his way to Glasgow, near Ninian's Church, Stirling, Mungo stayed with a man called Fergus. When Fergus died, Mungo took his corpse with him to Glasgow in a new cart pulled by two bulls. A representation of Fergus and the cart can be seen today painted on a pillar in Fergus's chapel in Mungo's Cathedral in Glasgow.

Glasgow grew where the Molendinar Burn runs into the Clyde (it now runs underground), at the first place where the river could be forded. In the sixth century, it was a sizeable town of halls, houses, storehouses, workshops, shops and stalls gathered about the line of the high street that still runs north from the river. Further north still, where Glasgow Royal Infirmary, Mungo's Cathedral and the Necropolis stand today, there was a glade on a high hill that had been sacred to the people of the old way for centuries.

The majority of the population of Glasgow still favoured the old way when Mungo arrived, although there was also a substantial Christian community in the town. Merlin and Languoreth would have heard about Mungo shortly after he arrived because one of the first things he did, as described by Jocelyn, was to desecrate the sacred hill of the Druids as a deliberate matter of policy. '[Mungo] surrendered the dead [Fergus] to that cemetery in which no man had as yet been laid. This was the first grave in that place . . .'[1]

This started a religious war. Mungo must have known this would happen. The Druids struck back and tried to remove the offending grave, but by the end of the year many who had tried were 'Punished, with some serious misfortune and some even with death'.

By the symbolic act of burying Fergus, under Christian rites, in the sacred grove of the Druids, Mungo challenged the power and influence of the old way and marked himself out as a man to be reckoned with.

It is difficult to avoid the conclusion that Tutgual, the king, a Christian sympathiser, was complicit in Mungo's plan. Mungo had connections with the royal house – it suited kings of an authoritarian bent to have a religious partner, and Christianity was the coming thing in the courts of Europe.

In France, Clovis I, the first of the Merovingian kings of the Franks, had converted to Christianity in 496 and, with the support of the Church, gone on to conquer the Alamanni, a neighbouring German people. When Merlin was born, during the reign of Clovis's son, Chlotar I, the power of the Roman church was spreading across France. It must have been well known in Strathclyde that association with a hierarchical religion, particularly one that did not encourage freethinking, bolstered the interests of kings. It must also have been known that this new religion was materially different from the old way in that it offered to cooperate with, not challenge, those in authority. This was, of course, at the expense of the people, but that would have been of no concern to a budding Church and state partnership that would, for the next 1,500 years, use a combination of temporal and spiritual power to impose its will, brooking no alternatives.

Mungo may have had the tacit backing of the king, but his hold on Christian support was not absolute. Jocelyn says that when Mungo arrived in Glasgow, he went to live with two brother monks, Anguen and Telleyr. I believe it would be wrong to imagine this as a threesome and more accurate to picture Mungo joining a Christian community divided between two factions. Mungo exacerbated these divisions when he set about uniting the Christians under his authority, with the zeal of a young man who was certain of the righteousness of his cause. Although Mungo was only in his late teens or early 20s at this time, he was a dynamic and single-minded man, which is what really counted. Telleyr represented the wing of the Christian party that was more tolerant of the beliefs of others and so naturally opposed to Mungo's more militant tendency. Mungo, however, found Anguen a brother spirit and altogether more biddable. In Jocelyn's words:

> Anguen received [Mungo] as an angel of the Lord, and prized him out of the most loving affection of his heart. With all reverence and veneration, he was subservient in obeying and submitting to his commands, even to the point of delivering up his [congregation] to him . . . However the other brother, who was called Telleyr, was very troublesome to [Mungo] . . . by secretly slandering his religion, frequently resisting him openly to his face, and treating him with insults and injustices.[2]

Anguen's support for Mungo was rewarded when he was 'enlarged in both matters of wealth and in the culture of the Christian religion'. That is, Anguen received material wealth and hereditary benefices.

(The Celtic Church allowed clerical marriage and inherited church offices until the twelfth century.) The intractable Telleyr, on the other hand, was to be made an example of. Mungo bided his time and planned his move: '. . . [T]he Lord of vengeance . . . did not for long allow the injury to his servant [Mungo].'

Telleyr was marked for death. What we would call a 'hit' was arranged. Telleyr had 'an accident at work':

> On a certain day, after many insults by which he had provoked the soul of [Mungo], [Telleyr] went out to his work. And because he was powerful in his physical strength, he placed on his shoulders a tree of great weight that exceeded the size of his strength. . . . And when he had gone but a little way, he struck his foot against a rock and fell to the ground, and thus was pressed down by his burden and died . . .[3]

This 'accident' might be accepted as a coincidence if it was the only occasion on which such a thing happened, but, as will be seen, this is far from the only time that someone who stands up to Mungo meets with a swift and violent end. Jocelyn makes what happened clear when he writes:

> When a foolish man perishes, a wise man will be more prudent, we plainly have enough proof in the case of this man [Telleyr] that we should beware of offending [Mungo], and we should not dare to inflict on [Mungo] trouble or harm or injury.[4]

In the whole circumstances, it is more likely that Mungo had Telleyr killed and that Jocelyn engaged in a rather clumsy cover-up.

Once Telleyr was disposed of, Mungo made a show of lamenting his death, to placate Telleyr's followers, and took care of the funeral arrangements to ensure there would be no Mark Antony-type speech over Telleyr's body. It is astounding that Jocelyn, in reporting these events, makes so little effort to disguise what was going on and leaves it clear that Mungo was not slow to order assassinations. Indeed, Jocelyn seems more concerned that his readers should not think Mungo was truly upset by the sudden, violent death of Telleyr. Hardly has he said Mungo mourned than he goes on to reassure his readers that, in effect, Telleyr had it coming. Jocelyn quotes Solomon: 'He that is perverse in his ways shall fall at once.' In Mungo's Glasgow, no one could say they had not been warned.

Jocelyn ignored his sources when it suited his book and changed the 'facts' when they did not match his commission, but this was mainly in connection with theology; ample evidence of Mungo's temporal crimes remains. Of course, Jocelyn did not see Telleyr's murder as a crime. To Jocelyn, Mungo was simply zealous in his faith. Mungo was to be 'zealous in his faith' many more times in the next 60 years.

CHAPTER ELEVEN

Morken the Chief

When the Angles erupted from their bridgehead on the east coast to dip 'their red and savage tongue in the western ocean', c.550, Merlin and Languoreth were ten years old and growing up on their father's lands of Cadzow and in his hall in the Royal Town of Partick. They could not have failed to hear of the success of the Angles or to appreciate that these Angle victories presaged danger for Strathclyde, so they must have been thrilled when news arrived that the Britons of the south had rallied under Emrys and fought back against the Angle invaders.

Merlin and Languoreth must also have heard of Anguen and Telleyr and the struggle in which they were engaged. As Morken was a prominent man in a relatively small population, it is even probable that they had seen both contenders. Given Morken and Telleyr's common opposition to Mungo, it is likely that Merlin and Languoreth would have been able to meet Telleyr when he conferred with their father.

In 552, Mungo became bishop of Glasgow and, soon afterwards, perhaps in the mid-550s, set about imposing his authority by force, when he organised a raid on Morken's property. Jocelyn says:

> The northern enemy [Morken], that is to say the prince
> of this world had placed his seat in those parts and was
> ruling in that place . . . [Mungo] . . . attacked the hall of
> that armed strong man and plundered his vessels . . .'

Morken was, in Mungo's Christian eyes, 'the prince of this world',
that is, in Christian cosmology, the Devil. In reality, he was a lord
of Strathclyde who simply opposed a way of life that was alien to
his culture. Morken would have delighted in a battle for plunder
or fame, but religious war as a concept would have been foreign to
him. He owned property in Partick, so we may fairly suppose the
hall that was attacked was there.

Mungo's lightning strike on Morken's hall demonstrated his
power (and brought him some vessels), but its main effect was
psychological. People were so frightened that some who had not
converted to Christianity ran to the living fountain of baptism
like thirsty hinds with kindled desire (and who can blame them?).
Others, who had been Christians and had thought better of it,
came back to the Church.

The attack on Morken's hall was the first blow in what was to be
a campaign of terror. Jocelyn would have us believe that Mungo's
preaching carried the day, but common sense and a broad reading
of his text makes it clear that Mungo had the help of an armed
mob. Mungo promoted his cause, 'until all the ends of that land
remembered', which suggests that he taught the people a lesson
they would not forget; not because the lesson was memorable, but
because the violent means by which it was taught could not be
forgotten.

If the king did not sanction this attack, he almost certainly gave
it his tacit approval, because Mungo is unlikely to have courted
the king's displeasure and risked being left alone to face Morken's
wrath.

Mungo was an able and ambitious politician. It cannot have escaped his notice that when Tutgual died there was a good chance that Rhydderch would succeed to the throne and that Rhydderch was married to Languoreth, daughter of the leader of the people of the old way. It would be surprising if Mungo did not have a candidate of his own in mind to succeed. If this were so, there would have been sound political reasons for neutralising Morken (lest he support Rhydderch when the time came). However, he underestimated Morken, Merlin and their people.

Jocelyn seems to have lost sight of the fact that what he is describing is gang warfare when he points to Mungo as the main cause of the civil unrest in Glasgow at this time. Those of the old way no doubt retaliated. If Merlin was in Partick when the attack occurred, as a son of the house, he doubtless tried to protect his father's retainers, although he was probably only in his early teens.

Mungo retained the initiative, spoke softly and carried a big stick. Morken and Merlin probably had to stay away from Partick for a time, at least until the mob had dispersed. No recourse could be expected from the king, because Mungo's momentum was great and the king was in his thrall. Having cowed opposition by a show of force, Mungo set about systematically ransacking and destroying the sacred places of the old way and replacing them with churches. Jocelyn continues:

> And so [Mungo] began to wage war on the temples of demons, to overturn the images, to build churches . . . to divide parishes into fixed allotments with measured boundaries, to ordain clergy, to dissolve incestuous and illicit marriages, and to change concubinage into lawful marriage.[2]

In effect, Mungo instigated a pogrom. This was no short-term local purge but a concerted and wide-ranging change in the social fabric. It started in Glasgow, but it would have been nonsensical to try to change the marriage laws in only one small town, so we must suppose much of Strathclyde was affected. Even if Morken's family home in Cadzow was allotted to a parish, it must be doubted whether a monk or priest would have been brave enough to try to impose himself there, far less insist on the dissolution of some warrior's marriage because it was entered into under non-Christian rites.

Merlin must have known by this time that religious toleration, as practised by the Romans, the Celts and the Telleyr Christians, was alien to Mungo's form of Christianity and realised that if he did not take steps to curb Mungo, the old culture of the Celts was in danger of extermination.

Celtic society was unique in many ways, but in economics it was similar to almost every other until the industrial revolution: primarily rural, with almost everyone working on the land and/ or being directly dependent upon agriculture. Farmers cooperated with their neighbours as occasion demanded and contributed to their chief in return for protection and other services. What was left over, they used to provide for their families. If the balance struck between the contribution to a chief and the portion retained by the farmer was fair, everyone was happy.

Mungo organised his community of monks as a collective and bound them 'as fellow workers in gathering in the harvest for the Master'[3] – a way of working similar to the agricultural collectivisation practised by Stalin and just as unsuccessful. Any surplus the monks created fell to their superiors in the monastic community to distribute, so, although Church leaders would have nothing 'of their own', they would have the surplus produced by innumerable others to distribute and deal with, as if it was their own. Jocelyn emphasises that the monks lived alone in single huts, but even as late as the twelfth century the Church was taking steps to eliminate marriage among Celtic clergy, so we may reasonably suppose that in Mungo's day many monks had wives or concubines and families to provide for. This situation was bound to cause economic tension. Whatever the reason, Mungo's economic plans fell apart, and he was reduced to stealing from the people of the old way:

> It happened at a certain time that [Mungo] was without any oxen, and from the want of these the land was left unploughed and fallow. When [Mungo] saw this, he lifted his eyes to the edge of the wood placed nearby and saw a herd of stags springing here and there. At once, he said a prayer, and with the mighty virtue of his words, he called them to him.[4]

Jocelyn says the stags came to him, which is obviously preposterous. The stags were yoked to ploughs 'in place of oxen to plough the earth', and they ploughed the fields of the Mungo Christians 'as if they were tame oxen and accustomed to agriculture'. Of course, no stags were involved, only tame oxen belonging to people of the old way. Mungo stole them. The stag reference, which Jocelyn distorted and used to inject magic into his story, originally signalled the fact that the victims of the theft were of the old way.

As we have briefly seen, different peoples used to be associated with different animals. The people of Caithness were associated with the cat and the *Epidii* of Argyll with the horse. The symbol of the Scots of Argyll was the boar. The old Roman name for Strathclyde was Damnonia,[5] from the Gaelic and Latin for stag. The people who lived in what became the Kingdom of Strathclyde were originally the people of the stag. This association with animals on the part of people of the old way was anathema to Christians, for whom animals, particularly horned animals, came to figure devils.

When Jocelyn says that Mungo called stags to him and that they acted the part of oxen, we may, unless minded to accept such nonsense, reasonably conclude that the Mungo Christians simply stole oxen belonging to people of the old way, people of the stag. The only surviving evidence relevant to this time was written by Christians, or at least censored by them over more than the last 1,000 years: they destroyed the rest. It is, therefore, easy to obtain a one-sided view of events, although, again, it is ironic that everything negative about Christians in this chapter is based on evidence which they chose to create and save. For Jocelyn, overt aggression on Mungo's part was a virtuous thing, because Mungo did what he did for the Christian Church. The theft of property belonging to another was justifiable on this basis.

If the accounts told and written by the people of the old way had survived, I do not doubt they would say they were not the pushovers that Jocelyn suggests they were and that they would contain accounts of the people of the old way raiding Christian properties and taking goods belonging to Christians.

We can reasonably suppose that the young Merlin was enthusiastic in whipping up opposition to Mungo's men when they stole the property of the people of the old way and that he orchestrated raids in return. Given he was a scholar and not primarily a man of action, it is likely he also damned Mungo and his bully boys with sharp invective.

By the late 560s, Languoreth and Rhydderch were married and had started a family. While she remained of the old way, she would have had to take care not to alienate too many Christians, as her husband had no automatic right to succeed to the throne and might need wide Christian support if he were to become king on his father's death. King Tutgual too, although he was increasingly in thrall to Mungo and his Christians, had to avoid showing them too much favour, lest he increase the civil unrest that was now rampant in his kingdom. Tutgual's policy was to ignore the growing communal lawlessness if he could, and only to intervene if he had to. A king's position was only secure if there was a substantial measure of consent to his rule in the kingdom. In the past, maintaining this consent had been a relatively straightforward matter, but that changed when Mungo arrived.

CHAPTER TWELVE

Cathen the Druid

The raids by the Mungo Christians led to civil disturbance, with gangs of Christians and supporters of the old way fighting in the streets. Those of the old way chose Morken as their leader, or, as Jocelyn puts it, 'a certain tyrant, who was called Morken . . . was persuaded by power, honour and riches to walk in great and wondrous matters above him.'[1] Morken was not, as Jocelyn says, king of the Cambrian kingdom; he was simply a high chief. The Cambrian reference is simply a confused reference to the Britons, whose successors, the modern Welsh, still use the appellation Cymry.

Merlin would have been expected to take a lead in the fighting, but he was never a great warrior and was probably of little use in this connection. Even at the Battle of Arderydd, fought when he was in his prime, he was not included among those who, according to Geoffrey's *Vita*, 'slew the opposing enemy with their hateful swords'.[2]

Morken appears to have been a bluff chief of men who felt bound to react when Mungo tried to constrict his way of life. It is reasonable to suppose, therefore, that when Jocelyn says Morken 'scorned and disdained [Mungo's] . . . life and teaching', it was the more scholarly Cathen the Druid, Morken's ally, and the young Merlin, his son, who took the lead. They scoffed at Mungo's 'signs as of magical images, and . . . considered all his deeds as nothing'.[3] This incensed Mungo. And it must have been particularly galling for him when his crops failed again and he had to ask the king to ask Morken to help him:

> [Mungo] at a certain time required grain for food for the brothers of the monastery, went to the king, and making known his need and the need of his household, he asked that Morken supply their need by coming to their aid out of his abundance.[4]

Morken refused to supply Mungo with grain and taunted him, pointing out that much as Mungo claimed to have a God on his side he still 'need[ed] all good things, even [his] necessary nourishment' from him, Morken. Morken went on – no doubt, to Mungo's fury – 'I, however, who seek neither the kingdom of God nor his justice, am increased with all prosperity and an abundance of all things smile on me . . . your faith is empty, and your preaching is false.' Merlin and Cathen probably had a hand in this speech.

The only account we have of what followed is suspect, because it was written by Jocelyn. Unsurprisingly, he gives Mungo the last word and throws in a preposterous miracle for good measure. At this remove, all we can do is read between the lines. Jocelyn says that after Morken scoffed at the Christians' failure to fend for themselves, he challenged Mungo:

> If, trusting in your God and without human hands, you are able to transfer to your dwelling all my coarse meal which is held in my storehouses that you see, I concede and give to you freely from my spirit and I will submit faithfully to your petitions concerning other things.[5]

This challenge is impossible to believe. It is, almost certainly, a clumsy fabrication invented to justify Mungo's subsequent actions.

After the above exchange, in which Morken, Cathen, Merlin and their supporters came out on top, Jocelyn says, 'Morken departed joyfully, as one who had mocked the holy man with such an agreement.' Mungo and his men fumed at the insults they had endured and, facing starvation, decided on drastic measures:

> When evening came, the saint lifted his eyes and hands towards heaven, and with a profusion of tears poured out a most devout prayer to the Lord. And in that same hour, when the tears rose up from the innermost bosom of the saint and flowed from his eyes, the River Clyde, which flowed near him, suddenly proceeded to swell up, by the command of Him who has the power in heaven and on earth, in the sea and over all the abyss. And overflowing its banks and encircling the storehouses of [Morken] that stood there, it lifted them up and dragged them into its channel. And with a great force, the river transported them to dry land, all the way up to the place [where the Molendinar Burn runs into the Clyde] where [Mungo] then was accustomed to spend time. . . . The water was able to transport the storehouses abounding with grain but not to moisten them. And when the crowd had seen that the servant of God had made such a sign in the name of the Lord, they said that the Lord is truly great and greatly to be praised who has so magnified his saint.[6]

The place where Mungo 'spent time' can only be Glasgow, and, as the grain went upriver, its starting point was almost certainly Partick, which means that Morken had warehouse property there.

The High Court, the supreme criminal court in Scotland, sits today where the Molendinar Burn runs into the River Clyde, but no jury that ever deliberated there, indeed no jury in the world (outside of Dayton, Tennessee), would believe that Mungo did not simply steal Morken's grain by force. To find out what really happened, it is necessary to apply common sense. Mungo and his people were starving. They looked to Morken and his people for help. Morken refused to help and humiliated Mungo. Mungo ended up with Morken's grain. Conclusion: Mungo stole Morken's grain.

The situation in the Partick–Glasgow area deteriorated further and rapidly after Mungo's raid on Morken's halls of grain. Tutgual the king knew he had allowed things to go too far and, as civil unrest grew, realised he had to do something about it. The status quo, however, now suited the Mungo Christians (they had the grain) and they were content to let matters rest. While they believed they could count upon the protection of the king, they put it about that Morken could well afford to 'share' his grain and was only angry because he was greedy (and because Mungo could conjure up miracles):

> However the aforementioned . . . Morken, although exceedingly rich and great in the eyes of men, yet being a vile slave of Mammon, bore ill the loss of his grain, as it seemed to him, and the sign that had occurred from heaven.[7]

Morken had to strike back if he was not to lose the respect of his men. He railed against Mungo, calling him a 'worker of evil' and promising to exact the most severe revenge if Mungo crossed his path. Morken did not need encouragement to feel aggrieved, but Jocelyn says that Cathen, Morken's counsellor, incited him against Mungo. Cathen is described as 'a certain most wicked man', which is simply, in this context, a way of saying Druid without using the word. Merlin, a volatile character, as he would demonstrate drastically in the next decade, must also have argued for swift and severe retaliation. According to Jocelyn, 'a spirit profuse with evil [that is, Morken] is more easily persuaded to join with him who embraces the same [that is, Cathen]'. Jocelyn goes on:

> For an impious leader [Morken], according to scripture, has impious men as his ministers. And very often he selects such men to be secret advisors to him, who impart venomous whispers into the ears of those who freely listen to iniquities and add to the fire of malice with the bellows of accusation by applying fuel of their own accord, so that it does not extinguish itself but flares up more abundantly.[8]

Cathen and Merlin were almost certainly among the 'impious men'.

There was now a real threat of civil war. (Indeed, a religion-inspired civil war was to break out within the decade.) Even Tutgual the king, who until this time had been reluctant to play an overt part in the troubles, decided he had to take matters in hand, and so, under his aegis, a meeting was arranged. It was now Mungo's turn to mock and scoff. This would have been especially galling for Morken because he knew that Mungo's people had been telling gullible people that Mungo's prayers had brought Morken's grain to his door. Jocelyn, though, naturally portrays Mungo in a flattering light: '[Mungo] wishing to extinguish malice with wisdom went into the presence of the ruler in the spirit of meekness rather than with the rod of severity.'[9]

It is easy to imagine how this must have exacerbated the anger of an already irate Morken, particularly when Mungo went on to, quite literally, patronise him, 'in the manner of a most merciful father' trying 'to amend the foolishness of a son'. I can only assume that Tutgual had insisted the men arrived unarmed, as what happened next was that Morken gave Mungo what in Glasgow today would be called 'a good kicking':

> However the man of Belial [Morken] after the fashion of
> a deaf adder that stops up its ears so that it cannot hear
> the voice of the wise enchanter, did not follow the word
> of warning and the counsel of salvation. On the contrary,
> urged on by a greater madness, Morken rushed at him,
> struck him down with his shoe, and threw him down
> lengthwise onto the floor.[10]

Mungo put the best face he could on this attack, and, 500 years later, Jocelyn backed him up: 'However the saint [Mungo], being raised up by the bystanders, endured with the greatest patience his injury and dishonour so that his teaching might be known by his patience.'

In truth, he had been shamed and he knew it. His standing, already undermined by his inability to feed his supporters, had now been crushed under Morken's feet. The balance of power had swayed in Morken's favour, although Mungo ran away rejoicing 'that he was counted worthy to suffer shame for the word of the Lord'. Jocelyn does not say so, but it is reasonable to suppose that Morken followed up his victory and recovered by force what was left of his grain.

The king must have been dismayed by these events and concerned at such a challenge to his authority. For one of his people to attack another at a meeting over which he presided undermined his position and opened him to a challenge for his throne. Fortunately for Tutgual, the cause of his problems was also his salvation. The religious differences in Strathclyde and the dissent and disruption they caused would not go away if another man was put in his place – another solution had to be found.

The Christians blamed Morken's temper and his principal adviser, Cathen the Druid, for what had happened to Mungo. Irrespective of the part Cathen played in Mungo's disgrace, Druids were a threat to Christian power, so the Mungo Christians, true to form, planned to assassinate Cathen. Some time after Morken assaulted Mungo, Cathen, 'the provoker of this sacrilege, mounted his horse . . . and he departed with delight as one who seemed to himself to have triumphed over the saint'.[11]

Jocelyn gives the impression that Cathen was hardly out of the door after Morken's assault before he was punished for his part in events, but this is unlikely. If the Christian mob was strong enough to take on Cathen at this time, why is there no mention of its attacking Morken, and why did Mungo so obviously slink off? It is likely that some time passed, enough for plans to be laid and men to be chosen to execute them. Mungo's assassins fell on Cathen, pulled him from his horse and killed him, although, Jocelyn says:

> But a judgment came from the face of the Lord so as to perform justice for the injury suffered by his servant . . . the steed on which [Cathen] sat fell down after striking its foot on I know not what kind of obstacle. And his rider fell backward before the gate of the king his lord, and having broken the neck that he had raised up with arrogance against the bishop of the Lord, Cathen died.[12]

I like the disingenuous line that says Cathen's horse struck its foot 'on I know not what kind of obstacle'.

Cathen and Morken complemented each other. Morken was, literally, the Great Chief, the man with the land, the grain, the money and the men to wield power. Cathen, as a Druid, no doubt provided most of the intelligence. Merlin must have known Cathen well. As a leading Druid, Merlin and Languoreth would have had a lot to learn from him when they were young. By the time the dispute between Morken and Mungo reached its climax with Morken kicking Mungo, Merlin was probably in his late teens.

Malory says that Merlin's teacher was a man called Blaise. He describes Merlin going to see 'his master Bleise [sic]',[13] providing him with information and asking him to keep a written record of Arthur's battles. Robert de Boron, writing at the turn of the twelfth century, says Blaise was not only Merlin's teacher but Merlin's mother's confessor. Unsurprisingly, this is the version taken up in *El Baladro del Sabio Merlin*, written in Spain c.1498, at the time of the Catholic monarchs Ferdinand and Isabella. Blaise is also said to have been present at Merlin's birth and death, which, by any reckoning would have made him a very old man. The majority view is that he was Merlin's teacher, or, as he is often described, Merlin's 'master'.

Scholars have tried to identify Blaise for generations. Professor Norma Lorre Goodrich says, 'the searching of one hundred years has failed to discover a personage of this name. Therefore, if the real Merlin is found one day, his lifelong companion will, hopefully, be beside him. The real name of this companion was probably not Blaise, but concealed, and intentionally so.'[14]

It has been suggested that Blaise was the Bishop of Troyes, who visited Britain in the early fifth century (too early for Merlin, according to almost every authority). After his death, the bishop was canonised as Saint Lupus (Latin for wolf). By this account, Merlin was a Breton, and as the Breton for wolf is *Blaidd*, apparently pronounced Blaiz, it is supposed that this Bishop of Troyes was Blaise, Merlin's mentor. Gerald of Wales, an obsequious churchman, later canonised, writing in the twelfth century, refers to a storyteller called Bledhericus, who, as the historian Ashley has suggested, may have been Blaise,[15] but Bledhericus does not sound like Blaise, and Bledhericus did not live within centuries of Merlin.

For me, Merlin's teacher is to be found by his side, and his real name was not Blaise. He was Cathen the Druid. Morken was a leading figure among the people of the old way and so must have had many friends among the Druids. Cathen can, at least, be placed next to Merlin in history and geographically. Merlin at his father's property in Partick, Cathen on the nearby White Island of the Druids. As Merlin's father's partner in opposition to the Mungo Christians, Cathen was of the right generation to be Merlin's teacher; as a Druid and a scholar, he was ideally suited to instruct Merlin in the old way. It would, in these circumstances, be surprising if Cathen was not Merlin's teacher, or, at least, one of his teachers.

There is, however, the matter of names. I criticised the Bledhericus theory because Bledhericus does not sound like Blaise, but then, neither does Cathen (whatever Cathen means). Translated into Scottish Gaelic, Cathen may have some 'cat' connection – cat is the same in both English and Gaelic – or it may be something to do with wild geese, as a wild goose is *Cathan* in Gaelic. (Irish soldiers who fought for the French in the seventeenth century were known as the Wild Geese.) It is perhaps more likely that Cathen was called by a name that had fighting connotations, because, in Gaelic, *Cath* means battle. Cathen, taken to mean the battler, makes sense (and throws light on the name the Wild Geese). It may be, perhaps, his name was taken from the Gaelic *Cathaighim*, which means provoking, accusing or fighting, any one of which describes Cathen perfectly.

I have concluded that Cathen was, at least, one of Merlin's teachers and the real man who went on to become the legendary and mysterious Blaise. The above evidence is more than I have been able to find in support of any other candidate, but the Scottish sources held still more. Jocelyn says that Cathen was, among other things: Morken's soldier; 'a certain most wicked man' who was in Morken's confidence and who incited him to hate and injure Mungo; perverse; a spirit profuse with evil; impious; venomous; a mocking loudmouth; a provoker of sacrilege; and (as if all of this was not enough) a man who would 'freely listen to iniquities and add to the fire of malice with the bellows of accusation by applying fuel of their own accord, so that it does not extinguish itself but flares up more abundantly'.[16] This is all contained in one chapter. It would not be surprising, given that this was the Christian view of Cathen, if Christians had a name for him other than the affectionate 'Battler'. What was Cathen to Christians if not a blasphemer? In Gaelic, this would have been *Blaisbheum*. In the seventh century, when stories of Merlin and Arthur were taken south and out of context to places where Gaelic was not spoken, the descriptive name Blasphemer might well have become simply a name, and later, on the tongues and by the pens of non-Gaelic speakers, the shortened name Blaise.

A map in Robert Paul's *Partick Anecdotes* shows an island marked 'The Whyt Inch' (White Island) in the middle of the River Clyde, near its junction with the River Kelvin, in 1800. The name of this island is remembered in the modern name of the nearby district of Whiteinch, at the north end of the Clyde Road Tunnel. The island was removed in the nineteenth century to allow large ships clear passage to Glasgow. The colour white is closely associated with the Druids.[17] Pliny the Elder, describing a Druidic ritual, wrote of a Druid clothed in a white robe cutting mistletoe from a tree with a golden sickle and allowing it to fall and be caught in a white cloth.[18]

There are many white-Druid connections in the Arthurian canon. Lancelot's father was King Ban, although Ban was not his real name, only the name by which he became known. He is often portrayed as a bookish man. *Ban* is the Gaelic word for white. This suggests Ban was a Druid, or, if not a Druid, a scholar, and so associated with the Druids.

In 397, a monk called Ninian founded one of the first Christian settlements in Scotland at Whithorn Priory in Galloway. The name

Whithorn, according to the conventional wisdom, refers to a white church that Ninian built there, *Candida Casa*: the White House. Buildings in the fourth century were often made of double-woven wattle walls, infilled with stones and rubble and then plastered on the outside and whitened. Many buildings were built like this. There is no reason to suppose that Ninian's church was especially white, or, at least, white enough to merit the name the White House. It is more likely that Ninian built his church upon a site revered by the people of the old way (as Mungo did in Glasgow, when he built his church and buried bodies on the Druids' sacred hill). If this is what Ninian did, he would have anticipated the advice of Pope Gregory to Augustine, when Augustine set off for England two centuries later. Gregory suggested that locations sacred to the people of the old way be taken over, the relics of saints added, the old precincts sprinkled with holy water and the whole place rededicated, 'because people come more readily to the places where they have been accustomed to pray'.

The policy adopted by Gregory led to many elements of the old way, including Druid-inspired place names (such as those involving the colour white), being forgotten and to their being replaced with a Christian alternative. In time, as the Druids and memories of their teaching were suppressed, place names that included 'white' came to be connected with Mary, the mother of Jesus, for obvious reasons: white connoted purity, and Mary was famous because of the story of the virgin birth.

Partick was a royal town in the sixth century, so many chiefs kept some establishment there, including Morken. It is inevitable that there would have been Druids there, too, and that they would have had some connection with the island in the middle of the Clyde that came to be called the White Island.

Because Cathen is so prominent in Jocelyn's *Life of Kentigern*, it is reasonable to infer that Cathen was an important Druid. The king had a capital base in Partick, and Morken and other chiefs had establishments there. In these circumstances, it makes sense to suppose that the prominent Druid Cathen had his base there too.

Mungo set up in Glasgow, and not in the more established Partick, which suggests that the old way was more firmly rooted in Partick and that initially the Christians found Glasgow a more amenable place. It makes sense to suppose that the Druids' main centre was on the White Island in the middle of the Clyde, and that it had been for centuries; it was such an obvious site.

In later life, Merlin retired to a house built for him by Languoreth, which stood on a hill near Partick. If Merlin walked out of this house and took the shortest route to the river, he would have ended up on its north bank, looking directly at the White Inch, the White Island of the Druids.

Morken did not survive Cathen for long. Soon after Cathen's assassination, Morken died from tumours in his feet. Small details like this cause of death lend credibility to Jocelyn's work as a source of evidence. If he had invented a death for Morken, we can be sure it would have involved something more exciting than tumours in his feet. Cathen met a violent death when 'a judgment came from the face of the Lord so as to perform justice for the injury suffered by his servant [Mungo]'. Cathen may have encouraged Morken to attack Mungo, but Morken was the one who kicked him. If Morken had not died in his bed but was a victim of violence, we can be sure Jocelyn would have said so. Alternatively, it would have been easy for Jocelyn to invent a gory end for Morken. It is to Jocelyn's credit that he did not take this course.[19]

Although Morken died in his bed of natural causes, it was said that his death was brought about by supernatural means. This, together with the memory of what had happened to Cathen, so frightened Morken's contemporaries that, for a time, Mungo was the main power in the land. With reference to this episode, Jocelyn refers to the 'sort of retribution [God] renders to the arrogant':

> For many days afterwards in his city of Glasgow and in his diocese, Kentigern lived in much quietness and had peace in his circuit, because the divine judgment shown to his persecutors supplied to others an incitement of fear, or reverence, or love, or obedience toward the saint of God. And this furnished an opportunity to do whatever he wished to the advantage of God.[20]

Mungo having an opportunity to do whatever he wished is a frightening prospect, but not everyone was cowed. After the death of Cathen and Morken, the troubles continued and the balance of power swayed:

> After some time had passed, certain sons of Belial [the name earlier attributed to Morken, so these certain sons included Merlin], the fruit of vipers of the kindred of the formerly mentioned . . . Morken, pricked by the sting of very bitter hatred and infected with the venom of the devil, met as one and took counsel that they would take [Mungo] by deception and kill him. . . . Several times they stretched out many snares for him in order to shoot arrows at him unexpectedly, but the Lord was a strong tower for him so that his enemies, the sons of iniquity, could not prevail against him.[21]

Although they were in the majority, the people of the old way had not, until the troubles caused by the Mungo Christians, spoken with one voice. They had always been notoriously individualistic and disinclined to fall in for long under anyone's authority. When a significant number of Tutgual's chiefs banded together in opposing Mungo, the king realised he too was in danger. He must have been aware that if Mungo was killed in retaliation for the assassination of Cathen, a religious civil war was a real and deadly prospect. One of the reasons the king had favoured Mungo, even though the Christians were not in the majority, was that Mungo's Christians presented a united front under his command. Even if many of them differed from Mungo doctrinally and temperamentally, they all remembered how he had assassinated Telleyr, so they did what they were told. This made Mungo a valuable supporter of the king. However, when Mungo lost his fear-factor and his illusion of invincibility, when Morken humiliated him, his Christian opponents had an opportunity to unite against him. Given Mungo's record of falling out with everyone he worked with unless they did what he told them to do, I suspect that many Glasgow Christians were tired of him and pleased to see him go. They must have realised that he had gone too far and that a peaceful compromise was not possible with Mungo about. With Mungo gone, they would have known that they had a chance to recover their position with the king.

With the hitherto disparate people of the old way united in opposition to him, and indeed bound together to kill him, it must have become clear to Mungo that his position was untenable. The king, ever a man to trim his sails to the prevailing wind, could see the way it was blowing now and deserted Mungo too. Tutgual arrived at a compromise that suited almost everyone, the main exceptions being Merlin and Mungo. He withdrew his support from Mungo and allowed him to be pushed into exile, but he continued to maintain Christians, albeit more moderate Christians, as his principal advisers.

Things were now too hot for Mungo in Glasgow. Jocelyn puts the best gloss he can on the facts:

> Accordingly, after being instructed by divine revelation, [Mungo] departed from those territories and headed eagerly

for the road which turned towards Wales, where at that
time the holy patron Dewi shone forth in his pontificate as
a star during Matins . . .[22]

Dewi was the saintly David of Wales, a man renowned for his
patience. Mungo fell out with him too.[23]

With Mungo in exile in Wales, Merlin may have expected
Strathclyde to go back to the way it had been before Mungo's
arrival, but that was impossible. The king was in the thrall of a
Christianity that offered a hierarchy that paralleled the aristocracy.
Christianity had the added advantage for Celtic kings that they
could avoid having to listen to innumerable Druids all with their
own opinions telling them what was good for the people. It was
much better for them to have a religion which told the people that
what was good for the king was good for them too.

Tutgual had good reason to want to maintain a unified kingdom
at this time. He was about to go to war. The Angles had not been
an immediate threat for almost 20 years because they had had their
hands full ensuring that the Britons who were subject to their rule
did not rise up against them and that the British aristocrats who
had run away stayed quiet in their fortress bolt-holes. They also had
to be wary that the one-time followers of Emrys, now under his
successor Gwenddolau, did not threaten them again.

The Emrys–Gwenddolau forces had established a small enclave
in south central Scotland. Being without a significant aristocracy,
the conduit through which Christianity tended to flow, many of
their people who had taken to Christianity reverted to their old
ways. By this action, they unwittingly set the scene for one of the
most important British battles, the Battle of Arderydd, in which
Merlin stepped firmly from the wings to the centre stage of British
history.

CHAPTER THIRTEEN

Uther Pendragon, Son of the Sky God

When Pascent son of Vortigern heard that Emrys was unwell and that his lieutenant Gwenddolau was in charge of the British army, he and his Scottish-Irish allies thought they would win an easy victory.

Merlin was about 20 years old at this time. Emrys, not being of the erstwhile ruling class, must have found himself short of educated men with administrative ability when he had taken charge, so, doubtless on the recommendation of his lieutenant Gwenddolau, he had invited Gwenddolau's distant cousin Merlin to join him.

Merlin was son of Morken son of Morydd son of Mor. Gwenddolau was son of Ceidio son of Garthwys son of Mor.[1] They shared a common great-grandfather, although some sources say that Mor was Gwenddolau's great-great-grandfather. This genealogy suggests that Gwenddolau was, like Merlin, one of a family of high chiefs, which also suggests he was unrelated to Emrys, who was of lowly social rank.

It is often suggested that Emrys and Gwenddolau were brothers. Later writers often invented relationships to lend coherence to their stories. Two contemporaries working together in a common cause would be described as brothers; if one was significantly younger than the other, a father-and-son relationship would be used. Geoffrey says that Arthur's father was 'Utherpendragon', the third son of the southern British king, Constantine – the other brothers being Constans, who went into the Church, and Aurelius Ambrosius (whom I have identified as Emrys).[2]

According to Geoffrey, Uther was called Utherpendragon, which he claims means 'a dragon's head',[3] because he had a dragon fashioned in gold that he kept with him when he went to war. This is desperate stuff. Emrys, as we have seen, was the first Pen Dragon. The title was needed because Emrys was not a king and had to be careful not to be seen to be seeking to supplant the royal family. It also has the virtue of making sense with reference to the place in which Emrys was active – at least by my account – the lands once occupied by the Sarmatian dragon soldiers.

Uther has consistently been taken to have been a first name. It has been said that, in Welsh, *Uthr*, it means 'terrible' and that 'Arthur the terrible' could have been mistakenly taken to mean Arthur son of Uther.[4] The general consensus is that Pendragon means not a dragon's head but chief dragon. The confusion surrounding Uther Pendragon arises, in part, because the first line in Malory's *Le Morte d'Arthur* is misleading on every level. In book one, chapter one, line one, Malory says, as regards the story of Arthur, 'It befell in the days of Uther Pendragon, when he was king of all England . . .'

In fact, by my reckoning, Arthur and Uther crossed paths only once, at the Battle of Arderydd, where Arthur was instrumental in bringing about Uther's defeat and death. Uther Pendragon was not a king, although he held the equivalent of royal powers, and although Emrys is sometimes described erroneously as a king, he was not one. The Pen Dragons did not reign over Angles, they killed them.

There were three Pen Dragons: Emrys; Emrys's lieutenant and successor, Gwenddolau son of Ceidio (Merlin's friend); and a warrior called Maelgwn, who, as a young man, fought at the Battle of Arderydd and who ended up, in the early seventh century, a pensioner living in Merlin's house. The dragon soldiers of the Pen Dragons were defeated and dissipated at Arderydd, so Maelgwn was Pen Dragon in little more than name. Only Emrys and Gwenddolau exercised real power as Pen Dragons.

To return to the Arderydd entry in the *Annales Cambriae* for the year 573, it couples Merlin's name with that of Gwenddolau: 'The Battle of Arderydd between the sons of Eliffer and Gwenddoleu son of Ceidio; in which battle Gwenddoleu fell; Merlin went mad.'

Ceidio is derived from the Latin *caelum*, sky, from which the French get *ciel* and we have in English celestial, and *dio*, from the Latin *deus*, god. That Gwenddolau was designated son of Ceidio – that is, son of the Sky God – suggests he was a man of the old way. This is corroborated by his friendship with Merlin and the fact that he went down fighting an allied army led by Strathclyde marching under Christian banners.

After Gwenddolau's death at the battle of Arderydd, the aristocracy reasserted itself and retook the lands of the Pen Dragons, while the forces that had fought under Emrys and Gwenddolau became landless men. Merlin, with many others, escaped into the Caledonian wood, where he was to remain in hiding for seven years.

As was always the case, both sides told stories about the circumstances surrounding the battle. Those told by the people of the old way survived in the oral tradition and in writing until, in time, they were censored into oblivion. Those told by the Christians were, of course, warped to suit the purposes of the Church, and this, coupled with the fact that within one or two centuries they were being told in the south of Britain, far from their roots, means they lost much that made them make sense. By the time they came to be used as sources for printed books, they had become garbled in the extreme.

What happened was this. Stories were told in the form of poems such as Y *Gododdin*, which runs to almost 100 verses and in which so many warriors were praised that some even had to share a verse. Families and friends paid to have their loved-one warrior commemorated in this way. Once these people died out, there was a natural tendency for poets to focus on the greatest heroes, and the greatest heroes in the century preceding the division of Britain by the Angles, which led the Britons of the south of Scotland to retire ignominiously to the south and west of Britain, were Emrys, Gwenddolau and Arthur.

To recap, with a view to understanding the 'Uther' in 'Utherpendragon', Emrys, the first Pen Dragon, fought the Angles in the 550s. Gwenddolau, the second Pen Dragon, fought the Angles in the 560s and early 570s. Maelgwn became Pen Dragon after Arderydd in 573, although by then there was no organised force for him to take over. As there were only two Pen Dragons of moment, it would have been natural for people living hundreds of years later to refer to Emrys as Pen Dragon and to Gwenddolau as the other Pen Dragon. In relation to 'other', the *Chambers English Dictionary* says, 'forms [include] . . . othur . . . othyr . . . othir . . . oother . . . other . . . [and] *uther*' [my emphasis]. The specifically Scottish version, according to the *Oxford English Dictionary*, is 'uthyre'.

Uther means other. The version that sounds most like the name given to Arthur's father by the conventional wisdom means what the dictionary says it means – and it is Scottish. We do not know how it was pronounced or how it was spelt in Geoffrey's source, so he can be excused for mistaking it for a first name. Gwenddolau was the other Pendragon, *Uther Pen Dragon*.

In later centuries, writers with flawed hindsight, when looking for a father for Arthur, mistook Gwenddolau for Arthur's father. As the three great heroes of people of the old way in the sixth century were Emrys, Gwenddolau and Arthur, it would have been a simple and understandable thing for a storyteller or writer to take it that the relationship between the three was familial, and that Gwenddolau, the *Uther Pendragon*, was Arthur's father.

There is circumstantial evidence placing Uther Pendragon in the south of Scotland. The Welsh poem 'Pa Gur', written in the thirteenth century after an eleventh-century original based on ancient oral tradition, refers to 'Mabon, son of Myrdon the servant of Uthyr Pendragon'.[5] Lochmaben is about 22 miles from the site of the Battle of Arderydd and Gwenddolau's fortress, the area in which, if I am correct, the *Uther Pendragon* was active.[6] The evidence contained in a Welsh poem, recorded by a poet who had no reason to invent a name with a Scottish connection, is, again, evidence contrary to the interest of the party providing it, although, in fairness, in the sixth century the distinction between Wales and Scotland was far different from today. The south of what is now Scotland was P Gaelic-speaking (Welsh-speaking).

Some time in the early 560s, when Merlin was in his early 20s, an Angle called Eopa approached Pascent and asked him what he would give him if he killed Emrys. According to Geoffrey's *Historia*, Pascent promised Eopa a thousand pounds of silver, promotion and eternal friendship. Eopa, who had learnt the language of the British and some skill in medicine, presented himself in the guise of a doctor monk in the town where Emrys lay on his sickbed and promised him a cure:

> He promised he would restore the King [Emrys] to health,
> if only the latter would swallow his medicines. Eopa was
> ordered to prepare a draught immediately. He mixed a
> potion and gave it to the King. Aurelius [Emrys] took it
> and drained it in one gulp.[7]

Emrys went to sleep believing he was about to recover his health:

> The poison ran quickly through his veins and the pores of
> his body; and thus death, which has the trick of sparing no
> man, came to him while he slept. Meanwhile the accursed
> traitor slipped away in the crowd and was nowhere to be
> found . . .'[8]

The assassin made his way back to his paymaster to claim his
captaincy and collect his pieces of silver, but he was too late.

Gwenddolau was out hunting Pascent when news was brought to
him that Emrys had been assassinated.[9] He called his counsellors to
him and asked for their advice. Merlin, ever impetuous in military
matters, urged Gwenddolau 'not to put off for a moment making
contact with the enemy'.[10] Gwenddolau doubted this advice but,
nevertheless, closed with the enemy. Pascent and his allies came
out to meet Gwenddolau:

> The moment the armies came in sight of each other, they
> drew up their lines of battle on either side, marched forward
> to make contact, and so began the fight . . . In the end,
> when much of the day had passed, [Gwenddolau] proved
> the stronger and won the victory, killing Gillomanius [the
> Irish-Scots leader] and Pascent in the process. The [enemy]
> turned and ran to their ships, and in their retreat they were
> cut down by the [Britons] who pursued them.[11]

When word got out that Emrys was dead, the Angles, under Octa
son of Hengist, broke the treaty that had been agreed with Emrys,
allied with the remnants of Pascent's army and sent across the

North Sea for reinforcements. When this massive army was ready, Octa fell upon and set about ravaging the land of the Britons. Gwenddolau, with Merlin as part of his army, set out to stop him.

When Gwenddolau and Octa met in pitched battle, the Angles took a defensive position; the Britons attacked. Gwenddolau's men were unable to break the Angle line by assault. Tired and weakened by their losses, they were driven back in flight and pursued by the Angles until they were able to take refuge on a steep hill as the sun set. The Angle army, which was by far the larger army, lay in wait until the morning, expecting to mop up the remains of a defeated foe, but, before dawn broke, Gwenddolau launched a surprise night attack on the Angle camp. The Britons butchered the main mass of enemy with 'might and main', captured their leaders and routed the rest.

According to Geoffrey, Uther/Gwenddolau then pacified Alclud (Clyde Rock), Dumbarton, on the Clyde, and the Scots, by which Geoffrey seems to mean the people north of the Forth-Clyde line. He then has his hero move to London! This is all nonsense, of course; no leader, in any of the three centuries following the departure of the Romans, no matter how powerful, blithely moved about the main island of Britain with such ease, far less exercised power in places as far apart as the Clyde and the Thames. Geoffrey had Arthur in London because London was the main city in England in the twelfth century, although not in the sixth.

It is more likely that after his victories, first against Pascent and his Angle and Scots allies, and then against the whole Angle forces combined, Gwenddolau was powerful enough to treat with the king of Strathclyde at Dumbarton and with the Scots king of Dalriada (Conall, Arthur's father's cousin). Given the seaborne invasion of the Isle of Man in which the Scots supplied ships, the king of Scots in issue is more likely to have been of Dalriada than the all-but-landlocked king of the Scots of Manau, Arthur's father, Aedan. Merlin, arriving back in his homeland as part of Gwenddolau's army, must have caused some disquiet among his family and friends. His close friendship with Gwenddolau was to lead to an open breach with Strathclyde within a decade and years in exile.

The only reason these kings entered into negotiations with the likes of Gwenddolau, the heir of the low-born Emrys and the leader of a maverick state, was that Gwenddolau was militarily strong at this time. Gwenddolau, like Napoleon at Tilsit, found the established powers prepared to work with him because they had to. Everyone must have known that, given the opportunity, they would combine and destroy him. That is what happened to Napoleon, and that is what happened to Gwenddolau.

All about Gwenddolau lay British kingdoms whose kings and lords resented and feared him, and the Angles remained a constant threat. The British aristocracy knew that Gwenddolau was the greatest war leader of the day, and more, they knew that if men like Gwenddolau could rise by merit alone, none of them was safe in his inherited place. The British lords, who favoured the old pre-Emrys regime, defied Gwenddolau, absented themselves from his lands and banded together as conspirators in foreign courts. Some, unable to face Gwenddolau in the field, barricaded themselves in fortresses and called upon Scottish mercenaries, the famous men of Manau, to help them in their fight.

Gwenddolau spent many debilitating years putting down rebellions. According to Geoffrey, the rebellious lords included Gorlois. In Geoffrey's fiction, Uther had fallen passionately in love with Gorlois's wife, Ygerna. Uther asked Merlin to help him, as Geoffrey puts it, 'have his way with Ygerna'.[12] Merlin changed Uther's shape to that of Gorlois and so enabled Uther to have sex with her:

'That night she conceived Arthur, the most famous of men, who subsequently won great renown by his outstanding bravery.'

This is all nonsense, of course. Uther did not change shape and have sex with Ygerna – well, not all of him, anyway. Neither was Arthur Uther/Gwenddolau's son. In later centuries, storytellers looked back and saw only the greatest warriors poking up through the mists of time: Emrys, Gwenddolau and, of course, Arthur. When they looked for a father for Arthur, they looked no further than Uther Pendragon. It did not matter that Uther Pendragon was Gwenddolau or that he was not Arthur's father. All that mattered was that Arthur had a father and that he was British. To have told the truth, that Arthur's father was Aedan, a Scot, would not have been acceptable. As the stories developed, Arthur was made less Scots and more British, and, eventually and ironically, English!

Arthur had no magical conception. The boy who was to become the hero, Arthur, was a young child living in Manau when Gwenddolau was seeking a wife. The place of this story in Geoffrey's narrative is instructive and suggests there is some truth behind it. It would have made sense for Gwenddolau to try to consolidate his position by a marriage alliance with some aristocratic family. If he did, it did not work.

Religion, as usual, was a constant source of strife. It is clear from his name, son of Ceidio – son of the Sky God – and from his friends, especially Merlin, that Gwenddolau was of the old way. The vehemence of the alliance ranged against him at Arderydd suggests not only political and social differences but religious differences too. Christianity tended to be imposed from the top down. When the traditional lords were replaced by Emrys and then Gwenddolau and other 'new men', this dashed the hopes of the Christians. People went back to the old way.

Gwenddolau and Merlin were constantly engaged in putting

down risings on the part of the traditional lords. Merlin was waging war on two fronts, in the south with Gwenddolau against the Angles and the rebel aristocrats, and in the north, in Strathclyde, against Mungo and his Christians.

In the late 560s, Gwenddolau became unwell, worn down by his efforts to hold his small fiefdom together. His illness affected him for a long time, during which his enemies actively stirred up his neighbours against him.

Gwenddolau and his people were not the only ones fighting the Angles. Octa, who had been Gwenddolau's prisoner, escaped, returned to the Angle land of Bernicia and called for reinforcements from Germany. When he was ready, the Angles fell once more on British lands. Even Geoffrey says that this attack was launched against Albany, that is, *Alba* - Scotland. Geoffrey provides corroboration for this when he says Loth of Lodonesia, Lot of the Lothians, led the British defence. Lot was, however, only the titular leader of an allied force that included Urien of Rheged in south-west Scotland and Gwallog of Ebruac in Yorkshire. These two would have proved difficult enough to control, but Lot's own contingent included a young man by the name of Mordred, who was a very terror.[13] He was to play a part in the deaths of Urien, Arthur and Merlin. Lot's allied army won battles at Ystrad Gwen and the Halls of Berwyn,[14] in what is now the north of England, but he lost several battles too because he was unable to get his army to follow orders and so was unable to win a conclusive victory.[15]

Emboldened by their successes against the Angles, even though they had suffered an equal number of defeats, the British saw an opportunity to attack Gwenddolau and close the ring of allied British kingdoms that encircled the great Angle bridgehead in the south-east of Scotland and the far north of England. The only break in the chain of allied lands lay about Caer Gwenddolau, Gwenddolau's fortress, because the British kings who had been prepared to work with Gwenddolau when he was relatively powerful were not prepared to accept him into their councils after they gained in confidence militarily and his health failed.

The British aim was to form a chain of allied kingdoms to surround the Angle land of Bernicia on the eastern shore before pressing the Angles back into the sea. Gwenddolau would have been pleased to join the alliance, but this was impossible. The exiled leaders of the southern Gododdin would have seen to that by working on the insecurity of their fellow aristocrats.

The freedom Gwenddolau represented also threatened the Church, so the Christians, eager to see a nest of the old way exterminated, found common cause with the exiles. The scene was set for the Arderydd campaign.

CHAPTER FOURTEEN

The Battle of Arderydd

The Battle of Arderydd was the last great pitched battle in which the people of the old way stood in arms against their Christian enemies, which alone would explain the frequent references to it in the most ancient surviving poems. It was more than that, though. It had a social objective – Gwenddolau, who was seen as an upstart lord, was to be crushed – and a military purpose, the closing of the last link in the chain of allied British states about the Angle bridgehead.

The Angle coup in 547 which had led to Emrys and Gwenddolau's revolution had weakened the grip of the traditional lords and allowed many people to revert to the old way. As Jocelyn says, albeit with reference to a similar situation that arose almost ten years later, 'the people of the countryside quickly neglected the way of the Lord, which [Mungo] had shown to them. And as dogs that return to their vomit, they lapsed into the rites of idolatry.'[1] Christianity originally spread from the lower social levels upwards until Constantine made it the state religion of the Roman Empire, after which people who professed to be Christians, being in positions of power, imposed their beliefs from the top down, until Christianity became the only acceptable religion in every court in Europe. In the sixth century, however, it was still only making inroads in Scotland.

The exiled Gododdin chiefs, those who had not come to an accommodation with either Emrys or Gwenddolau, used this revival of the old way as a lever to bring Christian influence to bear on their behalf. Their enemy, Gwenddolau, was of the old way, so they professed sympathy towards Christianity to win the support of Christian sympathisers such as Tutgual of Strathclyde. They were also free with constant reminders that if Gwenddolau was allowed to 'get away with it', traditional lords in Strathclyde and of the Gododdin would be next. A consensus developed: Gwenddolau should be destroyed, Christianity restored and the lands where he held sway divided among the exiles.

The Angles, worn out from fighting Lot and recently chastened by Gwenddolau, were content to allow the Britons to kill each other. Of the main players listed in the *Annales Cambriae* entry for 573, the only one we have not discussed so far is Eliffer. ('The Battle of Arderydd between the sons of Eliffer and Gwenddolau, son of Ceidio, in which battle Gwenddolau was killed. Merlin went mad.')

Eliffer was the daughter of Peredur, who was a high chief based in south-west Scotland. There is an inscription in the parish church at Llangollen, Wales, that, while primarily relevant to a St Collen, also refers to Ethni as the daughter of an Irish lord, when, at this time, the Irish and the Scots were synonymous.[2] As part of his campaign to please his southern bishop, in *Vita Merlini*, Geoffrey shamelessly transposed Peredur, a prince of south-west Scotland, to North Wales. Eliffer was married to Tutgual, king of the Strathclyde Britons. Their sons included Rhydderch and his youngest brother, a man with the unique name Ardderchddrud (obviously a name with the same root meaning as Arderydd).

It was Peredur who struck the first blow in the Arderydd campaign. His lands were contiguous with Gwenddolau's, so he was likely to be among the biggest beneficiaries if Gwenddolau was defeated. Peredur would have hoped to form the last link in the chain of allied British states surrounding the Angles.

The historian W.F. Skene identified the site of the Battle of Arderydd in 1865 using the works of the fourteenth-century Scottish historian John of Fordun, who says the battle was fought 'in the field between Liddel and Carwanolow'. There is a similar identification of the battle site in the *Vita Merlini Silvestris*, where Carwanolow is given as Carwannock. The River Liddel, in the Scottish borderlands, is easily identified. Carwanolow, Skene identified as Carwindlaw, a reference to a place he found in a survey of the Barony of Liddel. This survey also referred to a place called Arthuret, which Skene identified as two small hills, Arthuret Knowes, a mile from Longtown. He thought these hills marked the site of the Battle of Arderydd and concluded that Carwanolow and Carwindlaw were corruptions of Caerwenddolew, that is, Caer Gwenddolau, Gwenddolau's Fort.

When Skene visited Longtown, he found the coaching inn, The Graham Arms, boarded up, but he hired a dog cart and horse from an old coachman and his wife who were looking after the place and set off for Gwenddolau's Fort. Three miles north of Longtown, he crossed what he was told was the Carwinelow Burn, before passing south-east of Lower and Upper Moat farms and climbing the slope to what the locals called a Roman camp, but which he could see were the remains of an ancient British fort. There he found a massive earthen rampart surrounding the inner enclosure of what had once been a great fortress.

Given the location of this ancient fort, Skene's identification of the battlefield as at Arthuret Knowes cannot be correct. If the battle was fought at Arthuret Knowes (one mile north of Longtown, on the River Esk), the Knowes would be south of both Carwanolow and the Liddel Water, and not, as Fordun says, between them.

I set out to visit the site with my 14-year-old son in January 2006. In Longtown, we asked for directions to Carwinley, the most recent version of 'Caer Gwenddolau'. We were told there was no one place of that name, that the name covered a wide area of ground north of the town. Driving north from Longtown, over Skene's Carwinelow Burn, we passed the houses nearest the name Carwinley on our map and drove on to Lowmoat. A householder there directed us to the fort by a path that he said would enable us to avoid Highmoat Farm, where we could see a discouraging dog on a chain. This boggy route – it could hardly be called a path – took us along a derelict railway line that ran south of the Liddel Water. We walked in ankle-deep mud looking for a bend in the river that would give us a bearing until the going became too difficult and we were forced to climb the steep bank that lay to our right. At the top of this, we found woods, then a field and a path. When the path gave out, we kept going until we reached what appeared, even from a few yards away, to be a copse of slight trees and shrubs. My son ran ahead into this undergrowth ('Liddel Strength' on our map) and was soon calling back to me that he had found the ramparts and moat of a fort.

Two entrances break the outer rampart, one to the west and one to the east. Both lead to an inner rampart that surrounds an oval enclosure which contains a high, hemispherical mound that was the capitol of the fortress. The north side of the fortifications run along the edge of a steep cliff that falls down to the Liddel Water far below. Scotland begins on the far bank.

Skene and Nikolai Tolstoy picture the battlefield of Arderydd at Arthuret Knowes, south of Carwanolow, Caer Gwenddolau, and not between the fort and the Liddel Water, as Fordun says. Even if Carwanolow covered an area of ground, as local people said, there was still no way Arthuret Knowes could be between it and the Liddel Water.

I believe Skene was swayed by the belief that Arthuret, with its obvious Arthur connections, was derived from the same root as Arderydd. They are often held to be synonymous, but they are not.

Fordun is clear: the battle was fought between the Liddel Water and Carwanolow (Caer Gwenddolau). The *Vita Merlini Silvestris* says the same. The only field that lies between Caer Gwenddolau and the Liddel Water lies to the north-east of the fort. It is there, I believe, that the Battle of Arderydd was fought.

In 573, an allied British army of overwhelming power marched against Gwenddolau. Rhydderch son of Tutgual, king of Strathclyde, husband of Languoreth, representative of the most powerful of the allies, was in command.

Merlin's loyalties were divided. Rhydderch was his friend and brother-in-law and Strathclyde was his home, but Gwenddolau too was his friend, and Merlin had fought by his side since he was a young man. However, Strathclyde marched under Christian banners and Gwenddolau for the old way, so Merlin stood by Gwenddolau's side, one last time.

Merlin held land and other significant property in Strathclyde. His twin sister was the wife of the man most likely to succeed to the throne of Strathclyde, while Gwenddolau drew his strength from one small part of southern Scotland. His men were vastly outnumbered by the combined forces of all the kingdoms that surrounded them (except, of course, for the Angles). No one could have doubted but that Gwenddolau must be defeated. Still, Merlin sided with Gwenddolau.

The introduction to the Battle of Arderydd in Geoffrey's *Vita* is laconic: 'A time came when it happened that a quarrel arose among the princes of the realm.'[3] He does not say what this quarrel was about. To do so would have been politically dangerous, as it would have disclosed the fact that there was a viable alternative to Christianity.

The initial sparks of war sprang up when Peredur attacked Gwenddolau. The Angles had been cowed at Ystrad Gwen and the Halls of Berwyn, and Peredur and his allies saw an opportunity to turn upon and destroy Gwenddolau. He staged minor raids that increased in scale until war broke out and the land was laid waste.[4]

Even if Theodoric, king of the Angles of Bernicia, had not suffered recent reverses, he would have been mad not to stand back and watch two British armies tear each other to pieces.

Peredur was soon joined in his war by the armies of Strathclyde, the northern Gododdin, Rheged, Ebruac (York, North Pennines) and the exiled aristocrats of the southern Gododdin, the Bryneich. Marching with this allied army was a force of men from Manau, under their wily king, Aedan Mac Gabhran. Accompanying Aedan was his son, a young man of 15 years, who was about to fight in his first great battle. It was to be the first of many. His name was Arthur, and he was the martial wonder of the age.

Rhydderch's allied army seized the initiative and attacked Gwenddolau on his home ground, devastating the countryside as Gwenddolau's men, massively outnumbered, fell back to the gates of Caer Gwenddolau: 'throughout the cities they wasted the innocent people with fierce war'.[5]

The allies' main force, marching from the north, crossed the River Liddel upstream from Gwenddolau's fortress and, approaching along the south side of the river, met Gwenddolau's warriors on the field that lies between the fortress and the river.

When the armies met and joined in battle, 'on both sides alike men fell in the tragic slaughter'. Gwenddolau's war party, heavily outnumbered, went for an early knockout, with desperate charges that strove to break the enemy's shield wall. They were beaten back, until, in a do-or-die attack, Gwenddolau's brothers made a breakthrough:

> They slew the opposing enemy with their hateful swords, and three brothers of the prince [Gwenddolau] who had followed him through his wars, always fighting, cut down and broke the battle lines. Thence they rushed fiercely through the crowded ranks with such an attack that they soon fell killed. At this sight, Merlin . . . grieved and poured out sad complaints throughout the army . . .[6]

The *Vita* has Merlin speaking from the battlefield; this suggests that he played an active part in the fighting:

> 'O glorious youths, who now will stand by my side in arms, and with me will repel the chieftains coming to harm me, and the hosts rushing in upon me? Bold young men your audacity has taken from you your pleasant years and pleasant youth! You who so recently were rushing in arms through the troops, cutting down on every side those who resisted you, now are beating the ground and are red with red blood!'[7]

The flower of Gwenddolau's forces fell in the charge of the three princes, but the rest fell back in order, bringing the bodies of the three dead brothers with them. When Gwenddolau's army faltered and dropped back, Rhydderch's army, seeing its chance, advanced for the kill: 'The terrible fighting ceased not, the lines of battle clashed, foe fell to foe. Blood flowed on every side and the people of both nations died.'[8]

As was the way among Celts in the sixth century, warriors

looked for an opportunity to win individual distinction. According to a poem called 'Dialogue Between Merlin and Taliesin', written between the late thirteenth and early fourteenth century but based on much earlier sources, both oral and written, one young warrior fighting for Gwenddolau made his name at Arderydd:

> Swiftly came Maelgwn's men,
> Warriors ready for battle, for slaughter armed.
> For this battle, Arderydd, they have made
> A lifetime of preparation.[9]

Maelgwn was to take command of the remnants of the dragon soldiers who fought under Gwenddolau at Arderydd and to succeed him as the third and last Pen Dragon. Forty years later, he was to be found old, broken and looking for a place by Merlin's fire, but at Arderydd he came swiftly, ready for battle and armed for slaughter.

Still the army of Gwenddolau and Merlin held fast, until the best warriors in the allied army made their move and their shield wall was shattered: 'All together rushing in arms they fell upon [Gwenddolau's forces[10]] . . . and wounded them and cut them down, nor did they rest until the hostile battalions turned their backs and fled through unfrequented ways.'[11]

The best men of both the victorious and the defeated armies were to win everlasting fame in years to come under Arthur. The very name of the battle, Arderydd, is closely connected with him, and the local landmarks, the Arthuret Hills, which are associated with the battle, suggest not only that Arthur was present at the battle but also that he played a telling part in the fight.

Gwenddolau's army was broken and his routed men in full retreat, Merlin among them. The *Vita* says, 'Merlin called his companions out from the battle and bade them bury the brothers in a richly coloured chapel; and he bewailed the men and did not cease to pour out laments . . .'[12]

This is unlikely. These men died trying to breach a shield wall, and when they failed and their comrades fell back, their bodies are likely to have remained where they fell. Even if the bodies were recovered, it is unlikely that Merlin had time for lavish funeral arrangements. This passage in the *Vita* nevertheless highlights how close Merlin was to Gwenddolau's family.

Fearful losses always followed once a shield wall was broken. In his old age, reminiscing with Taliesin, Merlin would remember the loss of men they had both known. The 'Dialogue Between Merlin and Taliesin' has Merlin say:

> 'The slaughter was terrible,
> Shields shattered and bloody.'[13]

Geoffrey does not say that Gwenddolau was actively involved in the battle. He was unwell at this time, so perhaps he stayed in the fort or was carried to the field on a litter. He does not seem to have died in the battle, but, according to Geoffrey's *Historia*, along with 'some hundred men' after drinking poisoned water, or, and this is more likely, simply tainted water drunk when he was a fugitive after the battle.[14]

It is at this point that Geoffrey's insistence that Merlin was on the Christian side comes back to haunt him. How can he explain why Merlin runs off after the battle to spend years in exile in the Caledonian Wood? The story of Merlin's 'wilderness years' was one of the most famous of all the stories told about him in the oral tradition. Geoffrey could not miss it out, so he says that Merlin went off into the woods because he was distressed by the loss of so many friends in the battle, in particular by the deaths of Gwenddolau's brothers. But this would have been an unlikely reaction, even if they were friends. The more convincing scenario is that the brothers were on the losing side, the side of the old way, that Merlin was on their side and was now not only upset but also in danger. How else are we to make sense of the line in which

Merlin is given the following words? 'O glory of youth, who will now stand by my side in battle to turn back the princes who come to do me ill and their hordes that press upon me?'[15]

The three brothers were dead. Merlin had lost their support. Merlin had to face princes, plural, which suggests he was up against an alliance, which can only be the allied Britons under Rhydderch and Peredur. That Merlin's side needed to turn back those who came against him clearly suggests he was on the side that was on the defensive: Gwenddolau's side.

The most likely reason why someone would run off and hide in a wood after a battle is, of course, that he was on the losing side and running for his life, but, as the Christians won the battle, Geoffrey, trying to promote the idea of a Christian Merlin, has difficulty with this and so adopts the idea that Merlin went mad in the immediate aftermath of the battle (although this calumny was not directed at Merlin in his own lifetime until 30 years later, after he retired from court). By my reckoning, Merlin did not run away because he was mad; he ran away because he was not stupid. Gwenddolau was dead, his army was destroyed and the cause of the old way broken. Merlin was on the run: 'He departed secretly, and fled to the woods not wishing to be seen as he fled. He entered the wood and rejoiced to lie hidden under the ash trees.'[16]

In the wake of the battle, the aristocracy reasserted itself and retook the lands that had been theirs under Vortigern, while those who had fought under Emrys and Gwenddolau became landless men. Many of them doubtless escaped into the great wood with Merlin, as described here by the 'Dialogue':

> Seven score heroes, maddened by battle,
> To the forest of Celyddon they fled.
> Since I Myrddin, am second only to Taliesin,
> Let my words be heard as truth.[17]

It was seven years before Merlin came out of hiding.

Merlin cannot have failed to regret the death of his nephew, Languoreth's oldest son, who was probably only 15 years old and fighting in his first battle at the time. It would take the death of Tutgual the king and the imminent threat of an Angle invasion to bring Merlin back to the court of Strathclyde and power, when the very existence of the British was at stake, but never again was he to march in arms for the old way against the Christians. The strategic balance was struck at Arderydd. From then on, while Christianity would suffer tactical defeats, its rise was inexorable.

After Arderydd, the traditional chiefs of the southern Gododdin were restored to power. Peredur, no doubt, gained his share. Urien of Rheged became secure in the south-west and Strathclyde, and the people of Ebruac in the Pennines. Strathclyde, now the undisputed dominant power in west and central Scotland, found its writ running as far south as Cumbria.[18]

The greatest beneficiary of the Arderydd campaign was a Scot, Aedan Mac Gabhran, who had brought the men of Manau to fight for Rhydderch and discovered a warrior star among their number, his son, a 15 year old by the name of Arthur.

CHAPTER FIFTEEN

The Wilderness Years

Most of the survivors of Gwenddolau's shattered army, those who were not immediately caught and killed, probably returned to their homes. Others, who, like Merlin, were prize catches or who were simply determined to continue the fight or who had no home to return to would have had no option but to make the best of it in the forest. The figure 140 contained in the ancient poems, being the number of men and women who escaped with Merlin, need not be taken literally, although it seems sensible. Rhydderch's men set out in hot pursuit. As Rhydderch's warriors searched the woods, Merlin ran and hid and ran again. The poem 'The Greetings'[1] tells of Merlin 'Hidden from the dogs of Rhydderch the Faithful'.[2]

Merlin, doubtless distressed by the failure of his cause and the loss of so many of his friends, must have been especially saddened that, by going against her advice and fighting against her family in a battle in which her eldest son was killed, he had alienated Languoreth. Echoes of this time can be heard in poems inspired by ancient oral tradition:

> Sweet apple tree in the glade,
> Trodden is the earth around its base.

The men of Rhydderch see me not,
[Languoreth][3] no longer loves nor greets me
I am hated by Rhydderch's strongest scion.
I have despoiled both his son and daughter:
Death visits them all – why not me?
After Gwenddolau no one shall honour me,
No diversions attend me,
No fair women visit me.
Though at Arderydd I wore a golden torque
The swan-white woman despises me now.[4]

It has been supposed the 'scion' referred to above was Mungo, but Rhydderch's strongest scion is, for me, obviously, Languoreth. Languoreth is referred to, then the strongest scion, then Languoreth's children, then Languoreth again as the swan-white woman. How likely is it that Mungo should have had a place in this list (especially as, by my reckoning, Mungo had gone into exile in Wales two years before)? The despoliation of Rhydderch's son is easily explained. He died in the battle. The despoliation of Rhydderch and Languoreth's daughter, Merlin's niece, is inexplicable with reference to available evidence. Perhaps she followed her uncle Merlin into Gwenddolau's camp.

Merlin soon settled in the relative safety of the great Caledonian Wood that covered much of southern Scotland.[5] To begin with, times were hard. The *Vita* paints a rather gloomy picture of Merlin alone, struggling to exist on the meagre rations he can find in the forest: 'If, by chance, I find some navews [turnips] deep in the ground, the hungry swine and the voracious boars rush up and snatch them away from me as I dig them up from the turf.'[6]

To begin with, Merlin's band of followers must have been few in number, but in the weeks and months that followed, others must have joined them until a viable community formed in the forest. This community probably included a disproportionate number of Druids, as any Druid associated with Gwenddolau and Merlin would have known that, if captured, she or he would have had no chance of survival. The authority of the Christians did not extend far beyond the tree line, so they were relatively safe. If a traitor had given away the location of their camp, no force capable of catching them could have approached without being seen well in advance. In any event, they probably moved between several hideouts, although their main base was probably near Hart Fell.[7]

Many of Merlin's fellow fugitives would have had experience of living off the land, and there were always 'locals' to help them if need be. It would not have taken long before Merlin's band was comfortably placed. However, the mere ability to survive would not have been enough for Merlin, and although he was relatively safe and could have comforts such as books brought to him, he was out of political circulation and unable to return to his home. News that the Telleyr Christians were now in control in Strathclyde must have exacerbated the frustration of his political impotence.

Languoreth, too, would have had her problems. She would have been under suspicion because of her association with Merlin, although her husband's destruction of Gwenddolau would have stood her in good stead. It is ironic that the Christians probably judged Languoreth with reference to her brother and her husband, and not as an individual of moment in her own right. Because she was a woman, they missed the fact that she was more astute than her brother, more able than her husband and more dangerous than either of them. She was to be a main player in her own right in the events of the next four decades.

Because Languoreth's eldest son had died at the Battle of Arderydd, any sympathy she might have felt for Merlin because he was on the run for his life must have been tempered with fury at his stubborn refusal to accept her advice and his utter folly in coming out for Gwenddolau when it was clear to her, as it should have been clear to him, that Strathclyde and its allies were bound to prevail.

Rhydderch, too, must have felt antagonistic towards Merlin, even though they had been friends. He too had lost a son, and Merlin's gross lack of judgement when he took sides against the armies of Strathclyde had given Rhydderch's competitors for the crown ammunition to use against him. Even if Rhydderch had wanted to help Merlin at this time, it would have been difficult to do so without endangering his prospects of succeeding to the throne. Rhydderch had led the forces of Strathclyde against Gwenddolau and so had distanced himself from the rebellious Merlin, but his position as next in line for the throne was by no means secure.

Languoreth must have known that if her husband was to succeed his father, Tutgual, she could not afford to be too closely associated with her exiled brother. However, there were innumerable people of the old way whose business took them in and out of the forest, so she was able to stay in contact with Merlin in secret. Languoreth and Rhydderch knew that when Tutgual died they would need the support of the people of the old way and of as many of the different Christian factions as they could garner if Rhydderch was to be selected as the next king. They knew too that the Telleyr Christians would be challenged by the Mungo Christians when Tutgual died and that, regardless of who came out on top, Merlin's support would be vital to counter Christian influence.

Merlin must have known that ending his exile would not be easy. Mungo had been exiled because he had been a troublemaker. Merlin was in exile because he had risen in arms against his king. It would be much easier for Mungo to return than Merlin.

Mungo founded a monastery in North Wales after he disagreed with David and they parted company. Among his monks was Asaph, a young and ambitious monk who was not prepared to accept Mungo's authority without question. He and Mungo argued over who should be in charge, and when Asaph won, Mungo was forced to leave. Taking with him the monks who remained loyal to him, Mungo headed north and established a new monastery in Hoddam, Dumfriesshire.

The *Catholic Encyclopaedia*, Vol. VIII, says, after the Battle of Arderydd in 573:

> At the earnest appeal of King Roderick [*sic*], [Mungo] returned thither, accompanied by many of his Welsh disciples. For eight years, he fixed his see at Hoddam in Dumfriesshire, evangelising thence the districts of Galloway and Cumberland. About 581 he finally returned to Glasgow . . .

These 'eight years' do not make sense. We know that when Mungo was expelled from Strathclyde he went to live in Wales with David. We know too that Mungo disagreed with David and with a British chief, Melconde Galganu, and left to set up with Asaph, and that when he disagreed with Asaph he left to set up in Hoddam. Mungo was not an easy man to get along with, but even he would not have found it easy to disagree with so many people in such a short period of time that he would have eight years to spend in Hoddam. I agree with the *Catholic Encyclopaedia* that Mungo returned to Scotland after the Battle of Arderydd, but I cannot see that he was in Hoddam for more than two or three years. It follows that he left Scotland some time before the battle (573). He had left Strathclyde because he had fallen out with Tutgual, the king of Strathclyde, so the most likely date for his return is 580, when Tutgual died and Rhydderch came to the throne. This means that Mungo probably left Strathclyde for his Welsh exile in 572 and returned to Strathclyde eight years later, in 580, after having to spend two or three years biding his time in Hoddam.

Jocelyn's account of it is as follows:

> The holy patron Kentigern built his church at Holdelm and
> ordaining priests and clerics, he established his Episcopal
> seat there for some time for a certain reason. Afterwards
> being admonished by a divine revelation and being
> demanded by justice, he translated his seat to his city of
> Glasgow.[8]

When Jocelyn says that Mungo stayed at Hoddam 'for a certain
reason' and does not say what that reason was, we can be certain
it was not one that showed Mungo in a good light. Mungo stayed
at Hoddam because he was forbidden to return to Glasgow while
Tutgual was alive.

When, with the passage of time, it was safer for her to do so,
Languoreth arranged to meet Merlin face to face, probably near
Cadzow, away from the prying eyes of the court but far enough in
among the trees for Merlin to be able to escape if need be.

Languoreth's plan to put Rhydderch on the throne of Strathclyde
when his father, Tutgual, died suited Merlin. He had rebelled
against Tutgual, and he would not be allowed back to court, far less
back into a powerful position, while Tutgual was alive. Rhydderch
was Merlin's friend and brother-in-law. If he became king, Merlin's
position would be immediately strengthened. It was vital to Merlin
and Languoreth that Rhydderch be king.

Stories told during Merlin and Languoreth's lifetime were taken
south in the century after their death and used to create poems that
tell of their meetings in the woods. The poem 'Dialogue Between
Merlin and His Sister'[9] is probably the product of many hands,
each with access to different oral and written sources. We can be
sure the same censorship that applied to Geoffrey, the same career
considerations that influenced Jocelyn and the same dramatic
demands that restricted Malory influenced each contributor to this

poem, but it still allows some insight into events in the late 570s. The broad gist of the relationship between brother and sister is plain, and the wider political context can be made out, but the writer of the 'Dialogue' and later editors and censors do not appear to have entirely understood the material they were working with, so the details are confusing. This is understandable, because they were writing centuries after the events they were dealing with, in Wales, a foreign country, and in ignorance of the precise political context that occasioned the poem in the first place. Even if they had understood what had gone on, they could not have repeated it openly. In fairness to these writers, they were not intent on writing history but a popular entertainment.

The middle part of the 'Dialogue' is made up of rambling prophecies about who will succeed who, who will thrive and who will fail – medieval people seem to have had an insatiable appetite for prophecies. Once the prophecies are ignored (because they are almost all anachronistic impossibilities), only a little of the poem is left, and it is in this remainder that most of the relevant historical evidence is to be found.

I cannot see that Merlin and Languoreth met only once, at the end of Merlin's exile. I suspect they met many times between 573 and 580 and that these meetings have been conflated in the poem for dramatic purposes. The screenwriter William Goldman recommends coming into a scene as late as possible. This is exactly what happens in the 'Dialogue'; rather than bother with preliminary meetings, the poem addresses the meeting that took place immediately after Languoreth became queen in 580. However, in one verse, Languoreth says:

> 'I pine every time I leave my brother,
> Tears furrow my tired cheek . . .'[10]

This suggests several meetings before what purports to be the single meeting described in the poem.

In 580, Tutgual died and Rhydderch was chosen as the new king. When Languoreth became queen of Strathclyde, she slipped away in secret to visit Merlin in his exile in the woods:

> 'I have come hither to tell
> Of the jurisdiction I have in the North;
> Every region's beauty is known to me.'[11]

She told Merlin she was now a queen, with all the power that entailed, and that the whole kingdom was open to her, which might have been poetic licence but it did broadly reflect how her fortunes had improved. They discussed developments in Strathclyde and how to end Merlin's exile. Languoreth was realistic; she knew that bringing her brother back would be a delicate business and that her husband had to be careful not to overly favour the old way in the person of an exiled traitor. Although Rhydderch was now king of Strathclyde, the fact remained, in the Arderydd campaign, Merlin had taken up arms against the late king, Tutgual, and fought against the army of Strathclyde. He had also been and remained an inveterate enemy of Christianity and the Christians.

Languoreth reminded Merlin that she had advised him against allying himself with Gwenddolau. Merlin, who had refused to accept her advice at that time, now accepted he had been wrong and asked her what he should do next: 'Since the action at Arderydd . . . [Languoreth] and all that happened to me, dull of understanding I am, where shall I go for delight?'[12]

Languoreth had direct access to events in Strathclyde and first-hand knowledge of diplomatic exchanges. Merlin, stuck as he was in the woods, had no such direct access or first-hand knowledge, but he would have been kept informed by old soldiers from Gwenddolau's army who travelled in the forest and by the Druid network. The difference between Merlin and Languoreth was less the information available to them than their judgement and temperament. Languoreth's had proved to be better than her brother's, although it is unlikely that Merlin acknowledged this, even to himself; men do not tend to think that way. It is more likely he recognised that Languoreth, being a queen, held better cards than him.

Even the least-informed person in Strathclyde knew the Angles were massing in Bernicia and that it would not be long before they waged all-out war against the Britons. Languoreth and Merlin recognised that if the Britons stood divided, they would fall separately, and that the only way to survive was to unite in the face of their common foe. They also knew how difficult it would be to achieve this unity, given the loose and disparate nature of the British political system and the stubborn individualism engendered by Celtic culture. Externally, the people of Strathclyde were divided from their fellow Britons in the kingdom of the Gododdin. Internally, Strathclyde was divided between Christians and supporters of the old way.

The 'Dialogue' provides a glimpse of the politics of the day and allows cross-referencing which dates the episode it describes. Aedan Mac Gabhran's men of Manau had fought well at Arderydd, and after the battle Aedan's prestige and power had increased substantially. The 'Dialogue', through Merlin, touches on the circumstances that subsisted in central Scotland in the first few years that followed the Battle of Arderydd:

> 'Since Gwenddolau was slain at Arderydd
> You feel only fear, sister
> Merfyn Vrych, from the region of Manaw.'[13]

These lines, when set in their true time and place, are easily explained. Merlin's sister was Merfyn Vrych, that is, daughter of Morken.[14] Manau was centrally situated between Strathclyde, the land of the Picts and the lands of the Gododdin, and bordered Merlin and Languoreth's family lands of Cadzow. 'From the region of Manaw' does not mean that Languoreth was from the region of Manau but that Manau was the source of her fear. She was concerned that Manau would prove a threat.

But why should Languoreth be in danger from the region of Manau? This only makes sense when the political circumstances that subsisted after Arderydd are considered. Strathclyde had won a great victory, but it owed this, in no small part, to the men of Manau, who had fought under the titular command of Rhydderch but who had been brought to the field by their king, Aedan. After Arderydd, Aedan expanded his power north and west of Strathclyde. A force that had been an ally had become a potential threat. Aedan's son, the warlord Arthur Mac Aedan, was now in his late teens or 20 years old and had already won several battles that would contribute to his reputation as one of the greatest military men in history. Aedan was an ambitious and clever politician, Arthur was the best military leader of the day and the men of Manau were swiftly becoming Celtic Spartans. Languoreth had reason to be afraid of Manau. It is this fear on Languoreth's part to which Merlin refers when he says, in effect, I know that you have been worried about Manau ever since Arderydd.

A few verses later in this same poem, Languoreth asks Merlin who will be the leader of their cause, the cause of the old way, now that their father Morken is dead. Merlin says that Rhydderch will be – or, at least, should be – the next champion of the old way.

When Tutgual died, it became clear there was a chance that Merlin might return to court. Rhydderch was king and wanted Merlin back. Mungo was back, and Merlin was the only one who could stand up to him. The men of Manau and the Angles were also both a looming threat.

The ruins of Cadzow Castle, Hamilton, above the River Avon, on the site of the fortress that was Merlin's childhood home.

Representation in St Mungo's Cathedral, Glasgow, of the corpse of Fergus on the cart Mungo used to bring it to Glasgow.

The view information at Cadzow Castle, showing Ben Arthur.
The words are almost worn away by countless pointing fingers.

Hills of Dunipace, eastern hill.

The Capitol at Caer Gwenddolau.
The Battle of Arderydd (573) was fought near by.

Stained-glass window, Stobo Kirk, showing a Christian view
of the meeting of Merlin and Mungo Kentigern in 580.

The point at which the Pausayl Burn meets the Tweed, where Mungo and Merlin met in 580.

St Mungo's Cathedral, Glasgow, on the site of Mungo's church. Note the fish and the ring on the coat of arms on the lamp post.

The Druids' hill from the graveyard of
St Mungo's Cathedral, Glasgow.

St Mungo's Cathedral from the Druids' hill, now the Necropolis.

View of the top of the Druids' hill, now the Necropolis, Glasgow.

Apsley Street, Glasgow. View from Ardery Street.
Merlin's house was at the top of the hill.

Ardery Street, Glasgow.

Modern buildings on the site of Merlin's house.

The hill at Drumelzier, Dunipace, where Merlin was buried. The modern quarry buildings can be seen in the background.

Merlin says to Languoreth:

> 'Listen to rumours,
> Let the wind whistle in the valley,
> Seven years, as it was long since.'[15]

Tutgual's death, in 580, was seven years after the Battle of Arderydd. If I am correct, Merlin spent seven years in exile, until Rhydderch succeeded Tutgual. Merlin and Languoreth's priority, now that Rhydderch was king, was to maintain him on the throne. Merlin prophesies:

> 'The wind tells me
> Rhydderch Hael's standard cannot fall.'[16]

There then follows some of the vague and anachronistic prophecies that I have referred to. In amongst them is an obscure verse that includes the words, spoken by Merlin:

> 'Rhydderch Hael, while he is the enemy
> Of the Bardic city in Clyd
> Where will he come to the ford?'[17]

Rhydderch was new to the throne and had doubtless needed Christian support to ensure his succession. In these circumstances, Rhydderch had, at least, to appear to favour Christianity and to be against the old way in public. When he first came to the throne, he would have been bound to reward his supporters and, until he had consolidated his position, he would have been careful not to alienate the powers at court. Initially, this meant favouring Christian Glasgow at the expense of the Druids.

The 'Bardic city' on the Clyde was probably that hotbed of the old way, Partick, situated next to the Druids' island, Whiteinch, and the one-time home base of Morken and Cathen. The Christian stronghold was the newer and rapidly rising town of Glasgow.

Merlin asks when will Rhydderch cross over from the ecumenical ground he is standing on to the side of the old way, that is, come out openly as a supporter of the old way. Rhydderch, though, had no intention of coming out firmly on one side or the other. He was minded to use one side against the other and to control both.

It is much more likely that Languoreth encouraged her brother to meet the Christians halfway. She knew it would stand Rhydderch in good stead if he could show that he, and only he, could bring Merlin and Mungo to the negotiating table and the warring Christian and old-way factions together. If only Merlin would undertake to stand with the Christians behind the new king, Rhydderch, then he could return from exile.

Languoreth asks Merlin if he will allow the Christians a place in the community, but, for Merlin, compromise with the Christians is not an option:

> LANGUORETH: 'Who will there be to keep order?
> Will there be a church, and a portion for a priest?'

> MERLIN: 'There will be no portion for priest nor minstrel,
> nor repairing to the altar,
> Until the heaven falls to the earth.'[18]

Something has been lost in translation here. For minstrel we may read bard, and for bard we may read Druid. If this is not correct, then the insertion of minstrel, in the sense of entertainer, is nonsense. Reading these lines in context, I take them to mean that Merlin intended to rule alone, without recourse to either the Christian or Druidic parties.

Languoreth responds:

> 'My twin-brother, well you have answered me,
> Myrddin, son of Morvryn the skilful –
> Yet your tale is a sad one!'[19]

Once again, Merlin has refused to follow his sister's good advice.

This answer disappoints Languoreth, but she undertakes to tell her husband.

Merlin and Languoreth both foresaw the destruction the Angles would wreak across their land as they fought their way once more to the western sea. They were afraid that this time their destination would not be the Solway Firth, as it had been in the 550s, but the Firth of Clyde in the centre of Scotland. Such an expedition, if successful, would divide and destroy first the Gododdin lands and then Strathclyde. The Angles would then be perfectly perched to fall on Dalriada in the west or to consolidate again, south of the Antonine Wall, before attacking the Picts in the north. No one was safe.

Languoreth knew that the right thing to do was to put the survival of the community above personal preferences, but Mungo and Merlin did not see it that way. For both of them, it was all or nothing.

The 'Dialogue' ends with several verses of farewells in which, again, Languoreth urges Merlin to consider working with the Christians. When, again, he refuses, they agree to disagree.

Before they parted – Languoreth to report to Rhydderch; Merlin to continue his stubborn stance in the forest – Languoreth excused her past coldness towards him by reminding him that she had lost a son in a battle in which he had been active on the other side:

> 'My only brother, chide me not.
> Since the battle of Arderydd I have suffered.'[20]

Merlin consoled her in her grief and promised her that she need never fear his letting her down again:

> '[Languoreth], be not dissatisfied.
> Has not the burden been consigned to earth?

Everyone must give up what he loves.
While I live, I will not forsake you,
And until death will keep you in mind . . .'[21]

They needed each other. He needed her to help him get back to court. She needed him to be the king's first counsellor; she could not do this job herself – at least, not directly. She could, however, work through her husband and her brother.

There then follows a Christian imprecation from Languoreth:

'Swift the steed, free the winds
I commend my blameless brother
To God, the supreme ruler
Partake of the communion before thy death.'[22]

Merlin's response is unsurprising:

'I will not receive the communion
From excommunicated monks,
With their cloaks on their hips –
May God himself give me communion!'

We can safely assume that Languoreth's asking Merlin to take Christian communion was either self-censorship on the poet's part or the result of a later amendment gauged to show Languoreth, at least, in a Christian light. There was no particular prospect of Merlin's death at this time, and even less prospect of his converting to Christianity.

The reference to 'excommunicated monks, with their cloaks on their hips' and the assertion that he would take communion only from God himself smacks of ideas that would burgeon with the Reformation of the Christian Church, a century after the surviving manuscript versions of the poem were written. 'May God himself give me communion!' suggests a sidestepping of the organised church of his day and presages 'reformed' ideas. The reference to excommunicated monks may be a reference to monks of the Celtic

Church who were deprecated by the Roman Church that was in power in the late Middle Ages. That they had their habits about their waists suggests the rough-and-ready Celtic clergy.

> LANGUORETH: 'I will commend my blameless brother
> To the supreme Caer
> May God take care of Myrddin!'

> MERLIN: 'I too command my blameless sister
> To the supreme Caer . . .'[23]

This leave-taking is significant because it contains an echo of a ghost of a voice that speaks of a way of life that is now all but forgotten.

Languoreth left Merlin still in exile in the forest and returned to court in Strathclyde. The scene was set for her to take centre stage.

CHAPTER SIXTEEN

Battle Rejoined

In 580, the death of Tutgual king of Strathclyde removed the main obstacle preventing Mungo's return to Strathclyde. Kings in Strathclyde were not chosen by primogeniture but by tanistry, that is, a system by which a prospective king stood to be chosen from among the late king's closest male family members. Rhydderch was not an automatic choice to succeed his father, so he needed supporters. Given Mungo returned to Strathclyde at the same time as Rhydderch became king, it is reasonable to suppose that Mungo and Rhydderch came to an understanding and that Mungo, as the leader of one of the strongest Christian factions in Strathclyde, used his influence to buy his way back into favour. It would not have been as easy for Merlin to end his exile. Merlin's crime, open rebellion against his king, was more serious by far than Mungo's crime, being a general troublemaker. It would not have been acceptable to the moderate Christians if Rhydderch allowed his friend and brother-in-law back to court immediately upon taking the crown, although this would not have prevented Merlin using his influence on Rhydderch's behalf.

Weighing in Merlin's favour was the fact that the Angles were preparing to attack and Rhydderch knew he would need a united people if his kingdom was to survive. He knew, too, that less than ten years before, in the Arderydd campaign, two British armies, divided by religion, had torn each other to pieces and that nothing would give greater comfort to the Angles than for the Britons to engage again in civil war. Consequently, Rhydderch's policy upon taking the throne was to bring the various factions in his kingdom together to work as one under his aegis. Unfortunately for Rhydderch, Mungo was more interested in carrying on where he had left off: fighting the people of the old way and people he saw as heretic Christians. As Jocelyn puts it, '[Mungo] returned to fight against the ancient enemy and to drive him out of the boundaries of the north . . .'[1]

Jocelyn says that Rhydderch and an immense multitude filled with joy came out to meet Mungo, but, given Jocelyn was writing promotional material, this must be suspect. If looked at carefully, Jocelyn's account reveals something of what really happened:

> [Mungo] revealed his purpose, saying, 'Whoever envies the salvation of men and is against the word of God, I command them in virtue of that same word of God that they depart straightway and not to pour any impediment onto those who would believe.' Having spoken this much, a vast multitude of skeleton-like creatures, horrible in form and in aspect, quickly departed from that assemblage and fled from the sight of all.[2]

'Skeleton-like creatures' was, almost certainly, meant to describe Druids and others of the old way. It is likely that Mungo appeared before the new king and the assembled people and started a fight that led to those of the old way and perhaps some Christians who were opposed to Mungo storming out. It is unlikely that Mungo, newly returned from exile, was in a position to decide who should stay and who should go.

BATTLE REJOINED

The Telleyr Christians had been in power in Glasgow since the early 570s, when Mungo was sent into exile and Merlin joined Gwenddolau. They knew that Mungo would upset the delicate balance of tolerance that had subsisted between the people of the old way and the Telleyr Christians in the last years of Tutgual's reign. It was in their interest to have Merlin back at court as a counterbalance to Mungo. Languoreth wanted Merlin back. So too did Rhydderch, but he had to be careful. The only ones who did not want to end Merlin's exile were the Mungo Christians, who were outnumbered. When they recognised that Merlin was to be allowed to end his exile, they had to make the best of it and arranged to have Mungo made part of the delegation that was to be sent to meet him. According to the *Silvestris*, Mungo was the main mover in bringing Merlin back to Strathclyde, but the *Silvestris* is a biased source, and this is impossible to believe. In no circumstances does it make sense to suppose that, as the *Silvestris* says, Mungo went to the woods, met Merlin and at Merlin's behest forgave him for his sins: 'On a certain day, as [Mungo] was . . . praying in a thicket in the wilderness, it happened that a certain madman [Merlin³], naked and hairy and devoid of all worldly possessions crossed his path like a raging beast.'

This naked, hairy, raging and beastly Merlin is a clumsy fiction, as is the first statement attributed to him: 'I am a Christian.' Merlin is then said to confess that he was the cause of the 'slaughter of all the slain who were killed in the battle . . . which was fought in the plain that lies between Liddel and Carwannock' and that he is in exile in the forest as a penance for this sin. Mungo, we are told, felt sorry for Merlin and prayed to his god to help him, although all Mungo asks is that Merlin's misfortunes and sorrows be held to his credit when he dies and not that something should be done to ameliorate these misfortunes and sorrows in life.

The *Silvestris* does not say where this meeting took place, although it is traditionally held to have been near Stobo in south-central Scotland, some 50 miles by the oldest roads from Glasgow. (A beautiful little stained-glass window in Stobo Church represents the scene.) This is an understandable place for Mungo and Merlin to have met. Stobo lies between Glasgow-Partick and what was then the heart of the Caledonian forest, and the place where the Pausayl Burn runs into the River Tweed would have been easy to find.

In a later enhancement of the tradition that had grown about Merlin and Mungo's meeting near Stobo, the writer of the *Silvestris* says that Merlin died and was buried at this same place. The meeting point is now called Drumelzier. I believe that this was the *name* of the place where Merlin died and was buried but that these things happened far from Stobo. The real Drumelzier lies elsewhere.

Geoffrey's *Vita Merlini* contains a more instructive story. In this, Merlin is unhappy with his lot as he strives to live in deprived circumstances in the woods (he is portrayed as a madman in this version too). One day, Merlin was talking to himself, and 'The sound reached a passer-by, who turned aside towards the source of the speech he heard.'[4] When Merlin saw this traveller, he ran away and hid in the woods.

> Then this traveller fell in with another man, who was from the court of Rodarch [Rhydderch] . . . Rodarch's wife was Ganieda [Gwynedd/Languoreth] a beautiful woman with whom he lived most happily: she was Merlin's sister. Distressed by what had happened to her brother, she had sent retainers to the woods and the depths of the countryside to bring him back. It was one of these who came upon the traveller.
>
> The [queen's] messenger set off into the woods. He searched the deepest valleys, he crossed high mountains, and he penetrated the most secluded places, seeking his

man everywhere. There was a spring on the very top of a
certain mountain, surrounded on all sides by hazels and
dense thorns. Merlin had settled there, and from that place
he could watch the whole woodland and the running and
gambolling of the creatures of the wild . . . Thither the
messenger climbed, and with silent step went on up the
heights seeking the man. At last, he saw the fountain and
Merlin sitting on the grass behind it . . .[5]

The messenger attracted Merlin's attention by playing a harp. (Not
the easiest instrument to sneak up on someone with.) He sang of
Guendoloena (Gwendolyn), Merlin's wife, and of her grief at his
absence.

Of all the early sources, only the *Vita* mentions Merlin's wife,
Gwendolyn, but many have him involved with women. There are
dramatic reasons for this. Ancient romances, much like modern
romantic comedies, concentrate on the unmarried. Merlin was
indeed involved with many women in many different capacities
throughout his long life, but not necessarily romantically. To have
detailed his dealings with women accurately would have meant
showing them actively involved in innumerable pursuits, including
political and intellectual. This would have highlighted the more
prominent part that women played in life before Christianity
became prevalent. When women, such as Mordred's queen,
were unavoidably involved in events in Merlin's life, even if their
involvement was political, they were made 'safe' by reducing their
part to that of 'romantic interest' only.

Gwendolyn was, as one would expect:

Beautiful beyond goddesses in fairness; beyond the privet
petal; the rose in bloom; beyond the lilies of the field!
The splendour of spring shone in her alone, the beauty of
the stars was held in her two eyes, gold glittered in her
glorious hair.

But the messenger goes on to describe how this has all been ruined by Merlin's absence:

> All this has gone: gone the grace, the delicate bloom, the snowy splendour of her flesh. She is not what once she was, but worn with weeping. She knows not where the prince has gone, whether living still or dead. She lies sick with sorrow, faded utterly in the dissolution of long grief.

This business of a harp, a song and a pining wife is doubtless romantic nonsense, disguising what really happened. Merlin may have missed his wife, but there were vital political reasons that dictated his return to court.

It is possible, by reading the various accounts of this meeting as one and by considering them in their historical context, to work out what happened. The *Silvestris* is restricted to Mungo's meeting with Merlin in the woods. It is, of course, entirely gauged to glorify Mungo at Merlin's expense. Geoffrey's *Vita*, concerning the same meeting, does not name the king's emissary who encounters Merlin. It is doubtful this was Mungo and more likely it was simply one of the king's captains. If Mungo had been in charge, it is almost certain, given his record, that Merlin would not have made it back to court alive. Geoffrey's account is more detailed, although it is a plainly glamorised version of whatever truth lies behind it. The story Geoffrey tells is perhaps close to what the court heard: a version passed down and worked on over the centuries as part of the oral tradition before Geoffrey recorded it in writing. I have disregarded the 'Merlin was mad' theme in both accounts, because this was an invention of the late 590s gauged to undermine Merlin's credibility and authority. I have also disregarded the spurious romantic material concerning the distress of Merlin's wife and Languoreth, which is not to say that Gwendolyn and Languoreth were not distressed by Merlin's exile, only that he did not come back to court simply because his wife was missing him.

By 580, Languoreth's Christian father-in-law was dead and her husband was king. She was ideally placed to engineer Merlin's return. Even Mungo's presence could be turned to her advantage once the non-Mungo Christians decided that Merlin was useful to them too. Languoreth still had to be careful it did not become known that she, and, through her, Rhydderch, had been in contact with an exiled traitor during the reign of the late king. No king, far less a new king, would want to establish such a precedent, so Rhydderch and Languoreth's continuing contact with Merlin had to be kept quiet. Consequently, they pretended they did not know where Merlin was when the suggestion that he be asked to return was mooted and made a show of sending out men to search for him and of looking pleased and surprised when one of their men returned and reported to the court that he had been found. Mungo would have been understandably suspicious and wary.

According to Geoffrey, Languoreth's retainer found Merlin by a spring on the top of a mountain surrounded by hazel and dense thorns. Merlin was apparently asking himself at the time, 'How does it happen that the seasons are not all the same, distinguished only by their four numbers?' Unlike Jocelyn, for whom a recital of 'for God all things are possible' was enough, Merlin asked questions and sought explanations for the world around him. Of course, unless the retainer took shorthand and lay in the bushes noting what Merlin said, this is unlikely to be an entirely accurate report. It would be too much to suggest that when Merlin was found he was actually embroiled in the study of natural cycles, although it is possible. It is more likely that this was one of the ways in which Merlin filled his time when he was in exile and, knowing this, the writer added it to the scene in which Merlin is found.

One constant theme that runs through Merlin's life is his fascination with learning. He is consistently described observing and questioning and discussing his findings. Merlin was a scientist and a philosopher. Intellectual inactivity would have been abhorrent to him, and there is no reason to suppose he was unable to carry on with his scientific and philosophical work during his seven years in exile. Living away from towns, among friends, Merlin would have had books brought to him, and he would have had opportunities to talk to fellow Druids, scholars, bards and travellers from foreign lands who passed through the forest or who went out of their way to visit him.

If Geoffrey did not have a source that suggested Merlin was studious, why would he invent such a thing? The importance of this passage is that it reflects what Merlin was thought to be doing while in exile in the woods. In the twelfth century, when Geoffrey was writing, scientific activities were considered less dangerous than in later centuries, when Christians had recognised science as a serious threat to their hegemony and so something to be controlled and restricted. Consequently, Geoffrey portrayed Merlin as a scientist on the understanding that this would be considered no more than odd and exotic. Today, in a scientific age, the study of nature shows Merlin in a good light, but this was not Geoffrey's intention.

The last thing that Mungo wanted, so soon after his own return to court, was Merlin back in action. He opposed this at every turn, but he was in a difficult position as he too had only recently been in exile, and his influence, even among the Christians, was far from absolute. The Telleyr faction had always opposed him, but many other responsible Christians recognised the threat that Mungo now posed. This was no time for internal strife, but with Mungo about, discord was almost inevitable.

It was agreed that steps be taken to bring Merlin back to court. Mungo was not, as tradition suggests, the head of the delegation that went into the forest to negotiate with Merlin in this connection. This would make no sense. They were inveterate enemies. It is more likely that Mungo insisted he go along, and that this was allowed. Stobo/Drumelzier, where the Pausayl Burn ran into the River Tweed, was agreed as the meeting place. We can be certain that wherever the meeting took place it was not at Merlin's hideout, near Hart Fell, in the deep heart of the forest. He would have wanted to keep this secret. Merlin would have been naturally cautious until all was agreed and he was sure there was no trap. Stobo/Drumelzier was ideally situated; it was close enough to the edge of the forest to allow Merlin to escape if need be, while at the same time being readily accessible to those travelling from Glasgow-Partick. The negotiations were successful; indeed, they were probably formalities, the main matters having been agreed in advance. As Geoffrey says, 'Straightway they left the woods and came, rejoicing together, to the city of the king.'[6]

Mungo was back; Merlin was back. The scene was set for a struggle that in the next two years would change the history of Britain forever.

Geoffrey describes how Languoreth and Gwendolyn welcomed Merlin upon his return to court when his exile ended:

> So the queen was delighted by regaining her brother and the wife became glad over the return of her husband. They vied with each other in kissing him and they twined their arms about his neck, so great was the affection that moved them. The king also received him with such honour as was fitting, and the chieftains who thronged the palace rejoiced in the city.[7]

Merlin and Mungo agreed that unity amongst their kingdom and amongst the Britons was vital, but each thought that he alone should be the king's chief counsellor. The Telleyr Christians had reason to be afraid of Mungo and sympathised with Merlin. It was also clearly in Merlin's favour that he was Languoreth's brother. Consequently, Mungo's prospects of success in the long run were bleak, so he loosed the mob of his fanatic faction and set them to attack those who opposed him.

The *Vita* says this drove Merlin mad and that he wanted to run away, back to the woods: 'But when Merlin saw such great crowds of men present he was not able to endure them; he went mad again, and, filled anew with fury, he wanted to go to the woods, and he tried to get away by stealth.'[8]

Again, though, I rule out the reference to madness as a late libel.

Running away would only have played into Mungo's hands. Merlin was in a strong position, but, like Mungo, he knew they could never work together and that Rhydderch would have to choose. It is, therefore, more likely that when Mungo's men took to the streets, Merlin threatened to break off negotiations and leave town unless he got his way. This was therefore a negotiating ploy aimed at forcing Rhydderch's hand. Rhydderch consequently provided Merlin with a guard, but this was for his protection, not to prevent a mad Merlin running away.

Languoreth was also in on this ploy. She could not let it appear that Merlin's appointment as chief counsellor was a fait accompli, so she tried to make it look as if Merlin required to be persuaded to take charge. This would have given people time to get used to the idea that Merlin was the best man for the job.

Geoffrey, though, has Rhydderch placing Merlin under guard to ensure that he does not end negotiations and voluntarily go into exile, and then seeking to tempt Merlin with promises of power and wealth if he will stay at court:

> Then Rhydderch ordered [Merlin] to be restrained and a guard posted over him, and his madness to be softened with the cither; and he stood about him grieving, and with imploring words begged the man to be sensible and to stay with him, and not to long for the grove or to live like a wild beast, or to want to abide under the trees when he might hold a royal sceptre and rule over a warlike people. After that, he promised that he would give him many gifts, and he ordered people to bring him clothing and birds, dogs and swift horses, gold and shining gems . . . Every one of these things Rhydderch offered to the prophet and urged him to stay with him and leave the woods.[9]

If Merlin was truly mentally unwell, as his detractors say, why would the king offer him the power to act for him and to be answerable only to him? Why would the king tempt Merlin with such lavish gifts if he was mad? Looked at in context, it is clear that Rhydderch was desperate to establish a united front and wanted Merlin and Mungo to compromise, to pledge their followers to their king and go out together against the Angles.

The king's reference to a 'warlike' people is a strange thing for Rhydderch to say when tempting Merlin to take control. It is equivalent to a board of directors saying to a prospective manager, 'Come and run our company, the employees are really argumentative!' The 'warlike' reference only makes sense if being warlike was a positive consideration – that is, for example, when there was a war to wage.

Reading the *Vita*, it is difficult to believe it simply sprang as fully formed fiction from Geoffrey's head. I believe that the above passage was derived from one of Geoffrey's sources, perhaps one that came from St Asaph in Wales, where Geoffrey was bishop and where Mungo stayed when he was exiled from Strathclyde for the first time. Mungo knew Merlin; Geoffrey wrote about Merlin. Both were connected with St Asaph.

Merlin rejected the offers made by Rhydderch, saying:

> Let the dukes who are troubled by their own poverty have these, they who are not satisfied with a moderate amount but desire a great deal. To these gifts, I prefer the groves and broad oaks of Calidon, and the lofty mountains with green pastures at their feet. Those are the things that please me, not these of yours – take these away with you, King Rhydderch. My Caledonian forest rich in nuts, the forest that I prefer to everything else, shall have me.

By refusing the king's largesse and suggesting it be directed to the chiefs, Merlin won favour with the more materially minded and gave the impression that he had not returned to court for his own benefit. On the contrary, as he said, he much preferred to be left alone to enjoy the simple pleasures of nature. This was, of course, palpable nonsense, but it was also good politics. The king made a show of restraining Merlin, but this too was no more than a political pretence.

Mungo was not fooled. He knew that in a short time Merlin would soon be in charge, answerable only to the king. It was a make-or-break time for Mungo. He began to consider a drastic course.

Rhydderch played a noble but, perhaps, misguided part in these events. He believed that it did not matter if his kingdom was Christian or of the old way if it ceased to exist, and that a Merlin–Mungo axis was the only way to save it. Languoreth was more realistic. She knew there could be no Merlin–Mungo alliance and that one or the other had to be in charge. For Languoreth, there was no choice to be made. There was only Merlin.

CHAPTER SEVENTEEN

The Ring

Mungo knew that his most dangerous enemy was Languoreth, and that if he was to win the struggle in which he was locked with Merlin, he would have to break her bond with the king and end her influence on her brother's behalf. It was not the hot-headed Merlin but the hot-blooded Languoreth, when she took a young soldier in her husband's army as her lover, who gave Mungo his chance to bring her down.

Languoreth's affair gave rise to Glasgow's most famous story, although in the form in which it is known today, the true villain, Mungo, has been given the hero's part and the real hero, Merlin, expunged. To this mockery of history, a garnish of magic has been added until we have a story in which Mungo saves Languoreth from being found guilty of adultery by finding a missing ring inside a fish!

Every modern Glaswegian knows the story of the fish and the ring; it is commemorated on the city's coat of arms, official paperwork, buildings, buses and lamp posts. No Glaswegian child leaves primary school without being told at least an adulterated version (that is, a version without the adultery). There is even a nursery rhyme:

> There is the tree that never grew.
> There is the bird that never flew.
> There is the fish that never swam.
> There is the bell that never rang.

The tree, bird, fish and bell never grew, flew, swam or rang because they are only designs on Glasgow's armorial bearings. The fish is always shown with a ring in its mouth.

Alexandre Dumas used a version of the story of Languoreth's adultery as the basis for an adventure in which the Three Musketeers and D'Artagnan save their queen by recovering diamonds given to her by her husband and given by her to her lover. Jocelyn, who is the main source of the tale, wrote more than 500 years after Languoreth's death and 500 years before the fictional Musketeers, but the premise of the two stories is the same.

By Jocelyn's account, the scene is set after Mungo 'returned to his own place', Glasgow, following his time in exile in Wales, and found the queen, Languoreth, had given herself up to 'riches and delights' and had not kept 'faith with the royal chamber and marital couch as she ought or as is proper'. Jocelyn's Languoreth is a voluptuary engaged in adultery:

> For the abundance of riches and the fullness of her delights and the elevation of power accustomed her to serve the incentive and poultice of pleasure to the flesh. She turned her eyes onto a certain young soldier, who according to the rotten beauty of this rotting flesh seemed to her spring-like with a beautiful appearance and comely face and a form that was more handsome than many of her company at court. And as a man who was himself sufficiently ready and inclined for such homage, without any other goad he was easily made to sleep with her. . . .
>
> And as the days had passed on earth, the forbidden

pleasure repeated many times had become more pleasing
to both . . .

And she foolishly and shamelessly gave to her adulterer
a royal ring of gold that enclosed a precious gem, which
her legitimate husband himself had commended to her as
a special sign of his marital love.[1]

This 'opened the gate of suspicion' to enemies of the queen, and,
'A *faithful man of the king* [my emphasis] obtained certain knowledge
of the secret between the queen and the soldier, and he managed to
pour it by drops into the ears of the king.'

Rhydderch did not want to hear this news, probably because he
already knew of his wife's affair, but the informer pointed out to
the king that the ring he had given to Languoreth was now on the
soldier's hand, so Rhydderch could not avoid the issue. One day,
while out hunting, when the soldier lay down to rest and fell asleep,
the king took the ring from his finger and threw it into the River
Clyde. The soldier did not notice the ring was missing when he woke
up. Upon returning home, the king turned on the queen, reproached
her and demanded that she produce the ring he had given her.

She responded that she had placed it in a chest. Whereupon
the king, in the sight of his advisors, commanded that she
present it to him with all speed. Still being set with hope,
she entered her inner chamber as if to search for the ring,
but immediately directed a messenger to the soldier, and
made known to him the petition of the impassioned king
over the ring. And she sent word that he should quickly
send the ring to her. The soldier sends back word that he
had lost the ring and that he was ignorant of the place
where it had been lost.

He then fled from court, leaving Languoreth to face her husband's
wrath alone. Rhydderch, according to Jocelyn, threatened
Languoreth with public obloquy and a 'most shameful death':

> Clinging to your youthful adulterer, you have set me aside,
> the king your husband, although I made you the consort
> of my bed and mistress of my kingdom. You have acted in
> secret but I will act openly, and in the sight of the sun I will
> make known your dishonour and reveal your shamefulness
> in your face.

The king imprisoned the queen and there, in prison, she prayed to
the God of the Christians and called upon Mungo for help. When
Mungo heard the queen's plea for help, he ordered a servant to go
to the banks of the Clyde with a fish hook:

> and to cast the hook into the stream and bring back to him
> immediately the first fish that was baited and drawn out
> from the waters.
>
> The messenger fulfilled what the saint said and delivered
> into the presence of the man of God the fish he had
> captured, which is commonly called a salmon. [Mungo]
> requested that the fish before him be cut and gutted, and
> he discovered the above-mentioned ring in it. And at once,
> he sent it to the queen by that same messenger. When
> she saw it and took it back, her heart was filled with joy
> and her mouth with exaltation and thanksgiving.

The queen gave the ring to Rhydderch and was saved. Indeed, she
was seen as a victim:

> And so the king and all his court with him were made
> sad because of the injustices inflicted on the queen, and
> publicly he asked her for her pardon as he humbly kneeled.
> And he swore, if she so requested, the gravest vengeance
> or death or exile for those who would inflict accusations
> on her. But she, wisely understanding that mercy more
> than the censure of judgement was called for in respect
> to her accusers, desired to be merciful, just as it is proper
> indeed for one's fellow servant to be served.

And so the king and the queen and the informer were recalled into the grace of peace and mutual love for each other. And the queen, as fittingly as she was able, proceeded to the man of God and confessed her guilt to him. And making amends according to his decision, she zealously corrected her life for the future; for she restrained her feet from another such fall. Nevertheless she never revealed to anyone the sign by which the Lord magnified his mercy to her while her husband lived, but after his death she let it be known to all who wished.[2]

Once all the fabulous flummery in Jocelyn's version is ignored, the traditional story boils down to this: Languoreth committed adultery, was accused by a 'faithful man' and saved by Mungo. The faithful man who accused the queen is forgiven. (The only thing more suspicious than Mungo siding with Languoreth is that the 'faithful man' who accused the queen is not punished.)

The story is suspect not because a fish was taken from the Clyde and opened to reveal a missing ring; this, while unlikely, is possible. The story is suspect because Mungo sided with a woman accused of adultery – something which no one who knows anything about him could possibly believe. Not only does he not have a good word to say for any woman, he does not approve of sex (with them or without them), even within marriage. To Mungo, to enjoy sex was to 'serve the incentive and poultice of pleasure to the flesh'. To take pleasure in the body of someone of the opposite sex was to take pleasure in 'the rotten beauty of . . . rotting flesh'. How likely is it that such a man would sympathise with an adulterer?

Jocelyn makes much of Mungo's asceticism, claiming that he fasted for days, and when he ate, he ate only 'common and very light foods' and drank only non-alcoholic liquor. 'However if at any time it happened that he was . . . eating with the King, he refrained from abstaining with his customary rigor.'[3]

If Mungo ignored his beliefs to avoid offending the king, the source of patronage, it is unlikely he would do the same in order to side against the king. Mungo was not a man to choose an adulterous queen over a cuckold king. Whoever was the hero of this tale, it was not Mungo.

All the oddities in Jocelyn's version can be explained when events are placed in their correct historical context and the characters concerned recognised for who they really were. Jocelyn sets the scene soon after the end of Mungo's exile in Wales and Hoddam – that is, by my reckoning, in 580. Merlin returned from exile soon after Mungo. With Merlin back in action, Mungo knew he would have to fight for influence with the new king. Even if Mungo had been minded to conspire against the king by manufacturing a defence for a queen who had betrayed her husband, it does not make sense to suppose that he would have chosen this time to risk upsetting the fount from which all patronage flowed. Merlin too had to be careful not to fall foul of the king, but Languoreth was his sister, friend and ally, so he was bound to take her side, even if she was in the wrong – and, on this occasion, Languoreth was in the wrong. There can be little doubt but that Languoreth took one of her husband's soldiers as a lover. All the evidence points to adultery, and none suggests the queen was innocent of this offence against her marriage vows, except that she remained happily married to Rhydderch until his death 32 years later. One possible explanation for this is that her adultery never became known, but this cannot be; the legend has proved too popular and long lasting to suppose that it was not founded on common knowledge of events that actually occurred. It is impossible to believe that Rhydderch remained unaware of his wife's adultery.

Why, then, would he remain happily married to her? She was 40 years old at the time of her offence. She had already produced several children, and her child-bearing years would soon be over. Why would Rhydderch not use Languoreth's adultery to set her aside and marry a younger woman? What moved him to accept this affront? The evidence suggests that there were two reasons: Rhydderch loved Languoreth, and Rhydderch was gay.

There are five characters in the story of the ring: the king and queen (Rhydderch and Languoreth), the soldier lover, the informer and the hero. The identities of the king and queen are not disputed. The identity of the soldier lover is unimportant. Jocelyn's version of events has Mungo as the hero, but, as we have seen, there is reason to suppose this was not so.

The story only makes sense if Mungo was the 'faithful man of the king' who was forgiven when the queen was proved innocent. If this is correct, the most likely candidate for the hero is Merlin, the brother of the adulterous queen. Merlin is far more likely than Mungo to have sided with his sister, the queen.

Jocelyn deliberately describes events inaccurately, but his knowledge of the truth seeps through. When Jocelyn is really against someone, no calumny is too strong, and yet the informer, the villain, the man Mungo defeats in Jocelyn's story, is described as a faithful man. This suggests that Jocelyn was ambivalent about the informer, which would make sense if he and others knew the informer was Mungo.

When Jocelyn came to write his biography of Mungo, he set about the streets of Glasgow, and probably Partick too, looking for written and oral sources to add some solid substance to his work. One of the stories he heard was, almost certainly, the story of Languoreth's adultery. It had everything necessary to survive: sex in high social places, a trial and a happy ending. The only thing that could have consigned this story to oblivion was that Mungo was the villain. The problem, inherent in the story, was that Mungo was the queen's accuser, and everyone was rooting for the queen, even if she was an adulterer. A compromise that assuaged the people and the Christians was struck. The people could have their story, provided only that Mungo was made its hero. This was not a problem in principle; all Jocelyn had to do was delete the real hero and substitute Mungo. The problem in reality was that 'Mungo the hero' could not be easily grafted onto the body of evidence because this left Mungo siding with a sexual transgressor against her husband. Jocelyn persisted with his altered version of events. He made Mungo the hero and lived with the anomalies this threw up. He was confident that the illogical result of his work would not be questioned. He was right to be so confident. As far as I am aware, to date no one has questioned Mungo's being the hero of the story.

Jocelyn must have known that Mungo was the queen's accuser. He was not stupid, and so, just as he called Druids 'certain' men, he called the informer a 'faithful man of the king'. This was with a view to blunting what was an outrageous affront to local history and common sense. This also explains why, at the end of the story, after the queen is acquitted, the informer is forgiven. Jocelyn's idea was to minimise the fault of the informer because he knew, in reality, the informer was his hero Mungo.

The very fact that Mungo fits awkwardly into the hero's place in this story is a testimony to the historical truth that lies behind its plot line. If the Christians had invented this story, they would not have had their hero defend an adulterer and deceive a king. The evidence suggests the story existed before Christianity became almost all powerful in the written media, at least in the towns, in the seventh century. It also suggests the story was too deeply rooted to be obliterated, the most sensible inference being that it was as old as the late sixth century, when the characters it describes lived. If this is correct, then it is probable, contrary to Jocelyn, that

Merlin was the man who came to Languoreth's aid after Mungo accused her. Once this is recognised, the story can be seen to make sense.

The events upon which the story of the queen's adultery is based occurred in 580. The fish-and-the-ring element is a fanciful gloss, so I have ignored it. From one perspective, the story is relatively simple: woman commits adultery; woman accused of adultery; husband takes her back anyway. When looked at in its wider historical context, the story is somewhat more complex, because what happened was not a sixth-century soap opera but part of a political plan concocted by Mungo to destroy Languoreth and take power in Strathclyde.

When Rhydderch became king, the political complexion of Strathclyde changed, and men such as Mungo and Merlin were allowed to return from exile to vie again for the favour of the king.

Mungo was rightly concerned that Languoreth's influence with her husband would work in favour of her brother and to his own detriment. Mungo knew that to defeat Merlin he would have to remove Languoreth from the king's side, so he set about undermining her position. He, like everyone else, knew that Languoreth was involved in a sexual affair with a young soldier of the king's guard. The king knew this too but had decided to pretend ignorance. Frustration and a feeling of political impotence led Mungo to take the desperate gamble of exposing the queen to public reprehension with a view to forcing the king to put away Languoreth and her family.

He knew the king would not welcome being told officially that the queen was engaged in adultery, but he gambled that, to save face, the king would have no choice but to banish his wife and her brother, if not punish them even more severely. Mungo badly misjudged the tolerant attitude to sexual matters among the people of the old way and the nature of Rhydderch and Languoreth's relationship.

Mungo played the part of Claudius when he poured poison into the king's ear, but he found, as Jocelyn says, 'the king did not easily incline his ear or his soul to the one who reported his dishonour and the shame of his wife'.[4] This may mean the king did not want to believe what Mungo said but probably means that the king knew what was going on but did not want it made official, because then he would be bound to do something about it. Mungo made it official. We do not know with certainty what happened when he did. Jocelyn says that Rhydderch reproached Languoreth and had her imprisoned, and this may be true, but, if it is, it was either done for show or as the total punishment that Rhydderch felt it necessary to inflict. Languoreth was not banished, maimed or executed.

It was Merlin who spoke up on his sister's behalf and perhaps helped negotiate the solution to the problem, although this did not include any nonsense concerning rings and fish. His solution was to find the queen not guilty and to allow her accuser to escape punishment. He would have said, 'It will be as if nothing had happened,' which would have pleased Rhydderch, who had been content to ignore what Languoreth was up to. Of course, it could never have been as if nothing had happened.

Mungo's gamble had not paid off, and even though he escaped the direct consequences of his actions, he must have known that he had ruined any prospect he might have had of becoming the king's first counsellor.

If it is accepted that Languoreth committed adultery, that she was accused of this offence and that she was acquitted, as the evidence suggests, then the question arises, why did Rhydderch, a sixth-century king and warlord, not punish her severely? Even if Rhydderch's love for Languoreth was strong, she had taken a lover, and this must have reflected badly on him, certainly among the Christians in his kingdom, if not necessarily to the people of the old way. The queen's taking a lover must have been of some account, anyhow. If not, there would have been no point in her accuser accusing her.

I suspect that the truth is this – and this, I emphasise, is speculative. Languoreth took a lover because she liked sex and was not satisfied with her husband in that connection. The king understood why the queen had taken a lover, and, because he was a good man, sympathised with her. And I suspect the reason why Languoreth and her husband did not enjoy a good sex life is that Rhydderch was gay.

If I am right, it would explain why, after Languoreth and he had done their duty as king and queen by producing heirs, he was content to turn away while she sought sex elsewhere (although his kind nature had a part to play here). Rhydderch had pretended not to know the queen had taken a lover, even though he suspected it was probably an open secret. This would explain why, when Mungo accused her of adultery, the people did not turn on Languoreth shouting Jezebel and harlot. Instead, they accepted a situation they knew about and accepted as natural. When the queen was publicly accused, Rhydderch had no choice but to act aggrieved as a matter of form, but there was no possibility that he would permanently put Languoreth away. They had come to a happy way of living. The charge was found not proven and the queen was reinstated. It would, however, have been unjust to punish the accuser. After all, he had told the truth, and everyone knew it, but his 'card was marked'.

Just as Mungo's father had possibly been a gay man who was bound to play the part of a prince and marry a neighbouring princess, so too was Rhydderch bound to marry Languoreth although in a sexual connection this may not have been entirely to his taste. Rhydderch and Languoreth got on with it because they accepted their situation, they were both sensible and mature individuals and because, by the old way, sexuality was kept in perspective. This was in contrast to Taneu, Mungo's mother, who, as a Christian, found herself embroiled in a philosophy that did not like sex and particularly excoriated man-to-man sex (at least in public). Rhydderch and Languoreth had a happy life together. Taneu ended up alone.

If Rhydderch and Languoreth's marriage reminded Mungo of the failure of his parents' relationship, it would go some way towards explaining his misjudgement of the situation when he attacked Languoreth. As a Christian fanatic, he was ill equipped to judge the reaction of people who had grown up influenced by a philosophy that accentuated nature. I suspect the people understood the situation Rhydderch and Languoreth found themselves in and accepted it as part of life, as indeed it was. The people would have known that Rhydderch's being gay would not necessarily have stopped him being a good king, husband and father.

Obviously, there is no direct evidence that Rhydderch was gay. No such evidence could have survived, because the Church would never have countenanced such a thing being made public. 'Sulphurous fumes' which caused an intolerable stench came out of the bodies of gay men in Mungo's world. For Mungo, homosexuality was a 'detestable shameful crime'.[5] There is no way an openly gay man of ability and good nature would be recognised for all he was for many years to come.

Rhydderch was a good and just king. He was known as Rhydderch Hael, the generous, that is, a king who extended largesse to his people. In the first decade of his reign, he was titular leader of an alliance which, under the warlord Arthur, won the Great Angle War. In the ten years after this war, he reigned over a land that enjoyed peace and plenty and which was still remembered hundreds of years later.

There is one last item of evidence that I would pray in aid of this line. In Adamnan's *Life of Columba*, Rhydderch is mentioned only once, when he sent a man called Luigbe moccu Min to Columba to ask if his enemies would kill him. Columba 'questioned Luigbe about the king [Rhydderch] and the kingdom and his people' and then told him that Rhydderch would die in his bed 'at home on his own pillow'.[6] What is this about?

First, there was no prophecy. Adamnan wrote long after both Columba and Rhydderch were dead, with the benefit of hindsight. He knew, when he wrote, that Rhydderch had died peacefully at home. It could be that, knowing this, he simply made up a prophecy to impress the simple. Alternatively, there could be more to it than this. Why, if Columba could prophesy, did he have to ask Luigbe for information about Rhydderch and his kingdom and his people? What was he told that led him to conclude that Rhydderch would die in his bed? It can only have been that the king was not of a warlike nature. We can at least infer from this passage that Rhydderch was not a warrior. (Columba made similar prophesies about men who were entirely warriors – these, he said, would not die in their beds but in battle.)

Geoffrey, too, in his *Vita*, tells the story of the queen's adultery. He has Merlin as the queen's accuser, although he makes no mention of Mungo or of any ring and instead plumps for the story of the triple death. According to Geoffrey, Languoreth presented Merlin with the same boy, in three guises, on three occasions, and asked him to prophesy his death. When Merlin came up with three different and ostensibly self-contradictory predictions, all relevant to the same boy, his authority was undermined.

By Geoffrey's account, Rhydderch concluded that because Merlin was wrong about the boy's death, Languoreth must have been falsely accused by him. In the next paragraph, Languoreth's eyes are brimming with tears and she is incongruously begging Merlin to remain with her and not to go back to the woods. She has clearly forgiven him his grievous wrong, although there has been no explanation as to her reasons.

The internal inconsistencies in Geoffrey's *Vita* occur because the story of the triple death and the story of the queen's adultery were both well-known Merlin tales that Geoffrey was anxious to include, but not as they actually happened.[7] Geoffrey, because of sloppiness, laziness or arrogance, is content to have Merlin and Languoreth enemies in one story and friends in the next without explaining how they came to be reconciled. If Mungo, not Merlin, accused the queen of adultery, Merlin and Languoreth would always have been friends, and no change of tack in their affections or subsequent explanation of any reconciliation would be needed.

Geoffrey places the story at a time that fits exactly with events in Strathclyde in c.580. Merlin has just returned from exile, and the queen, Languoreth, is 'glad to have her brother back again'. Why, in these circumstances, would Merlin accuse his sister of adultery? This is never explained.

Having turned the truth on its head, Geoffrey has to make a violent change of tack and have the queen forgive her brother because of the next event he describes, the story of the stag army. The internal dynamics of this story, as we will see, demand that Languoreth and Merlin are friends.

In the *Vita Merlini Silvestris*, lastly, Merlin accuses a queen of adultery, but this queen is not Languoreth.

The only common feature in these three accounts is the figure of an adulterous queen. On two occasions, she is identified as Languoreth. In the third, she has become the wife of Mordred, Merlin's inveterate enemy and final nemesis. Mordred and his wife, whose actual identity I will be discussing later, will be party to the deaths of both Arthur and Merlin.

Mungo's attack, then, failed to strike home and left Mungo seriously weakened. This did not mean that the Christian cause was failing. There were Christians other than Mungo, and many of them did not want either Mungo or Merlin in power. The race for the kingdom's charge was not yet run.

CHAPTER EIGHTEEN

The Army of Stags

Although his prospects of advancement had been blighted, Mungo, as well as the Telleyr Christians, still had enough influence to prevent Rhydderch and Languoreth making Merlin prime counsellor in Strathclyde. Hot-headed as always, Merlin tried to force the issue by presenting the king and queen with the ultimatum that either they promoted him or he would withdraw not only his support but his person. When this did not work, to demonstrate his power, Merlin increased the stakes by having the people of the old way rise in arms to present an overt threat to the king's peace, all with a view to his achieving his ultimate ambition: control of Strathclyde subject only to the authority of the king. Geoffrey buried these events deep in the *Vita*, but, once again, when this is set in its right time and place and decoded, a sensible version of events emerges. Of all the stories Geoffrey tells, this one is, perhaps, the most deeply buried in allegory.

When Merlin threatened to break off negotiations and take himself off into voluntary exile, Geoffrey rehearses his tableau of Merlin going off to the woods while Languoreth tries to talk him out of it. Languoreth brings in Gwendolyn, Merlin's wife, to try

227

to change his mind, but he refuses her too. She then asks Merlin what Gwendolyn is to do if he leaves her alone again. Merlin's answer is the gift equivalent of a Pyrrhic victory:

> 'I shall remain clear of both of you and undestroyed by love. So, let her have her due chance of marriage and choose of her own accord, whom she shall wed. But let the man who weds her take care he never gets in my path or comes near me. Let him tread another road. For should it chance he meets me, he may feel my flashing sword . . .' He finished speaking, and, saying farewell to each of them as he went, set out for the woods he loved: no one stopped him.'[1]

Despite Merlin's warning and without apparently being divorced, Gwendolyn becomes engaged to be married and sets the day for her wedding (c.582). When this news is brought to Merlin in his forest fastness, he is, again, as almost always, engaged in scholarly enquiries:

> It was night, and the horned moon was shining brightly; all the lights of the vault of heaven were glittering. The air had an extra clarity, for a bitterly cold north wind had blown away the clouds, absorbed the mists on its drying breath and left the sky serene again. The prophet [Merlin] was watching the stars in their courses from a high hill.[2]

Geoffrey, rather contradictorily, has Merlin say, 'Yet I bear no grudge. She may marry now the time is right, and with my permission enjoy a new husband. When tomorrow dawns, I will go and take with me the present I promised her when I left.'

Internal consistency is not Geoffrey's strength. His Merlin is content that his ex-wife remarry while, at the same time, being intent upon killing her husband if she does. This is but one example among many of the absurdities that Geoffrey is reduced to writing as he attempts to adapt the truth to suit the prejudices of his patrons. It gets worse:

> So saying, [Merlin] set off round all the woods and clearings, and organised a herd of stags into a single line; . . . He seated himself on a stag, and at the coming of the day he set off, driving his lines before him. So, he came with speed to the place of [Gwendolyn's] wedding. Arriving there, he made the stags stand quietly outside the gates, then shouted, 'Gwendolyn, Gwendolyn, come out! What presents are looking for you!' Gwendolyn came quickly, all smiles, and was astonished to see a man riding a stag and it obeying him, astonished that so many animals of the wild could be brought together and that he alone was driving them before him like a shepherd accustomed to taking his sheep to pasture. The bridegroom was standing at a high window, looking in amazement at the rider on his seat; and he broke into a laugh. When . . . [Merlin] saw him and realised who he was, he promptly wrenched off the horns of the stag he rode. He whirled the horns round and threw them at the bridegroom. He crushed the bridegroom's head right in, knocking him lifeless, and drove his spirit to the winds. In a moment, the prophet dug his heels into his stag and set it flying and was on his way back to the woods. The incident brought out retainers from every corner, and they followed the bard in hot pursuit across country. But he went at such a pace that he would have reached the forest unscathed had it not been for a river in his path. While his beast was bounding across the torrent, Merlin slipped and fell into the fast current. The servants ranged themselves along the bank and captured him as he swam. They brought him home, bound him and handed him over to his sister.[3]

Having killed his ex-wife's prospective new husband, and having been captured in the act, Merlin is taken not to the king, as might be expected if Geoffrey had simply invented his story, but to Languoreth. This suggests that Geoffrey was relying upon some source which had Languoreth the main mover in the episode. Languoreth treats Merlin kindly but still he proves intractable, even refusing 'to taste the fine meals prepared for him'.

This passage in Geoffrey's *Vita* goes nowhere. In captivity, Merlin, apparently, proves his worth to Rhydderch by, among other things, disclosing the dishonesty of one of the king's lieutenants, although Geoffrey's narrative is vague and it is hard to tell who this person is. Eventually, Geoffrey, sinking under the weight of the nonsense he is writing, faces the inevitable, abandons any pretence of presenting a sensible or coherent story and resorts to a few prophecies to entertain his twelfth-century audience.

Again, when the evidence in the *Vita* is placed in its historical context and considered with reference to common sense and human nature, without magic or romance, all becomes clear.

In 580, Merlin came back to Glasgow-Partick and became embroiled again with Mungo. Mungo, convinced with good reason that Languoreth was influencing the king against him and in Merlin's favour, decided to eliminate Languoreth by accusing her of adultery. When his attack failed to strike home, Mungo was left seriously weakened, but Merlin was still unable to take advantage of Mungo's discomfiture because there was more than one Christian faction active in the kingdom. The moderate Telleyr party, which was no friend of Mungo's, and which had been in charge when Mungo and Merlin were in exile, stayed in control by playing the part of the compromise party.

The Angles were massing to attack. Rhydderch was doing all he could to unite his riven kingdom to face them. Merlin and Mungo could see what Rhydderch could not: that they would never work together and that one of them had to go. Rhydderch and Languoreth tried to broker a peace between the rival factions, but both Merlin and Mungo remained obdurate. Without the support of all of the Christian factions and the people of the old way, Rhydderch could not present the united front he needed to form an alliance fit to face the Angles. He offered Merlin wealth and power if he would stay and work with Mungo, but not the place of principal counsellor which Merlin coveted. Dissatisfied, Merlin threatened to break off negotiations but only as a negotiating ploy gauged to derive further concessions from the king.

Merlin's wife was not involved, at least, not in the way Geoffrey describes. Geoffrey was using Homer's old trick. The *Iliad* would have made more sense if Achilles and Agamemnon had argued over strategy and not a woman, but this would not have pleased Homer's audience, so he introduced Briseis as a love interest and made her the cause of the strife around which the story revolved. Geoffrey did the same thing when he brought in Gwendolyn, Merlin's wife, to personalise his story. In fact, when Merlin raised the stag army, it was not personal – it was strictly business.

Ruling out romantic elements, I proceeded on the basis that, whatever the story was about, it did not involve Merlin's wife's love life. It is more likely that Languoreth appealed to Merlin's love of his people. When the references to Merlin's wife are read as references to Merlin's people, events begin to make sense. Geoffrey has Languoreth encourage Merlin to stay with reference to his wife and ask, if he leaves, should Gwendolyn find another husband, remain as if a widow or go with him? It makes more sense to suppose that Languoreth told Merlin his people wanted him to stay and asked him, if he leaves, should they find another leader, remain leaderless or go with him?

When I saw through Geoffrey's deliberate obfuscation, I

understood what had actually happened. The real issue was whether the kingdom would be guided by Merlin in accordance with the old way or by the tenets of Christianity. This depended upon whether Rhydderch chose Merlin or a Christian as his chief counsellor. For Gwendolyn's hand in marriage, we should read the prize of primacy in Strathclyde. Geoffrey could not bring himself to allow that there was once a time when there was an alternative to Christianity, and that the old way could realistically have returned in force, so he ignored history and plumped for romance by reducing what were complex political issues to a marital dispute between Merlin and his wife. According to Geoffrey, the question was not whether Merlin would work with Mungo but whether Merlin would stay with his wife. Stuck with this nonsense, he has Merlin give his wife permission to go her own way and remarry if she so chooses, while, at the same time, warning her that he will kill the man she takes as a husband. Remove the romance and look at the politics and it all becomes clear.

The romantic passages are easily decoded: Merlin actually said to the king that he could favour the Christians at his expense, but if he did there would be trouble. There was no romantic dispute. There was no bridegroom. There was only a Christian threat to Merlin's ambition and a consequent threat by Merlin to resort to arms if he did not get his way. Rhydderch dared not side with Merlin lest he lose Christian support, so when Merlin's threat to break off negotiations did not work as he had planned, his bluff was called and he had to go.

The story of the stag army is not an idle fancy invented by Geoffrey. It is too convoluted for that. If Geoffrey had invented it, I do not doubt he would have written something more coherent. The history behind this, literally, fabulous fiction makes clear how Geoffrey's convoluted tale came to be and why he dared not say what had really happened. The clue is in the coded reference to stags – a device we have already seen in relation to Mungo in Jocelyn's *Life of Kentigern*.

Obviously, stags do not form ranks obedient to command, just as they do not behave as oxen and plough the land when told to do so, even by Mungo. In both cases, stags relate to the people of Damnonia, the old Roman name for Strathclyde. The people of Caithness were associated with the cat, the *Epidii* (cognate with Latin *equus*) of Argyll with the horse, the Scots of Argyll with the boar – and the people of Strathclyde with the stag. The name Damnonia derives from the Gaelic, Latin and Sanskrit for stag.[4] 'Damh – . . . stag, so Irish, Old Irish *dam*, . . . Latin *dâma*, *damma*, deer; . . . Sanskrit *damya* . . .'[5] Damnonia has been confused with Dumnonia, an area in the south-west of England. This was a convenient coincidence used to confuse the facts by some who were minded to move the Arthurian canon south.

There was a real 'stag army', but it was an army of people of the old way and of Damnonia. It was not only a non-Christian army; it was an anti-Christian army – something that Geoffrey dared not make clear. His patrons would not have been pleased if he had drawn attention to the fact that it was possible to bring armies to bear against the Church, as this might have encouraged the people to think they could do the same. Geoffrey's solution was simple; he deleted references to the old way and the challenge it presented and substituted a safe fantasy involving 'love and marriage' and an animal army. Instead of a real army of men engaged in real-life politics, Geoffrey wrote preposterously of an army of stags. His source material probably referred to the old way, and to the people of Strathclyde, Damnonia, as the people of the stag. These *Damnonii* – the warriors of the stag, the stag warriors – became, in time, simply stags in Geoffrey's book.

Having spurned a chance of 'administering the law in cities

and ruling over a warrior people',[6] when Rhydderch tried to bribe him to stay at court, Merlin left the court to engage in scientific and scholarly pursuits. When the news was brought to him, not that Gwendolyn was to be married but that Rhydderch was about to appoint a Christian to take charge in Strathclyde, Merlin was forced to take military action. Merlin was not good at military action.

He raised an army from among the warriors of the old way, the *Damnonii*, the stags, or, as Geoffrey puts it, he 'set off round all the woods and clearings, and organised a herd of stags into a single line'. Merlin's standard was probably raised at Cadzow, where he had his home base and which was conveniently located on the Clyde and easily accessible to the great Caledonian Wood, where Merlin had until recently been in hiding. The malcontent men and women of the south who had favoured the late Gwenddolau cannot have failed to ride north to join him. There is also reason to believe that this army included women, because Geoffrey says Merlin led not only a herd of stags, which, as we have seen, were warriors of the old way, but also a contingent of female deer and 'she-goats'. The stag army marched on Rhydderch's Royal Town of Partick, although they cannot have intended to overthrow the king; that would have been counterproductive and foolhardy, because that would have put Merlin up against Languoreth.

Languoreth had been more politically astute than her brother. She had seen that, if Merlin absented himself from court, the Telleyr Christians would take advantage and, worse still, Mungo might recover lost ground.

Mungo's influence had been weakened by many years in exile and further weakened when he tried and failed to bring Languoreth down. Were it not for the threat of both civil war and war with the Angles, we may suppose that Rhydderch would have exiled or killed Mungo when he accused Languoreth, although, of course, Languoreth was guilty, and this knowledge might have stayed Rhydderch's hand. The people of the old way opposed Mungo, and many, even in the ranks of the Christians, saw him as an enemy. When Merlin's army approached the capital, Mungo was perilously isolated.

Merlin led this army to the very walls of Partick, and there called out a challenge to the Christians. It is revealing that Geoffrey says Merlin made his army stand quietly outside the gates. This was a show of force, not a rebellion. Merlin was there to take charge of the kingdom under the king, not to divide it in civil war. Panic ensued inside the walls, where all were amazed at Merlin's audacity in raising the warriors of the old way. The Christians, who until then had been on the brink of power, laughed down at Merlin from the walls, but everything had changed. Geoffrey's nonsense about Merlin striking down the bridegroom with the horns of a stag can be ignored, although the hopes of the Christians were crushed, like the bridegroom's head.

Merlin had demonstrated his power, but this was not enough to have him immediately appointed the king's principal counsellor. Merlin might have taken power by *coup de main*, but this would not have brought him control of a united kingdom. The inescapable fact was that the Angles were poised to attack, and a disunited kingdom would certainly fall. This was why Rhydderch and Languoreth had been so keen to reach a compromise solution in the first place. According to Geoffrey, Merlin had no sooner struck his blow than he had to fly for his life, only to be captured and brought back to Languoreth - not to the king, but to Languoreth. The evidence shows that Merlin stymied the prospects of the Christians by a show of force but was unable to eradicate their influence.

This is where Languoreth came in. She embroiled Merlin in more negotiations, but this time, with Mungo sidelined and with the Christians cowed by Merlin's army, she was in a position to force through her preferred option. Merlin was not captured and physically bound. He was entangled in Languoreth's diplomacy. Languoreth had Merlin, and the rest of them, 'tied up in knots'. Still, it was not easy for her. Merlin had an army which, albeit standing quietly by, was ever likely to spark a civil war that would, in due course - whoever won - lead to the annihilation of the Britons at the hands of the Angles. The stag army simply broke the diplomatic logjam and allowed those who were minded to compromise to reach agreement. This was what Languoreth had wanted all along.

So it was that Merlin became principal counsellor to the king, with the proviso that he work with the Telleyr Christians for the common good. This internal alliance was formed just in time. Within two years, the Angles would be on the borders of Strathclyde. By that time, external alliances too would have been forged, and one man to lead them all would have come to the fore: Arthur. Merlin may have ended up Rhydderch's first minister, but I suspect that the real power lay with Languoreth. This is what Geoffrey means when he says that Merlin was captured and brought before Languoreth.

Mungo was sent into exile again. This time, he went to Rome and stayed there while the Great Angle War was waged. When it was over, he came back more powerful than he had ever been before.

CHAPTER NINETEEN

Rome

The Great Angle War that would determine whether the Celtic nations, the Britons, Scots and Picts, would stand or fall before the invading Angles was about to begin. Mungo envisioned a victory for the Angles, as God's punishment for the way he had been treated. Geoffrey says in his *Vita*:

> The betrayed Lord will betray Britain to foreign nations who are of the pagan sect and ignorant of God. And the island will be emptied of its native people, and the religion of Christian law in the island will be destroyed until its predetermined time.[1]

Leaving his Christian betrayers and enemies of the old way to their fate at the hands of the Angles, and Strathclyde 'blighted . . . by the heathen', Mungo set off for Rome. He knew that if he had led a united Church, he could have beaten Merlin and the people of the old way and made his support vital to the king. Consequently, when exiled for a second time, he set out to tap in to the fount from which most Christian blessings flowed and the only irresistible force in the Christian world.

Before the people of Strathclyde were ready to fight, Merlin had no choice but to allow the Christians, now predominantly Telleyr

Christians, a substantial place in the kingdom's affairs. Two other conditions also applied: Strathclyde had to form an alliance with the Gododdin British and the Britons, Picts and Scots of Manau, and a leader had to be found.

Merlin, no doubt remembering Emrys and how once before, when all seemed lost, a war chief who was not a king had risen and turned the Angle tide, and also the part Arthur had played at Arderydd on Merlin's darkest day and the series of victories Arthur had won in the years that followed, brought the allied kings to accept the situation was so dangerous that no one but the best man available should lead the army. This could only have been Arthur. As Nennius tells us:

> Then it was, that . . . Arthur, with all the kings and military force of Britain, fought against the [Angles].[2] And though there were many more noble than himself, yet he was twelve times chosen their commander, and was as often conqueror.[3]

Arthur was in his early 20s when the Great Angle War broke out. He was the son of Aedan, king of Scots, so there were many 'more noble' than he, in that they were of higher rank, but none more formidable and none, like him, undefeated. It is evidence of how dire was the plight of the Britons and their allies that they were prepared to allow a man who was not a king, and a Scot to boot, to lead them. They made the right choice. In battle after battle in the middle years of the 580s, Arthur made a name that still rings around the world. When the Great Angle War ended with the Battle of Badon in 588, Arthur was recognised as the warlord's warlord. His story is legend, but it should and will be history.

Mungo did not return to Strathclyde until the Great Angle War was over. Jocelyn says he went to Rome 'seven times',[4] but 'seven' is a stock figure and means only several or many times. Given

Mungo's age, the distance and difficulty of the journey and the absence of any evidence concerning actions in Britain during the 580s, I suspect that Mungo only went to Rome once, twice at most, and certainly not seven times.

Ostensibly, Mungo visited Rome because, in Strathclyde, 'different rites had emerged at different times that were contrary to the form of the Holy Roman Church and to the ordinances of the holy fathers'.[5] The Christians of Scotland were part of the Celtic, not the Roman, Church, and the different rites to which Jocelyn refers were not innovations but ancient. The Church in Scotland had been using rites contrary to those of Rome for centuries, but this had not bothered Mungo until he lost power in Strathclyde for the second time. Mungo's real motive in journeying to Rome was to seek the favour of the pope, for the authority this could bring him. Just before he left Rome for the last time, Mungo obtained the support he sought from Pope Gregory I, Gregory the Great, a man Bertrand Russell described as an astute statesman, 'masterful, and very well aware of what can be achieved in the complex and changing world in which he [had] to operate'.[6] Russell says that, before Gregory I, 'the bishop of Rome, although acknowledged as the greatest man in the [Christian] hierarchy, was not regarded as having jurisdiction outside his own diocese.'[7] By the time of Gregory's death in 604, the papacy was well on its way to the primacy it enjoys today.

During Gregory's papacy, the Church consolidated its position and spread its influence into hitherto untouched parts of Western Europe. Gregory disseminated his views and boosted his authority, and that of the papacy, through an extensive correspondence. He promoted his version of Christianity by sending instructions to other bishops and advice to secular leaders in far-flung places, including Seville, Marseilles, Sardinia, Ravenna, Dalmatia,

Syracuse, Byzantium and Antioch. He was in regular contact with the Franks, who had converted to the Roman form of Christianity in the late fifth century, and the king of the Visigoths, who became Roman Christian during Gregory's papacy. He even wrote to the Lombards, who were threatening Rome at the time. They too adopted Gregory's form of his faith shortly after his death. He really was Gregory the Great.

Gregory was astute in the extreme in recognising how useful those who held temporal power could be to the Church, so he looked for common ground upon which they could meet and work together, provided the Church was the senior partner. He kick-started a process that would see the religious and the lay worlds welded together in the impregnable form that came to be known as Medieval Christendom. Kings were allowed to retain that which was Caesar's, buttressed by what passed for moral authority, provided by the Church, on condition that the Church was allowed to use that authority to call upon kings to impose its will. If Gregory gave Mungo the advice he gave to other bishops, he would have told him not to criticise kings but to keep them ever aware of the hellfire that awaited them if they did not do what the Church required of them.

Gregory and Mungo were ideal allies. They were both vehemently opposed to the old way and determined to exterminate it. They were both, to say the least, unhappy about human sexuality. For Merlin, Languoreth and the people of the old way, sex was a natural thing to be enjoyed by all concerned. For Gregory, sex was a necessary evil and its attractions a threat to the power of the male-only clergy. By its acts the Church limited and by its teachings the Church circumscribed the place of women within its communion and in the secular worlds in which it held sway. Women were increasingly treated as second-class citizens as the first millennium wore on because men like Gregory minimised the contribution they made in Christianity's first few centuries, so reducing their value as individuals. Gregory contributed to this injustice by deliberately misinterpreting passages in the Bible to try to prove that Mary Magdalene, who was certainly a friend and follower of Jesus, if not his wife, was a common prostitute. Gregory propagated this view to such an extent that many Christians today still believe it to be true.

In Rome, Mungo 'laid bare his entire life' to Gregory and sought his advice and support. Gregory told him in 'what areas Britain was in need of amendment'. He also refused to recognise Mungo's authority as bishop of Glasgow because Roman forms had not been followed at his elevation. When Gregory reconfirmed Mungo as a bishop, he effectively established his personal supremacy and that of the bishop of Rome. Put bluntly, Mungo arrived in Rome a Celtic Christian and left Rome a Roman Christian.

Gregory's sending Augustine to convert the Angles of Kent to his form of Christianity in 597 is a landmark event in English history, but a similar event, Gregory's sending Mungo to act as his agent in Strathclyde, is almost unknown in Scotland.

When he got back to Strathclyde, Mungo claimed, as Gregory had claimed, that the status of the priestly class was null, because it did not derive from the pope. Mungo said that his confirmation by the pope gave him the power to make priests and that those whom he did not invest were not truly priests. Not everyone agreed with this, but Mungo had the power of the Roman Church behind him, and they did not stand a chance.

The Christian leader, Columba, was corresponding with Gregory while Mungo was in Rome. Columba, who was active in the north-west of Scotland, was allowed to go his own way by Aedan, king of Scots, and so had no occasion to visit Rome and no incentive to change the form in which he practised his religion. Although Columba remained a Celtic Christian until his death, he could not afford to ignore the power of Rome, so, when Mungo returned to Glasgow, Columba travelled from Iona, south by sea, to Glasgow, to visit him. It is indicative of the authority that Mungo's time in Rome had brought him that the aged and ailing Columba – he was to die within two years – came to Glasgow to visit Mungo.

This meeting enables Mungo's return to Glasgow to be dated to between 590, when Gregory became pope, and 597, when Columba died. It would be unreasonable to suppose that the first thing Gregory did when he became pope was to deal with affairs in Scotland, so, if we allow that Mungo remained in Rome for some time after Gregory's elevation, and if we allow time for his return journey and for him to settle again and retake power in Strathclyde, say three or four years in total, then Mungo returned from Rome c.594 and met Columba in, perhaps, the following year.

Mungo was now armed with the imprimatur of the most powerful branch of the Christian Church, the one most likely to come out on top in the internecine struggle that was raging among Christians at this time. From Jocelyn's account, we know that he also had with him the materials needed to bolster his authority: books of fixed rules, grants of rights, relics of saints and hard treasure that could be displayed to awe the simple or melted down to bribe the venal:

> The holy bishop [Mungo] with apostolic absolution and blessing went back to his home carrying with him rules, codes of canons, and many other books of sacred scripture, as well as privileges and many pledges of saints, and ornaments for the church and other things that pertained to adorning the House of the Lord. And he caused his own household to rejoice at his return, both because of the holy offerings and the presents.[8]

These 'presents' that so obviously impressed Mungo's followers would also have tempted the chiefs of Strathclyde, if not to convert, at least to argue in favour of allowing Mungo back and into an influential position.

The Telleyr Christians and the people of the old way must have looked upon Mungo's return with trepidation. The former had nothing to compare with the connections Mungo now enjoyed or the spectacle of gifts he brandished, and they were soon eclipsed.

Given Mungo's past record, Rhydderch too must have had reservations when he heard that Mungo was on his way back to Strathclyde, but he had to welcome him because he could not afford to ignore the benefits that would accrue to his kingdom if he adopted what was becoming the standard form of Christianity in Europe, or the potential for religious war if he took an individual tack. Reaching an accommodation with Mungo would have been tempting for any king. Rhydderch knew of the advances that Christianity, particularly Roman Christianity, had made on the mainland of Europe and was aware of the increasing hold it had on many of his people. No doubt, he also appreciated that if he accepted Mungo's Christianity, he would be part of an organisation that promoted the power of kings, provided only that a king allowed the Church to reign in spiritual things. Mungo and his Roman form of Christianity could offer friendly contacts with other Christian kings and make Rhydderch a member of a powerful and growing power bloc.

This must have seemed a good deal to many kings, even to a man of the old way such as Rhydderch. Many chiefs were already predisposed to accepting a hierarchical religion. The daunting fact that the non-aristocratic Emrys had usurped the position of the traditional chiefs in c.550 was within living memory. More recently, in the 580s, Arthur, who was not a king, had commanded kings in the Great Angle War. While the choice of Arthur to lead the allied army against the Angles had seemed a good idea when the situation was so desperate that no one cared who led it, provided they led it to victory, now that the war was over, many of the established chiefs were concerned that they had set a dangerous precedent when they set Arthur above kings. These chiefs would have been susceptible to Mungo's Gregorian policy and attracted by the idea that a rigidly enforced social structure, paralleled by a powerful and hierarchical Church, would ensure their status. As they succumbed to the temptations Mungo presented, the chiefs became less sympathetic to Merlin. These temptations included bribes, the promise of bribes, the chance to be a part of something big and the attraction of following the prevailing fashion on the Continental mainland.

Chiefs under the Celtic system were contracted with their people. An individual might show his or her chief respect but would not think the chief inherently better than him or her. The respect the chief engendered depended upon his qualities. This was an obvious disadvantage for all too many chiefs. They much preferred a system where men and women were treated with 'respect' in accordance with their titles.

The chiefs were won away from Merlin and the old way. It is easy to see why this might have been. Merlin had supported Emrys and Gwenddolau and had championed Arthur as warlord chief of the allied army in the Great Angle War, even though Arthur was not a king. While being an expedient and successful policy, this principle now threatened the security of the chieftain class, so they, aided and abetted by the Mungo Roman Christians, reacted. The result was the dissolution of the relatively broad-based Celtic community founded on the old way and the rise (in Scotland) of the Roman Church, the successor of the empire.

The power and influence of Merlin's people, at its peak in

Mungo's absence during the Great Angle Wars, was broken by the combined might of Mungo and Rome. Soon they were barely able to maintain a public presence or to celebrate their beliefs openly without ridicule or attack. Merlin still enjoyed the protection of the king and queen, but he no longer had a telling effect upon events. His position at the end of the Great Angle Wars was akin to that of Churchill at the end of the Second World War when, despite his wartime service and the popular affection in which he was held, the political tide swept him out of power.

Scotland had been devastated by war, plague and famine for the best part of a decade, and although, after the war was over, there had been a period of abundance, the people must have retained an innate sense of insecurity. In such circumstances, joining the substantial-sounding Roman Christians must have seemed attractive to the people of Strathclyde.

For a time, there was no outright violence, as everyone enjoyed the benefits of the bounty that followed the end of the war. Merlin and his people attended the king's court and gave counsel, as did the Telleyr Christians and the Mungo Christians. Merlin devoted some of his time to study and wide-ranging discussions with fellow Druids, Christians and visitors to the court. I suspect that, given his nature, Merlin was anxious to gain access to the books Mungo had brought back from Rome, although it is impossible to believe that Mungo would have let Merlin read them. No doubt, Merlin's Telleyr Christian friends told him what these books contained.

Within a century, the process that Mungo had started would overwhelm the Celtic Church of Columba and the Telleyr Christians and set the scene for their destruction at the Synod of Whitby. The Christian rites that Mungo promoted soon became the accepted rituals of the court and, increasingly, the general populace. Merlin, and those who shared his opinions, could only rail in vain against the flowing of this Christian tide. Before long, their opposition was reduced to impotent and futile protest.

During the Great Angle Wars, the Telleyr Christians and the people of the old way were allies, and Merlin's people would have had free access to their sacred places, the Necropolis hill included. Mungo, of course, took a different stance when he was back in power. Tension increased until the two parties ended up engaged in what, in Glasgow, would be called 'a slanging match'. The only source of evidence for this event is clearly partisan in its representation of Merlin; indeed, it shows the writer of the *Silvestris* with his gloves off. His bias is almost palpable:

> Now this madman, as it is said [Merlin], afterwards came out of the wilderness and sat on a certain steep crag which rises on the other side of Molendinar Burn, overlooking Glasgow, to the north of the church of that place. On many occasions, he disturbed St Kentigern [Mungo] and his clergy with horrifying shrieks, as they were singing the divine office.

Looking at events in their historical context, we can see what happened. Merlin, his fellow Druids and others of the old way walked east from Partick to the time-hallowed hill next to Mungo's church in Glasgow to celebrate life, as their predecessors had done for 1,000 years. There, they clashed with the Mungo Christians, and Mungo's Christians prevailed in the end. His church is now St Mungo's Cathedral, and what was once a beautiful grove of trees is now an awesome graveyard. This event was but one instance of an ongoing struggle that was fought out on the hills, in groves of trees, in the streets and in the halls of chiefs, and which continued for more than 1,000 years.

CHAPTER TWENTY

Twilight of the Druids

By the beginning of the seventh century, many of Merlin and Languoreth's supporters, particularly the warriors who had fought in the Great Angle War, were old, and the new generation of chiefs was less sympathetic to the old way and increasingly turning towards Christianity. Mungo was in poor health, but he was still active, and his now Roman churchmen were making advances at the expense of the Telleyr Christians and the other Christian parties in Glasgow.

Merlin was 60 years old at the turn of the century and must have longed to step away from the struggle with Mungo and be left alone to research and write. He must have realised that the old way was being eclipsed as a force in the community and doubted he could do anything about it. He had beaten Mungo at the time of the Arderydd campaign only to find other Christians in power. He had beaten Mungo again, ten years later, and gone on to win a great war, and now, ten years later still, Mungo was back in charge, re-armed and stronger than ever.

Merlin cannot have failed to conclude that the tide of history was running with the Christians, and that all he could do was step back and trust that the old way would keep on surviving until the tide turned back again. He cannot have imagined that the Christian Church would be in the ascendant for 1,000 years. He must have believed that, within a short time, perhaps a few hundred years, or a few decades even, toleration would return and the old way would be allowed to flourish in the open again. After all, toleration in matters of religion had been the norm throughout the preceding 1,000 years. The Romans had allowed people to follow their consciences during the time of the Republic and the Empire, provided they did not undermine the social structure. It was only in recent years, with the advent of Christianity, that some people had started to impose their beliefs on other people. This concept was entirely alien to Merlin. He must have believed that such a practice was unnatural and that consequently it would not, could not and should not survive for long.

Mungo was ruthless following his return from Rome. He won over the Christian priests and undermined Rhydderch by winning over many of his chiefs to Christianity, or, at least, to self-serving support of Mungo's policies.

There comes a time in every king's reign when courtiers, particularly among the younger generation, begin to think ahead to the next reign. Rhydderch was an old man at the turn of the century. His most likely heir was the vile and unstable Constantine, who, until Mungo's return, was considered a pariah and an untrustworthy renegade by Christians. In the next few years, Constantine became the Mungo Christian candidate for the throne. With his influence waning and his awful son's prospects improving, Rhydderch and Languoreth were effectively neutralised. There was a real danger that if it came to an open clash, Mungo would have enough financial, diplomatic and political influence to depose Rhydderch and put Constantine on the throne – then again, maybe not. Neither side wanted to find out.

No one was allowed to stand in Mungo's way, not this time. This was to be third time lucky. Following Jocelyn's account of Mungo's return from Rome is a chapter headed, 'What [Mungo] knew concerning the two clerics through a revelation of the spirit; and what happened to them which he himself prophesied?'[1]

Once the revelatory and prophetic passages in this chapter are disregarded as fabulous nonsense with no basis in reality, we can see, in what is left, how Mungo's ruthless ambition brought him power in Strathclyde. Although the surviving evidence relates only to Mungo's Christian victims, it may safely be taken that Merlin and the other leaders of the people of the old way were in at least as much danger as Mungo's Christian opponents.

Mungo changed the basis on which the Church in Glasgow stood. He wanted to ensure that the line of authority ran downwards, from the pope, through him, to the local priests. Given the pope was far away and had greater matters to concern him than events in Scotland, this meant that Mungo was in charge, and, more to the point, that he could not be ejected for a third time without Roman Christianity being repudiated.

Jocelyn allowed evidence of Mungo's antagonism towards women and homosexuals to stand in the *Life* because this was standard Christian fare in the twelfth century. Being against women and gay men was a good thing in Jocelyn's and Mungo's philosophy. It is, however, surprising that so much other damning material remains in Jocelyn's book. This can only be because not only did Jocelyn think being misogynistic and anti-gay was acceptable, but that killing people who differed from the religious norm was a good thing too. No dissenting voices were to be allowed:

> There was presented to [Mungo] among others for advancement to the priesthood a certain cleric of graceful form, great eloquence, and much learning. He was also

> a Britain by race but he had been educated in Gaul.
> When the saint [Mungo] saw this man, he summoned
> the archdeacon and commanded him to be removed
> immediately and to be separated from the clergy. For to
> the eyes of the saint, a sulphurous flame had seemed to
> come out from the bosom of that cleric and to pour into
> his nostrils an intolerable stench. By this vision which was
> revealed by the Spirit, he perceived what vice laboured in
> his body. For as was then made clear to the man of God
> alone [Mungo] but afterwards to all the others, the cleric
> was accustomed to that most detestable shameful crime
> for which divine vengeance overthrew the sons of unbelief
> in Pentapolis and destroyed them by fire and brimstone.[2]

This was year zero for the Roman form of Christianity in Scotland.
The graceful and eloquent cleric clearly already held a place of
moment in the old hierarchy. Under Mungo's new regime, he had
to submit himself for approval and acceptance. Everyone seems
to have thought that this graceful cleric was a worthy man of wide
learning and good standing who would be an asset to the Christian
community, excepting only 'the man of God', that is, Mungo. No
one saw any problem with this man until Mungo decided he was
unfit to be a priest, and the rest followed like sheep. This eloquent
cleric, who until then had been a valued member of the community,
was suddenly vilified as homosexual.

This is a common tactic of tyrants. Accuse one man of something
and the rest will fall into line lest they too are accused. It works best
when the charge is untrue, because then no one is safe:

> And the saint [Mungo] said to those surrounding him, 'If
> the sacred canons forbid women because of the weakness
> of their sex, which is in no way in default, to be advanced
> to priestly order, by how much more ought those men
> be shut out from so sacred an order and duty who are

perverters of their own sex and abusers of nature, who in contempt of the creator, with insult to themselves and in injury to all creatures, despoil that with which they are created and born, and clothe themselves as female. Nowhere do we read of a more grave vengeance being selected for censure than against that monstrous race of men in whom that detestable shameful crime consumed the original matter. Not only did it overthrow those cities with all their inhabitants with fire because of their burning lust and with brimstone on account of the stench of that abhorrent crime, but in truth it also turned them into a place horrible to see, filled with brimstone and pitch and an intolerable stench that received no living thing into itself, indeed having trees on its banks which displayed fruit outwardly healthy but inwardly full of smoke and ashes, and manifesting an image of the certain punishments of the lower world.[3]

Mungo was against gay rights.

In context, given the time and the circumstances, it is probable that the cleric's real problem was not that he was gay – if indeed he was – but that he was a man of substance, learned and eloquent, and so a potential challenge to Mungo's authority and that of the Church (the two were now one and the same). Being gay or a transvestite was a sin in the eyes of Mungo's Christians, so Mungo used this to have this learned man ostracised.

Having rejected this man as a priest, Mungo then had him killed, or, as Jocelyn says, in a passage that is as laconic as it is deadly, 'After this, the above-mentioned cleric went on his way and as rumour had it, he perished and was taken with sudden death.'

Hardly had Mungo disposed of the graceful cleric than an 'eloquent pilgrim' also brooked Mungo's wrath to his cost:

And when the holy man [Mungo] completed the office

[Church rituals] and had returned to his home, a certain cleric, who was a most eloquent pilgrim, met him among the others. Looking at this man, the man of God laid a burning eye upon him. And he inquired who he was, and where he was from and for what reason he had come into these parts. And he answered that he was a preacher of the truth and taught the way of God in truth, and he claimed that he had come into those parts for the salvation of souls. But when the saint conversed with him in speech, he convicted him of being made drunk with the venom of the Pelagian pestilence. Therefore wishing that he would return rather than perish, Kentigern refuted and admonished him earnestly that he renounce that ruinous sect, but he found his heart stony towards conversion.[4]

The very description 'eloquent pilgrim' suggests a learned and far-travelled man who was not afraid to speak out. Unfortunately for him, speaking out – worse still, speaking out eloquently – was dangerous if Mungo was about. The accusation against the eloquent pilgrim was of heresy:

Then the saint [Mungo] commanded him to be expelled from his diocese and denounced him as a son of death and that the death of both of his persons [spirit and body] was at the door. Also he remembered that saying of the Apostle, Shun the man who is a heretic after the second admonition, knowing that he who is such is destroyed.[5]

Mungo's gang of subservient Christians did what they were told, shunned the eloquent pilgrim and expelled him from Strathclyde. The eloquent pilgrim must have been glad to go (no doubt as fast as he could). Before he had got far, though, assassins sent by Mungo caught up with him and killed him. Lest it be thought this conclusion is unfair, I will quote Jocelyn in full:

> The same son of Gehenna [Hell] after being expelled, departed from those boundaries, and as he tried to cross a river he was choked by the waters and descended into Tartarus [Hell again]. And so this showed, being most worthy of faith and by such plain proof, the veracity of the prophecy of the most holy man.

Is it a simple coincidence that a pilgrim and therefore a seasoned traveller should drown in a river immediately after falling out with Mungo? Just as Telleyr had fallen victim to an accident at work after disagreeing with Mungo, and just as the graceful cleric had met a sudden death, this eloquent pilgrim drowned crossing a river. The common factor is inescapable. Mungo had these three rivals killed.

By contrast with the graceful cleric, the eloquent pilgrim was an outsider. I suspect he was called in to take on Mungo after Mungo had crushed all internal opposition. He was accused of heresy, which only means that he did not agree with Mungo.

I suspect these two assassinations are but illustrative instances of what was a reign of terror inflicted by Mungo upon his fellow Christians. It would be naive to believe that only one challenger was smeared and one dissenter murdered.

In the late 590s, it became increasingly difficult and dangerous for Merlin to continue living in Partick. He was the subject of verbal and perhaps physical abuse when he was out among the town's people who had converted to Mungo's new form of Christianity. Eventually, he found living there intolerable. Even if he was the brother-in-law of the king, he could always have an accident at work like Telleyr, meet with sudden death like the graceful cleric or fall in a stream and drown like the eloquent pilgrim.

Merlin's last hope died with Arthur in 596. Merlin knew that if even Arthur could be betrayed and killed, he too was in danger.

Merlin decided to remove himself, if not from harm's way, then at least from direct public attention. He moved out of Partick proper to continue his scientific endeavours in peace in a fine house on the slopes of nearby Partickhill.

CHAPTER TWENTY-ONE

The Harrowing of Galloway

In the 590s, the Telleyr Christians lost ground to Mungo's Roman Christianity, with all it had to offer in prestige, connections and wealth, until Mungo stood supreme in the Christian ranks. Then, having quelled local and imported opposition, Mungo turned his attention beyond the boundaries of Strathclyde towards the extermination of the non-Christian Picts in the south-west. Jocelyn says:

> Then the soldier of God burned with the fire of the Holy Spirit . . . And after he had amended his own nearby areas, namely his diocese, he advanced further and purified the country of the Picts, which is now called Galwiethia [Galloway], and the surrounding area from the filthiness of idolatry and the contagion of heretical doctrine. And as a sanctuary of wondrous songs, he led back to the rule of truth, and corrected, as he was able, whatever he found contrary to Christian faith and wholesome doctrine.[1]

The description of Galloway of the Picts as a sanctuary of songs suggests its people were of the old way and so ripe for the pogrom that Mungo's men were to inflict upon them.

The power of Strathclyde had increased significantly after the Arderydd campaign and again at the end of the Great Angle War, by which time Strathclyde's rule extended over the English border. This, however, left it strategically exposed to the remnants of the Angle kingdom of Bernicia to the east and the southern Picts to the west. If the Angles were to attack Strathclyde again, Galloway would be like a dagger at Rhydderch's back. In 596, Arthur had defeated the Picts in the north, so Rhydderch was free to turn south towards Galloway.

Jocelyn's account of the expedition against the southern Picts is slanted in favour of the Mungo Christians and gives the impression that the campaign was primarily a religious exercise. It was not. There were sensible political reasons for Rhydderch's invasion. The Mungo Christians merely followed in the wake of the army of Strathclyde because the old way was powerful in the south-west and they wanted to stamp it out. They destroyed the churches of Christian sects they did not agree with and desecrated the groves of the old way:

> For he [Mungo] sought Albania and there, with excessive sweat and certain unbearable measures, he was many times set before death by the snares of the barbarians, but he stood fearless in the faith. He converted, with the Lord working with him and giving virtue to the voice of his preaching, that country from the worship of idols and the profane rites of idolatry, which are almost equivalent, to the linen of faith, to ecclesiastical customs, and to the regulations of the canons. For he raised up many churches there and after erecting them he dedicated them and ordained priests and clerics and consecrated many of his disciples as bishops. Also he founded many monasteries in these parts, and he entrusted those to fathers whom he had ordained from his disciples.[2]

The leading Druid in the south-west was Taliesin, one-time bard of the great king Urien of Rheged who had been assassinated on the orders of the same Mordred who had betrayed Arthur and brought about his death in 596. Little of Taliesin's work survives, and even less is known about his life, but he must have had some significant influence on the conduct of the people of Rheged during his lifetime because he is remembered even today as Taliesin, Chief of Bards, one of the three 'Baptismal Bards of the Isle of Britain'. Taliesin's power base was destroyed in the Harrowing of Galloway in 598, after which he became a wanderer, ending up at Merlin's home more than ten years later.

Merlin, whose own power was waning, was unable to help his old friend when the Mungo Christians marching in the wake of the army of Strathclyde set about wresting Galloway 'from the filthiness of idolatry and the contagion of heretical doctrine'. Behind these words lies an ominous truth. When Mungo found people living 'contrary to Christian faith and wholesome doctrine', he set about correcting them and leading them to his idea of the truth. This was always a bloody business, particularly when Mungo 'burned with the fire of the Holy Spirit'.

Mungo, although by then a very old and sick man, went with the army. The people of Galloway fought back against the invaders, and when the army of Strathclyde carried the day in the open field, they continued the fight using guerrilla tactics. The warriors of Strathclyde, having defeated Galloway's army, wore down its resistance, destroyed its towns and fields and drove off its stock.

After this came the storm-clerics of the Mungo Christians, murdering and converting in the army's wake 'with excessive sweat and certain unbearable measures'. Mungo offered salvation in the next world, although the people of Galloway had not known they needed it until then. They knew a good life from a bad one, and that was that. Mungo, on the other hand, said Hell was waiting for those who did not convert and that just leading a good life would not do; one had to act in accordance with the forms of the Church too. This fear factor coupled with force factor was enough to produce converts, although the Christians never entirely stamped out disbelievers, even when they took to burning them in the sixteenth century.

Those who did not believe in the teachings of the Church were 'the enemies of the human race, the powers of the shadows of the world'. It mattered not that someone might believe in something 'better'; this was a meaningless concept to Churchmen to whom the 'truth' had been revealed and who brooked no dispute. This form of fanaticism is what Merlin had to put up with. How could he argue sensibly with people who brandished this sort of ideology?

After the harrowing of Galloway, Mungo returned to Glasgow to prepare the handover of power to the next generation, although, we must assume, he retained the ultimate sanctions in his own hands.

This was the last time Mungo journeyed far from home. After Galloway, Mungo turned his attentions outside of Scotland and sent out:

> from his own household those who he knew were strong
> in faith, fervent in the charity of God, notable in doctrine,
> and sublime in religion to the islands that were far away
> towards the Orkneys, Norway and Iceland, to declare to
> them the name of the Lord and the faith of Jesus Christ . . .
> [because Mungo] was now an old dried up bone and could
> not go to them himself, Kentigern wished that this work
> be fulfilled through his disciples.[3]

Mungo was about to retire from the active day-to-day running of the Church.

In the east, the sybaritic Mynyddawg Mwynfawr, king of the Gododdin, called warriors to his hall and then hesitated over-long before launching an attack on the Angles. For a year, his army feasted and drank before heading south to annihilation in the disastrous drunken debacle that was the Battle of Catterick. The Druid Aneirin recorded this event in unsparing detail in his poem Y *Gododdin*:

> Short were their lives, made drunk by pure mead,
> Mynyddawg's band . . . For a feast of mead they gave their
> lives . . .[4]
>
> . . .
>
> Before their grey hairs came their slaughter.
> Of Mynyddawg's men, great is the grief, of three hundred,
> but one man returned.[5]

Of course, Aneirin was the one man who returned, although this is almost certainly poetic licence. The Battle of Catterick was a crushing defeat for the Britons; the only positive thing that came out of it was the poem. In this, we have the only contemporary reference to Merlin to survive. It was written in the Edinburgh area c.600, two years after the battle. Its weight as evidence of Merlin's existence in central Scotland at this time is enhanced by the fact that Merlin is mentioned only in passing. The primary purpose of Y *Gododdin* was to praise the numerous heroes whose families and friends had paid Aneirin to write of their heroism. Merlin is not so glorified. Indeed, the one line in almost a hundred verses in which he is mentioned is rather mundane. Among verse after verse of magnificent poetry in which the martial prowess of hero after hero is extolled, Aneirin says Merlin made a monetary contribution: 'Myrddin of song, sharing the best part of his wealth, our strength and support.'

Merlin was 60 years old at this time and probably no longer inclined to go campaigning again, so he sent money. Merlin too was about to step back from centre stage.

CHAPTER TWENTY-TWO

Madman

Mungo left Merlin with no safe place to be in Glasgow or Partick, so, about the turn of the sixth century, Merlin retired from public life and became a pensioner of the king. He must have known that if the old way went down to defeat, people would face a dark age in which reason, tolerance and dissent would be stymied. With hindsight, we can see the old way was soon to be crushed, and, although never obliterated, the ideas that had served the Celts for millennia would be all but lost.

Languoreth encouraged Merlin not to step back from the troubles but to stand and fight; however, when she realised she could not change his mind, she did everything she could to make his life in retirement congenial. In this, at least, she had Merlin's full cooperation. Intellectually steeped in nature, Merlin naturally liked physical comforts. He was able to claim that, although he was able to provide for himself, just in case winter made things difficult, it would be helpful if Languoreth built him a house and an observatory and provided him with servants, secretaries and supplies. Geoffrey's *Vita* has him saying the following:

> 'But lest I lack food in winter you might build me a house
> in the woods and have servants in it to wait on me and

> prepare me food . . . Before the other buildings build me
> remote one with seventy doors and as many windows
> through which I may watch fire-breathing Phoebus and
> Venus and the stars gliding from the heavens by night,
> all of whom shall show me what is going to happen to
> the people of the kingdom. And let the same number of
> scribes be at hand, trained to take my dictation, and let
> them be attentive to record my prophecy on their tablets.
> You too are to come often, dear sister, and then you can
> relieve my hunger with food and drink.'[1]

Merlin negotiated with Languoreth, but no agreement would have been possible without Rhydderch's approval. Rhydderch must have known that Augustine, Pope Gregory's emissary, had arrived in Kent in 596 to convert the southern Britons. For Rhydderch, it was time to compromise. By agreeing to the deal that Languoreth had worked out with Merlin, Rhydderch ensured Merlin's safety while still catering to the demands of the Mungo Christians. Mungo agreed to leave Merlin alone – in reality, not to have Merlin killed. Merlin agreed to leave Partick and not to cause trouble.

I believe that this is when the defamatory term 'Madman' crystallised in relation to Merlin. By the turn of the sixth century, the old way was in retreat, and Merlin had been sidelined. The Mungo Christians who hated and feared Merlin were unwilling to kill him and risk the displeasure of the king, so they assuaged their fear and found an outlet for their enmity by purporting to treat him as a joke, a figure they could laugh at and taunt with impunity.

As the years passed, people would have become used to Merlin living away from the main run of affairs. They would have seen his observatory on top of its hill as a strange house 'with seventy doors and as many windows'. This, of course, would have made no sense to them and simply confirmed their view of Merlin as an old fool. They scoffed at and mocked Merlin, from a distance, and called him a madman. As the Mungo Christians and their successors controlled the main media from then on, this name stuck. (The name Lailoken, Chief of Druids, by which his friends knew him and which is most commonly found sourced in Scotland, survived, but only just.)

In the twelfth century, rational thinkers such as the philosopher and teacher Abelard began to take on the Church in debate. Such men frightened the authorities, not because of the ideas they espoused – most people would have had no idea what Abelard and his fellows were talking about – but because in debate they frequently mocked and made fools of the clerics the establishment put up against them to propagate the party line. In his novel *The Name of the Rose*, Umberto Eco took up this theme when he suggested that the one thing the medieval Church feared was not rational debate, which could always be stifled, but being laughed at. The danger, as the Church knew, was that once an institution became laughable, it could no longer put the fear of God into people. The authorities knew that as long as Merlin could be treated as a figure of fun, a madman, it was less likely that people would be tempted by his ideas.

The most likely course of events is this. In the early 600s, Merlin moved out of Partick to his new home. At this time, he would have been known by his given first name and by the name of his father; he would have been 'X son of Y'. After Mungo's character-assassination squad got to work, Merlin began to be called 'X the madman', that is, *Mer Duine*. Eventually, and probably after his death, his given name was dropped or forgotten and he was referred to simply as the Madman. Later, this became Myrddin. Later still, as we have seen, with the influence of French, in which Myrddin smacks of *merde*, the euphemism Merlin was adopted.

Merlin continued his scholarly work at his house on the hill using all the resources Languoreth had provided for him. The import of this work was lost on those who reported it. By their account, Merlin spoke of future events as if he was a prophet, although to them his prophecies were obscure and quite unintelligible. Those who relied on revelation would, of course, be disadvantaged when they considered the fruits of experiment and rational thought.

Later writers were unable to understand the nature of Merlin's studies. They thought of them in supernatural terms and called what he said prophesising because this was something they understood. There was no official effort to understand – on the contrary, the authorities in Christendom deprecated free and rational thought. As Augustine's namesake Saint Augustine of Hippo said:

> There is another form of temptation, even more fraught
> with danger. This is the disease of curiosity . . . It is this
> which drives us to try to discover the secrets of nature,
> those secrets which are beyond our understanding, which
> can avail us nothing and which man should not wish to
> learn.[2]

Merlin's scientific enquiries had no prospect of success against such a mindset backed by temporal power. Science in the Western world had developed spectacularly since the age of Pericles in the fifth century BCE, but 1,000 years later an intellectual climate change took place and humanity in the West entered an academic ice age that would last until the advent of printing. It is frustrating that we do not have access to the material available to the writer of the *Silvestris*, whose sources 'remembered certain worthless words [of Merlin's] and entrusted them to writing'. The available evidence suggests a Merlin researching, thinking and reaching conclusions and of these being written down for his and others' future reference. All now destroyed or lost, of course.

For the early seventh-century state to grow in power, it required a state religion. The old way, with its emphasis on individualism, questioning and challenging authority, was by its very nature the antithesis of a state religion. Strathclyde was faced with a choice – Christian or non-Christian – but it was not a real choice. Christianity, by this time, was almost certain to win. Saying that, Mungo's supporters and Merlin's supporters could not have been sure of this as they continued to clash in the streets even after Merlin stepped back from the fray. Sometimes one side won and sometimes the other, but the struggle in which they were engaged was not to be won on the streets of Glasgow or Partick. It was part of a wider struggle being waged across Europe, as people sought security amidst the uncertainty that followed the fall of Rome in the West.

Rome had ruled for centuries. When Rome fell, many forms of Christianity vied for power, but only one inherited the old framework and structures of the Empire and with a single-minded ruthlessness submerged all other versions of Christianity to win the day. Arianism and Pelagianism, like the old way, like Merlin, retreated into the shadows of history. The Dark Ages were about to begin.

CHAPTER TWENTY-THREE

Ardery Street

In 2000, my then nine-year-old son and I were planning a trip to the Highlands of Scotland to visit the place from where, I believe, our family left for Ireland in the 1600s.

In the early seventeenth century, during the reign of James VI of Scotland (James I of Great Britain), the Protestants, who were in the ascendant in the recently united kingdoms of Scotland and England, decided to dilute the influence of the native, mainly Catholic, Irish by encouraging Protestants, particularly poor Scottish Protestants, to emigrate to Ireland. My family, in the Ardrey line, was part of this plantation of Protestant Scots. Like most of their brethren, they settled in the north of Ireland. They were farm-labourers and small-shopkeepers in County Tyrone until the 1870s, when my great-grandfather, David, emigrated from Ireland to Scotland. His first address when he arrived in Scotland was McLean Street, Plantation, Glasgow.

It was while looking for McLean Street in *Bartholomew's Glasgow Streetfinder Atlas* 20 years ago that I first came across Ardery Street, across the Clyde, on the north bank. (It is spelt 'Ardrey' Street in the index, but 'Ardery' Street on the street sign, so I will call it Ardery Street throughout.) This find was only a curiosity at that time, and I did not visit Ardery Street because, beyond the coincidence of names, I did not think there would be anything of interest there to see.

I changed my mind after my National Library find in 2000. The index in the *Streetfinder Atlas* told me Ardery Street was on page 34, box S11, but there was no Ardery Street to be found in this box, so I telephoned the local police station for help. The duty officer told me where it was and explained its absence from the map, saying, 'It is only 3 ft long, but it has a Masonic Hall in it.'[1]

In December 2003, on my way home from a consultation in Paisley, I turned out of my way, north through the Clyde Tunnel at Whiteinch, where the White Island of Cathen the Druid had been, and along Dumbarton Road to see Ardery Street and to scout the lie of the land. I had attended Glasgow University, on neighbouring Gilmorehill, for five years, so I knew the area, but during this time I had hardly thought about the relationship of the rivers that lay nearby or the rise and fall of the land. Far less had I thought about the way the place had looked in the sixth century.

Ignoring the modern buildings, I pictured Partick as it was then. Situated where the Kelvin runs into the Clyde, Partick provided a place to ford the Kelvin and to run a ferry across the Clyde to Govan. It was an obvious place for a settlement. The land between the rivers and Partickhill, west of the town, would have been cleared of trees to allow the townspeople to see travellers from the north and west at a distance. Aedan Mac Gabhran, Arthur's father, and the war-band of Manau were based only a few miles to the north, and the Picts were within striking distance just beyond them, so we may be certain that Partick was fortified, probably with a palisade.[2] The rivers provided protection on the southern and eastern approaches.

Driving west along Dumbarton Road, I turned right into Apsley

Street, which runs straight uphill. Ardery Street is immediately to the right. It is rather longer than the '3 ft' my police informant said it was, but the Masonic Hall he had promised was there. The rest of the street is edged by tenement flats.

Today, Partick is famous as the home of Partick Thistle Football Club and the comedian and actor Billy Connolly when he was a child. Billy Connolly has joked that, when he was growing up, Partick was a quaint little fishing village on the Clyde, when in reality it was an amorphous part of the big city and covered in Glasgow tenements. There was, however, a time when Partick was a small village, although no one knows when it was first settled or why it was given a name that means 'Little Woodland'.

In 1136, David I, king of Scots, gave Partick to the see of Glasgow. It was there, in the bishop's palace, in about 1180, that the bishop of Glasgow instructed Jocelyn of Furness to write a biography of Mungo.

Dumbarton was Rhydderch's primary military base, because it commanded the approaches to the Clyde. Partick, which was more conveniently placed to serve as an administrative centre, was often his main centre of government. The land about Partick was a royal demesne. Rhydderch the king lived there in what was known as 'the Royal House at Pertnech'. Where the king had a royal house, many chiefs would have houses or halls of their own. Morken, Merlin's father, was one such chief:

> The village of Partick was of very ancient date, for King Morken, traditionally associated with St Mungo . . . had a residence at Pertmet, which is supposed to be Partick, and in the chartulary of Glasgow mention is early and frequently made of Perdeyc or Perthik.[3]

Merlin's father lived in Partick and had storehouses there. It was from these storehouses that Mungo stole grain in the 560s. Partick, like almost every other name in first-millennium Scotland, had more than one spelling. To the above Pertique, Pertmet, Perdeyc and Perthick, we can add Perthic, Pertnech, Parthick, Perdeye, Perthee, Pertia, Perthwick, Perehic, Perthnic, Prewye, Pertaic and Pertick (this last name is still used by local people today). I use the accepted modern version, Partick.

After Merlin was driven from Partick town by the hostility of the Mungo Christians about the turn of the sixth century, he ceased to be seen as an immediate threat and instead became the subject of Christian ridicule. They called him a madman. This suggests that Merlin was neither out of sight nor out of mind. By my reckoning, Merlin did not go far but set up home nearby, close enough to be thought of, by those who did not understand what he was about, as the local fool on the hill. Merlin had to get out of town, but when he left he was not entirely without power and influence and still had potential for causing trouble. This enabled him to negotiate an agreement that would provide him with peace and security in his old age and which would not require him to go into exile.

I suspect he put it to Languoreth and Rhydderch that it was a necessary condition that not only must he be allowed to continue with his scholarly work, he must also be provided with the means to that end. Part of this was his building with 70 doors and windows.

Clearly, Merlin was not simply concerned with eking out a living over the winter months, because, although he had specific demands relevant to his personal life (a house and servants), he gave priority to his professional, Druidic life. The building with seventy doors and windows is obviously an observatory – Geoffrey says as much in his *Vita*. It was to be remote from the other buildings and its purpose was to afford a view of the Sun, Venus and the stars (probably from the top of nearby Partickhill). Having covered his personal requirements, he turned to his professional staff: 'Let there be as many secretaries trained to record what I say, and let them concentrate on committing my prophetic song to paper.'[4]

Merlin encouraged Languoreth to visit him often, which, taken literally, means his house was located somewhere where frequent visits were possible:

> 'Come here often yourself, dear sister, and you will be able to stay my hunger with food and drink.' . . . His sister obeyed him, for she built the hall as prescribed and the other houses and all else he had commanded her. . . . Then [in winter] the queen would often come to visit him, happy to serve him both food and drink. He would dine from the varied dishes, and soon after rise, with a compliment to his sister; then he would wander through the house gazing at the stars, and sing in this manner of the future that he knew would be . . .[5]

At Merlin's behest, Languoreth had a large living complex built for him somewhere outside Partick, far enough away to avoid Merlin antagonising the Christians who had taken over the town but close enough for Languoreth, who was about 60 years old when the house was built, to visit Merlin often.

It is noteworthy that it was Languoreth and not the king who built Merlin his new home. Perhaps the king distanced himself from Merlin for political reasons, but, of course, Merlin's complex could not have been built if the king had objected. Rhydderch could retain the support of the Christians, or at least deflect their opposition, if he allowed his wife to be the prime mover in the arrangement made with Merlin. No one, however, would doubt that Merlin was in reality the king's pensioner and under his protection.

Local names and the oral tradition maintained Partick's royal connections for centuries until some of them came to be preserved as street names. In *Partick Anecdotes*, Robert M. Paul, a Partick man, drew upon evidence gleaned from Partick people who had played a part in the oral history of their area. (That is, they grew up before radio and TV.) Paul's sources, including local tradition, led him to conclude:

> The kings of Strathclyde had a castle at the mouth of the Kelvin and may well have had a hunting lodge in the hilly area to the north of Whiteinch. This is supported by . . . local place names. There was a short road behind Balshagray School, which was called the Rotten Row. This comes from the Gaelic *Rat-an Righ* – the road of the king – and may well have been part of a road leading to a hunting lodge.[6]

Oral history in the Partick area retained a memory of two places: the place where the king lived, the old fortified town itself, and some other place in the hilly area north of Whiteinch. Paul thinks this other place may have been a hunting lodge. This, though, can be ignored. Hunting lodge is a description that tends to be used when no other use is known and the place is away from main centres of population. The local tourist board in the Hamilton area has described the sixth-century fort at Cadzow, where Merlin's family had their home, as a hunting lodge of kings. It is a default position when nothing else is known. In any event, it seemed to me that a building less than a kilometre from the town was 'too close to home' to be a king's hunting lodge, so, as I know nothing about hunting, I contacted someone who did, to be told that, all other things being equal, a hunting lodge should be placed as far from a town as practical. This other place was no hunting lodge. If it had been, what was it that led to its survival in the oral tradition into the nineteenth century?

Robert M. Paul says that this 'hunting lodge' was in the hilly area north of Whiteinch. The modern Whiteinch lies about the northern entrance to the Clyde Tunnel, although the island (*inch*) from which it took its name was in the middle of the Clyde, near its junction with the Kelvin. If a line were to be drawn from Apsley Street, off which Ardery Street runs, to the river, it would cut across where the White Island was before it was removed to allow shipping upriver to Glasgow. It was here that Merlin's mentor Cathen the Druid lived. Ardery Street is directly north of where the White Island once was, and Rotten Row is well placed to service Ardery Street, whether there was a hunting lodge or a house there.

Tradition has its place as evidence, but it is notoriously unreliable unless the foundation upon which it is based is known, allowing the weight to be given to it to be judged. Paul gleans from the local people that there was some memorable building north of Whiteinch. The evidence he provides is consistent with this building being on or around the site where Ardery Street is today. If Merlin lived there for the last 20 years of his life, that would have made it more memorable than any hunting lodge.

In a remarkable passage in the last chapter of the *Life of Kentigern*, Jocelyn steps away from his hero, Mungo, and writes about 'a certain man' he calls Lailoken, that is, Merlin (see Chapter 25). Rhydderch, the king, is dying, but in the last year of his life, he:

> [S]tayed for a longer time than usual in a royal village which is called Pertnech [Partick]. A certain foolish man, who was called Laleocen [Merlin], lived at his court, and he received his necessary sustenance and garments from the bountifulness of the king.[7]

In 612, the year he died, Rhydderch visited Merlin at Partick. Rhydderch and Merlin were friends, they had been friends for more than 60 years, so it was natural that, as Rhydderch's life drew to an end, he would visit Merlin one last time.

If the observatory was remote from the main house and, being an observatory, high on a hill, the house where Merlin lived was probably on the hill's lower slopes. There are certain obviously advantageous places to build houses. Modern Apsley Street runs along the line of what was once the drive to Apsley House, which lay halfway up the hill on the south-facing side, to catch the sun. Ardery Street runs off Apsley Street. Apsley House is now gone; only the street name remains as a reminder of its location. Traditional Glasgow tenements now cover most of the hill. It is, I think, possible to see where a house would have been built. At the top of Apsley Street, there seems to me to be a relatively flat area of ground on what is otherwise a sloping hillside. If this is where Apsley House stood, those who knew about these things probably chose the site for some good reasons. If we suppose the builders chose the most agreeable site the hill had to offer, by virtue of the lie of the land, then we may suppose this land was much the same centuries before when, I believe, Merlin had his house built on the same spot. Unless there were some material differences in the landscape in Merlin's day, and I can know of no reason why this might be, Apsley House was probably built where Merlin had his house.

We know that Merlin was living in the vicinity of Partick in 612 because this is where Rhydderch came to visit him. Ardery Street is just over half a mile from the sixth-century Royal Town of Partick. The existence of Merlin's house was remembered in the oral tradition long after the fact that it was Merlin's house was forgotten. The Ardery/Apsley Street area works with the evidence.

One of the earliest references to Merlin has him at the Battle of Arderydd. Merlin had many Partick connections. There is an Ardery Street in Partick. There is, therefore, a coincidence of names, at the very least. Today, by my rough count, there are approximately 10,000 streets in Glasgow. Only one is called Ardery Street. One of the first references to Merlin has him at Arderydd. What are the chances it is a simple coincidence that Ardery Street is the name of the place where the evidence suggests Merlin once had his house. I believe Merlin's home in his last years was where Ardery Street is today.

CHAPTER TWENTY-FOUR

Stonehenge

Geoffrey says in his *Historia Regum Brittaniae* that Merlin built Stonehenge using stones brought from Ireland. Wace closely followed Geoffrey when, in c.1160, he said, 'Merlin arranged the rocks in order, side by side . . . in English the name of the place is Stonehenge.'[1]

The most famous of many stone circles in Scotland is Callanish, on the Isle of Lewis in the Outer Hebrides, but, of course, the most famous stone circle in the world, the only one on which lintels remain, is Stonehenge. It is widely accepted that such sites were used for astronomical purposes and that those surviving are only a tiny minority of the innumerable circles that once were common all over Britain.

In 1999, near the great stone circle of Avebury, twenty miles from Stonehenge, the remains of six to eight concentric rings of post-holes, up to six feet deep, were found. These are thought to have held oak pillars up to sixteen feet high. According to archaeologist Michael Pitts:

> 'There are [in this find] big implications for Stonehenge. If there were lots of timber structures like, or even bigger than, Stonehenge around at the same time, then Stonehenge is

no longer something weird or unique. It becomes part of
the religious scenery of the time.'[2]

The size and setting of the post-holes suggests that the pillars
they held were too thick and too close-set to be roof supports.
Archaeologists believe they formed a freestanding 'woodhenge',
and that there may have been 40 similar structures in the vicinity.

These truly ancient creations predated Merlin by millennia;
Callanish was built about 1800 BCE and the first phase of
Stonehenge was constructed approximately 5,000 years ago. When
the inspiration required to build great circles of stone waned, many
of the ways in which they were used must have been forgotten,
but, as the movements of celestial bodies, especially the Sun,
remained vital to survival, it is likely that succeeding generations
retained something of their ancestors' knowledge. Even if they
did not, circles of stone or wood were obviously useful tools for
someone interested in astronomy, so there is no need for any direct
connection to any inventive progenitor.

Lacunae in the record make it impossible to trace a line of
descent from the builders of Stonehenge, Callanish and other
circles to any later time, far less to a time as relatively recent as the
first millennium CE, but, given the obvious usefulness of a circle of
markers, there is nothing to suppose that later people intent upon
making sense of their environment did not use methods similar to
those used in earlier times.

The first of the 'Frequently Asked Questions' on English
Heritage's Stonehenge website is: did the Druids build Stonehenge?
The answer, of course, is no: 'The stones were built by three different
cultures, Windmill, First Wessex and the Beakers.'

The Beaker people flourished from about 2500–2000 BCE. They
are believed to have been Sun-worshippers, like the Druids. It is
possible that this coincidence, perhaps continuity, of religious beliefs

was paralleled by a continuity of method. It may be that not only did these ancient peoples and the Druids worship the sun but that they also strove to understand its movements using similar techniques. Of course, Sun worship is probably the earliest and most enduring form of worship, and there is no need for a theological connection between one community of Sun-worshippers and another; nor is there a need for a connection between the techniques used by one people and those used by another. It is possible that peoples separated by millennia decided separately to try to understand the movement of celestial bodies and used similar means to achieve this end. Of course, a vast number of circles remained for millennia and were available to provide inspiration and to be used as templates, if necessary.

Egyptians of the earliest dynasties buried their dead in pyramids. Later dynasties used rock tombs. Early inhabitants of Britain built massive stone circles. Their successors, like the later Egyptians, were less ambitious. They used wood to create woodhenges. Almost all of the enormous number of stone circles that once covered Britain have disappeared. The great wooden circles, which must have been far more numerous, given they were easier to build, are only now being discovered.

The confusion, deliberate or otherwise, that led Geoffrey and others to claim that Merlin built Stonehenge becomes explicable when Geoffrey's likely source material is considered. It is probable that Geoffrey knew the story of Merlin building Stonehenge from the oral tradition and used it when he wrote his preposterous account of it in his *Historia*.

Later, after he gained access to source material contained in St Asaph, Geoffrey probably found out about Merlin's house and used this knowledge when he wrote *Vita Merlini*. I do not know if he realised, when he read the description of Merlin's observatory that led him to write of 70 doors and 70 windows, that it was this structure that had led to the confusion that created the oral story which resulted in his recording that Merlin built Stonehenge. If he did, it was too late to do anything about it.

The *Vita* is firmly set in Scotland and does not say that Merlin went south to build Stonehenge. By the time he came to write it, Geoffrey knew better because, by this time, he had access to the St Asaph sources.

The 'house' that Languoreth built for Merlin is described by Geoffrey in his *Vita* as a complex (reference is made to other buildings), big enough to accommodate numerous servants, and 'in the woods', which simply means not in the town.

Merlin insisted that priority be given to another construction. This was to be 'remote' from the other buildings and to have 70 doors and 70 windows, through which Merlin could watch 'fire-breathing Phoebus' (the Sun), Venus and the stars. To use this other construction, Merlin required 70 secretaries (for which we may read 'many secretaries'). Everything was to be built somewhere close enough to Languoreth's home to allow her to 'come often' to visit him. This other construction is obviously an observatory, from which Merlin intended to study the movements of the planets and stars.

The construction of Stonehenge required the concerted efforts of whole peoples over millennia, and, no doubt, different people at different times used it for different purposes, but the general consensus is that Stonehenge was used as a tool to measure and interpret the movements of bodies visible in the sky. Merlin's observatory had this same purpose, but it was a one-off construction, for one man to use. It was probably made of wood (stone would have taken too long to erect and would have been too expensive). It was probably circular, or of several concentric circles, with lintels to steady the pillars, making it look to an ill-informed eye as if it had numerous doors and windows. Uninformed observers, which would be just about everyone, would not have described it with reference to its purpose, because almost no one would have known anything of astronomy. They would have described it as it appeared to them and tried to make a connection with something familiar. The observer would have seen a round structure with lots of openings that looked like doors or windows.

In the *History of the English* by Henry of Huntingdon, c.1130, there is an account of Stonehenge that presages Geoffrey's account of Merlin's many doored and windowed observatory. Henry, in describing Stonehenge, writes, 'Stones of remarkable size are raised up *like gates* . . .'[3] (my emphasis). This chimes happily with Geoffrey's doors-and-windows description of Merlin's observatory. Henry looked at Stonehenge and saw openings that looked like gates. Geoffrey's original source looked at Merlin's observatory and saw openings that looked like doors and windows.

This small observatory would have left little or no trace in the archaeological record. The Mungo Christians and their successors, with their anti-science bent, would certainly have destroyed any written astronomical records. In the absence of archaeological and written records, the only evidence to survive relevant to Merlin's observatory would have been in the oral tradition. By the time this percolated down to the fifteenth century, the description of Merlin's observatory would be very different from the structure that had once actually existed.

Few, if any, of the people of Partick would have heard of Stonehenge, but they would have known something of Merlin's observatory and been able to pass this on. When they did, and the story made its way south, it would have reminded southern listeners of a place many would have heard of that was also described as having many doors and many windows: Stonehenge. It would not have taken much for the place that Merlin built, perhaps described as 'like Stonehenge', to become simply Stonehenge and for the story to grow that Merlin built Stonehenge. This had two results: the protagonist Merlin appeared more magical, and the audience was pleased and enthralled to have a solution to the mystery of Stonehenge. This is the story that Geoffrey told in his *Historia* and dropped when he came to write the *Vita*.

Merlin's observatory either fell into ruin or was destroyed by superstitious Mungo Christians after he and Languoreth died. A place where questions were asked was a challenge to Mungo Christians, who specialised in giving answers untrammelled by experimental findings or reason. Whether it deteriorated or was destroyed, its memory remained. People still talked about Merlin after he died; if they had not, we would not know his name today, because the Christian establishment that did so much to obliterate or warp his memory would not have invented him. In the locale where he lived, the people remembered the site of his house and passed on stories about him until Jocelyn, 500 years later, could not omit him from his record. The local people told of a house, because they had no word for observatory, and of the fact it had innumerable doors, because this was strange and memorable and would impress a listener. I believe this is the place to which Robert Paul refers in his *Partick Anecdotes*.

CHAPTER TWENTY-FIVE

'Rhydderch is Dying'

Merlin's reputation must have drawn Druids and other scholars to him, and these probably included some of the more intellectually curious Christians, perhaps some old friends from among the Telleyr Christians, although they would have had to watch their step under Mungo's regime. Something akin to a school must have grown on Merlin's hill, despite the danger.

Mungo's Christianity was in the ascendant, but he was elderly and infirm. In 604, when he was seventy-six years old, he retired to the seaside, to an unknown place called Lothwerverd, where he remained until his death eight years later.[1] Although he remained the titular head of the most powerful Christian faction in Strathclyde, the day-to-day running of his Church fell to younger, more physically able men as his health continued to deteriorate. In a sad and unsparing passage, Jocelyn describes Mungo in the last few years of his life:

> The blessed Kentigern, being worn out with extreme old age, knew from the abundant fissures in his earthly body that its destruction was imminent . . . And because of his great age and because he was touched with infirmity, numerous joints in the whole of his body were almost totally decayed and loosened. And he supported his chin

and jaws with a certain cloth of linen that he wrapped over the middle of his head and under his chin, not too loose or too tight. . . .

Therefore as much as his strength was present, he impressed upon his own disciples, as they gathered around him, concerning the observance of holy devotion, the keeping of mutual charity and peace, the grace of hospitality, and the perseverance of prayers and holy readings.[2]

So far, so good, but . . . there is always a 'but' with Mungo:

But before all things, he gave to them and left short yet strong decrees to beware all evil appearances of simoniacal wickedness and to flee the communion and fellowship of all heretics and schismatics, and to steadfastly guard the decrees of the holy fathers and especially every precept and custom of Holy Mother church. . . . And he brought himself onto his noble stony bed. Then one voice of lamentation sounded far and wide, and then the grief of mourning covered the extremities of all as if with a horror of confusion.

In early chapters of his *Life of Kentigern*, Jocelyn makes much of the privations Mungo was said to have inflicted upon himself to demonstrate his holiness. This was standard stuff in almost every sanctimonious hagiography because it made it easier to convince believers that their religious leaders shared their often-appalling daily lot and that the privations they suffered in life would stand them in good stead when they were dead. There is, however, reason to doubt whether Mungo was quite the ascetic his supporters would have us believe and to suspect that reports of his strict personal regime were no more than propaganda built on a few ostentatious examples presented for public consumption. If Mungo was so averse to bodily comforts and resigned to suffer (for whatever reason), the question arises, why did he retire to the side of the sea in his old age? Why not stay in Glasgow and suffer it out?

It is fascinating to see Jocelyn twisting and turning his sources, working them to create the picture he was bound to present to the world while, at the same time, leaving material in play from which the truth can be deduced. As Mungo lies on his sickbed, stony or otherwise, attended by his monks, an 'ethereal messenger' arrives and tells him:

> Tomorrow you will depart from this mortal body into continuous life . . . And since your whole life in this world has been a continual martyrdom, it is pleasing to the Lord that you should have a more tender passage into death than other men. Therefore, suffer a hot bath to be prepared for you on the next day, and when you have entered into it, you will fall asleep in the Lord without grievous anguish, and you will rest in peace with him.[3]

There is no talk of a return to Glasgow.

According to Jocelyn, Mungo's god required him to live a hard life for more than 80 years and then allowed him one warm bath, just before he died, as a special treat. The circumstances of the death of an important man like Mungo would have been talked about by those who were present, and it would have been difficult, if not impossible, to conceal the fact that he died in a warm bath, so Jocelyn was bound to come up with a miracle. Mungo had arthritis. A bath would have helped him. It is unlikely that his death-bath was the first time he had sought such comfort. Who can blame him? The problem was, while they could get away with it, his followers had been putting it about that Mungo bathed in cold streams. It is all rather sad.

The matter of the bath is, however, but a slight deceit. What was to follow was horrifically inhuman. Mungo's monks approached him and asked that they be allowed to die with him: '. . . request from the Lord that it may be given to us to travel with you from this valley of tears to the joy of your Lord.'[4]

Mungo agreed to his followers' requests. He prayed and was told, 'For it will be for you as you desire concerning the disciples who have requested passage with you.'

Mungo, close to death:

> Entered into a small vessel filled with hot water after having first sanctified it by the sign of salvation, and a crowd of brothers surrounded him and waited the end of the affair. And when the saint had embraced a little rest in it, he raised his hands and his eyes to heaven, bowed his head, and surrendered his spirit.[5]

In the next passage, there is a description of what amounts to a Jonesville-type mass suicide by some of Mungo's more fanatical followers. After Mungo died, before the water even grew tepid, his more fanatical supporters entered into his bath and took their own lives. The less committed were content with less drastic measures: 'The water of that bath was given out to diverse persons in diverse places, and health was granted in many ways to many with sicknesses by drinking it or by sprinkling it on them.'

Mungo was buried on the right side of the altar under a stone in the church he had built at the foot of what is now the Glasgow Necropolis and what had been the Druids' hill. The followers who had committed suicide after his death were buried nearby.

Jocelyn adds on a hundred years to Mungo's life when he says that Mungo was 'one hundred eighty-five years old' when he died. By my reckoning, Mungo was born c.528 and died c.612. A life of 85 or 86 years is probably more accurate.

Remarkably, Jocelyn does not end his biography with the death of Mungo but with Merlin. Indeed, the last chapter in Jocelyn's

Life of Kentigern is headed 'Concerning the prophecy of a certain man', when 'certain man' is meant to be read as 'a Druid' by those in the know. Jocelyn calls Merlin Laleocen. He was, perhaps, using the book 'in Scottic style' he found in Glasgow market when he first set out to fulfil his bishop's commission as his source for this last chapter, although Merlin, or, as he would have been known in Strathclyde, Lailoken, was vital in the oral tradition. Jocelyn's source, whatever it was, obviously told a different story from the one he was bound to tell to please his patron in his *Life of Kentigern*.

The people of Glasgow knew their Mungo and their Merlin, although they also knew what was acceptable and what was not acceptable to the authorities. Jocelyn was, perhaps, impelled by popular demand to include Merlin in his writings, just as Geoffrey says demand for more about Merlin led to his inserting (spurious) prophecies in his *Historia*. It is probable that Jocelyn inserted something of Merlin towards the end of his biography of Mungo because the first audience reaction was dismay that Merlin was missing. Everyone in Glasgow knew how closely linked Mungo and Merlin were. It would have struck them as odd that there was no open reference to Merlin, so, I believe, the last chapter was added as a sop to public opinion. It may be, however, that Jocelyn, despite being deep in his master's thrall, retained some small integrity and had something of the writer-artist in him after all, adding Merlin of his own volition:

> In the same year that Saint Kentigern was released from the affairs of men . . . King Rederech . . . stayed for a longer time than usual in a royal village which is called Pertnech. A certain foolish man, who was called Laleocen, lived at his court, and he received his necessary sustenance and garments from the bountifulness of the king . . .

after the burial of Saint Kentigern, this man was himself afflicted with the most severe mourning, and he would not receive any comfort from anyone. When they sought why he grieved so inconsolably, he answered that his lord King Rederech and another of the first men of the land, named Morthec, would not be long in this life after the death of [Mungo] but that they would succumb to fate in that present year and die. The deaths of those whom he mentioned that followed in that year clearly proved that the words of the fool were not spoken foolishly, but rather they were spoken prophetically . . . Therefore in the same year in which the holy bishop Kentigern died, both the king and the chief died as had been prophesied, and they were buried in Glasgow.[6]

Using the name Laleocen, Jocelyn identifies Merlin as Rhydderch's pensioner, a man who subsisted on 'the bountifulness of the king'. This accurately describes Merlin's position. In addition, Jocelyn is bound to present Merlin as a fool because this was the line laid down by those in power in his day, but the people knew the truth from the oral tradition and even Jocelyn, having said what he had to say, does not carry on with the pretence that Merlin was a madman but says that, on the contrary, he did not speak foolishly.

It is surprising that so soon after Mungo's death, the story turns not to the sadness of the people at his passing but to the individual distress of a man who is called a fool. In what can only be described as an affront to Mungo's memory, Jocelyn says that Merlin was in deep mourning after Mungo's burial not because Mungo was dead but because Rhydderch and an unsung chief called Morthec are about to die. This is unusual in the extreme: the last chapter of a biography of Mungo and his greatest enemy is its hero.

Languoreth accompanied Rhydderch to Merlin's home, but when Rhydderch left, she remained behind. She would not have done this when her husband was unwell without some good reason to detain her. Merlin and Languoreth conferred with Taliesin, whom Merlin had called to his side. Doubtless many others attended, because Rhydderch's death would change everything. When news arrived that Rhydderch was failing fast, Languoreth left to be with him.

Languoreth arrived too late; by the time she got to Rhydderch's side, he was dead and the court was in mourning. In the words of Geoffrey's *Vita*:

> She collapsed in tears into the arms of her friends, tearing her hair and crying out: 'Weep with me, women, the death of Rhydderch.[7] Mourn for a man whose like earth has not been known to produce before in our age. He was a lover of peace, for he so administered a warrior people that there was no violence between man and man . . . Will the fair flesh and royal limbs indeed be hidden under the cold stone, and you become but dusty bones? Yet so it is . . .[8]

Languoreth was 72 years old when Rhydderch died. She had been at the centre of events for more than 50 years, but after the death of Rhydderch there was no place at court for her, so she went to live with her brother in the house she had built for him. Any hopes she might have harboured in middle age that she might play the part of a Celtic Livia ended when her son Constantine turned out to be not Tiberius but Caligula:

> Therefore I take leave of you – you noble chiefs, you high walls and household gods, you my sweet children, and all that is of this world. I shall live in the woods by the side of my brother . . . with my black cloak around me.

Merlin and Languoreth knew, when Rhydderch died, they would be easy prey for the Mungo Christians and Rhydderch's most likely successor, Languoreth's son, the unstable and ferocious Constantine. Merlin would have been naturally concerned for his safety and that of Languoreth, and to ensure that the old way was not forgotten. These considerations must have figured large in their discussions with Taliesin and other allies.

As always, once the magical material and talk of prophecies are put aside, the remaining evidence in Geoffrey's *Vita*, that which is not inherently unlikely or internally contradictory, presents a plausible picture. Geoffrey says that Taliesin came to Partick at Merlin's behest because Merlin wanted to know 'what winds and rain-storms were'.[9] This cannot be taken at face value. The king was dying and times were dangerous; Merlin is hardly likely to have called Taliesin to his side to talk about the weather. It appears to me that Geoffrey has put together various exchanges in numerous connections and created one great composite conversation, just as a modern film director would. According to Geoffrey, Merlin and Taliesin talked about scientific matters in the main, but this must be suspect because politics must have been their primary concern. Geoffrey would have considered sixth-century politics to be both too dangerous for him and too boring for his audience. Instead, so we are told, Merlin and Taliesin discussed science.

Geoffrey describes Merlin and Taliesin's conversation. This does not involve, as one might expect, casting dark spells, mixing noxious potions, fighting fictional beasts, conversing with non-existent beings (like demons) or inanimate things (like plants and trees), but science. Geoffrey does not even have Merlin travelling to faraway places and meeting strange people, as he preposterously has Arthur fighting Danes and Norwegians before going to France to beat the Romans; instead, Geoffrey describes Merlin talking to the like-minded Taliesin about things that can only have mystified a medieval audience. Why? If Geoffrey did not simply invent the exchanges he attributes to Merlin and Taliesin, he must have had access to sources that are now lost, perhaps through Geoffrey's St Asaph connection.

The two friends talked about astronomy ('Heaven . . . embellished with stars . . . is set above and envelops everything in the way a nutshell encloses a nut'), audiology ('Air is said to be fitted for the production of sounds'), oceanography, ('[The seas are] divided . . . into different types, to facilitate the development of natural forms from out of it by production over a long period'), before returning to meteorology ('With the help of the sun, the clouds are filled like water-skins by the rivers through the operation of a mysterious law. Then, when driven by the force of the winds, they rise on high into the upper atmosphere and discharge the water they have taken up . . .').

We may infer that the evidence available to Geoffrey suggested Merlin was a man who engaged in scientific enquiry. If Geoffrey had material relevant to Merlin and unrelated material relevant to scientific enquiry, why would he connect one to the other, rather than invent some marvellous magical happenings to entertain his audience? After all, magical miracles and prophecies were what the people wanted most.

Geoffrey's unexpected account of their conversation suggests that he was working from a trustworthy source, and, I suspect, a source that originated in Scotland, where the events in question took place (although it may be that this source material came into Geoffrey's hands indirectly through his St Asaph connection). The geographical evidence has always been thought to relate to southern Britain, but when it is closely considered, it can be seen that it relates to northern Britain, where Merlin lived. When Geoffrey has Merlin and Taliesin discuss geography, he has them say:

> Close to this island [Britain] lies Thanet, which is rich in many things – but lacks dangerous snakes; and it is an antidote to poison to drink wine in which Thanet earth has been mixed.

Our ocean also divides the Orkneys from us. These islands, separated by the flowing tides, number thirty-three. Twenty of them are un-worked, the rest cultivated.

Thule [Iceland] gets its name, 'Furthest Thule', through the sun, on account of the solstice or stop which the summer sun makes there. At that point, the sun's rays turn away so as to provide no illumination beyond. The sun thus takes away the daylight, so that ever through the endless night the air begets shadows, and in addition its coldness makes the sea hard and sluggishly un-navigable by ships.

The island which after ours is held to be superior to all is Ireland, for its happy fertility. It is larger; it possesses no bees, no birds (save a very few), and is entirely unsuitable for snakes to breed in. . . .

Scotland is the only country bounded on the north by the Orkneys, on the north-west by Iceland (Thule) and on the west by Ireland. This much is indisputable. Thanet, however, is more contentious. The conventional wisdom says Thanet is the island now called Thanet at the extreme east of the Thames estuary. (This is no longer an island; the channel that used to run from about Margate to about Ramsgate has silted up.) This makes no sense. Why, if the island of Britain was being described from a southern viewpoint, would anyone mention tiny Thanet near the Thames and omit the Isle of Wight or Anglesey?

I suspect the Isle of Thanet in eastern Kent only got its name because it was deliberately misidentified as Geoffrey's Isle of Thanet by those minded to set the scene in the far south of Britain. Alternatively, the position of the island described is similar to that of Lindisfarne. Lindisfarne, off the east coast near the modern Scotland–England border, is still a tidal island and is so close to land that when the tide is out it can be reached by a causeway. It would be reasonable to suppose that early invaders would have used islands such as Thanet in Kent and Lindisfarne in similar ways, as secure bases from which to launch raiding parties and later, as they became more established, as headquarters. If this is so, it would explain a name which is associated with the rank of Thane, a rank made most famous in Shakespeare's *Macbeth* (Macbeth was, for example, Thane of Cawdor). In any event, when considered in the wider context as detailed by Geoffrey, Lindisfarne is more likely to have been Geoffrey's Thanet than the present place of that name in Kent.

Merlin and Taliesin talked about the great events that had occurred in their lives – in particular, the turning point in their fortunes: the time when they lost their champion, Arthur. Naturally, because they were old men, but with some cause, they did not think things were as good as they used to be when they were young. Merlin says:

> 'My dearest friend – how great a burden has the kingdom borne since then, with the pact broken, so that it is not what it once was. Through unhappy circumstances, the nobles have been led away and turned to rend each other's vitals. They upset everything, and so prosperity has left the country: all goodness has gone. Those who live in the cities will abandon their walls in despair. For the Saxon [Angle], warlike and ferocious, descends on us, savagely overthrows our cities and ourselves once more.'

The above passage exactly reflects circumstances in the late sixth and early seventh centuries. After the Great Angle War, the 'peace dividend' led to a short time of plenty, before the aristocrats started to fight among themselves again. Geoffrey does not say what this pact was, but if, as I believe, this conversation took place near the end of Rhydderch's reign, *c*.612, it was the pact of mutual tolerance between the Telleyr Christians and Merlin's people that had bound the people of Strathclyde to each other during the Great Angle

War. It would have been foolhardy of Geoffrey to expand upon this pact, because it highlighted the existence of the old way, and Geoffrey was not a man to take challenging or courageous steps.

At the time when Merlin and Taliesin met, c. 612–15, the Angles had recovered both confidence and strength and were about to start a campaign that would cut Britain in two, so laying the foundations for the modern nations that share the main British island today.

CHAPTER TWENTY-SIX

The Dark Heart

After Rhydderch's death, Merlin and Languoreth met Taliesin to decide how best to protect the people of the old way. There were others present, but Geoffrey does not mention them. To have done so would have smacked of hard politics and made his narrative less audience-friendly. Much of what follows is taken from Geoffrey's *Vita*, which, although an entertainment, does not read as if it sprang fully formed from Geoffrey's head – too much is obviously based on some real historical source. No writer of pure fiction would have his hero decline to lead the resistance to an evil foe because he is too old.

Rhydderch's death raised the question of the succession. Languoreth and Rhydderch's oldest son had been killed at the Battle of Arderydd. Their second son, Constantine, was 52 years old when his father died. Recognising and fearing Constantine's faults, the Druids and the chiefs of the old way gathered at Merlin's house to offer him their support if he would take the throne. Civil war would have followed if Merlin had agreed to their request, and this at a time when an Angle threat was hanging over the heads of all the Celtic people of Scotland, Britons, Scots and Picts alike. Even were this not the case, even Merlin was not so lacking in judgement as to believe that it was possible for him to take charge of the kingdom.

Geoffrey's description of these events is deliberately obscured in allegory and can only be understood when Geoffrey's references to an underground spring are understood to be references to the old way. When Geoffrey says that Merlin heard that a new spring had broken out and 'streams of pure water were . . . gushing out, running far down the valley and swirling noisily as they rippled their way across the pastures', he is really saying that word was spreading of an upsurge of confidence among those of the old way.

Following this passage, Geoffrey goes on at length about various streams before getting back to the point: 'Previously these waters were flowing underground through lightless caverns . . .'[1] The waters that had been flowing underground clearly stand for the old way, which had been driven underground.

> The story was spreading everywhere about the new spring which had broken out in the woods of Calidon . . . Consequently, chieftains and other leaders soon came to see and to congratulate the prophet [Merlin] . . . They told him in detail how matters stood in the country; and he was asked to resume his kingly position and continue his previous fair administration of his people.
>
> But he said, 'Young men, at my time of life this cannot be demanded of me. I am now reaching old age, and it so enfeebles my limbs that with my slackened strength I can scarcely get across the fields . . . I will not reign again.'

Taliesin concurred, urged the chiefs not to tempt Merlin to civil war and recommended they prepare to fight the Angles: 'Away to defend your cities! . . . You have acclaimed our friend [Merlin] enough.' The chiefs had no alternative but to accept this advice.

The new king was chosen by tanistry, that is, from among the senior male members of the royal family. Merlin was the brother-in-law of the king, but Constantine was the late king's son and so had a better claim. Merlin was in his 70s; Constantine was 20 years younger. Merlin had the support of the people of the old way; Constantine had the power of the Christians behind him. Merlin had been inactive for years; it was to Constantine and his Mungo Christian allies that chiefs were turning. Everything weighed against Merlin.

Merlin's refusal to challenge Constantine was sound sense, from which we may safely infer he acted with the advice of Languoreth. If he had been unsuccessful, which was the most likely result, Constantine would have had him killed. As matters turned out, all Merlin did was buy a little time.

The way was clear for Constantine, the Christian candidate.

Apart from Taliesin and Languoreth, only one other person is identified as having been part of Merlin's household: Maelgwn,[2] an old soldier. Taliesin and Maelgwn were probably representative of the two main classes of people, Druids and warriors, who gathered about Merlin.

Maelgwn must have been an important man because Geoffrey says he was mad, which only means he held views that differed from Geoffrey's patrons' views and was someone to be feared:

> A madman came up to [Merlin and Taliesin] unexpectedly . . . He filled the forest air with a terrible noise, made threatening gestures and foamed at the mouth like a wild boar. . . . [Taliesin] realised who he was, and gave a deep sigh, saying: 'This was not how he once looked when we were in the flower of our youth. At that time, he was a strong handsome soldier, in whom the nobility of royal descent was patent . . . I was considered to be lucky, and I was, to have such good friends.[3]

The 'noise . . . threatening gestures and foam[ing] at the mouth' can be ignored as propaganda. When this is deleted, what is left is all too human. Taliesin remembered Maelgwn because he had fought beside him and Merlin at Arderydd, almost 40 years before, as depicted in the 'Dialogue Between Merlin and Taliesin':

> Swiftly came Maelgwn's men,
> Warriors ready for battle, for slaughter armed.
> For this battle, Arderydd, they have made
> A lifetime of preparation.[4]

Maelgwn is representative of the warriors of the old way, the men who had fought side by side with Scots and Picts and, indeed, Telleyr Christians against the Angles too many years ago. As they neared the end of their lives, they must have realised that the time of the old way was gone, at least for their lifetimes. Merlin's home would have been a natural focal point for such men and women. The Mungo Christians would not have liked this, but the people of the old way were still a force and could not be easily put aside.

Emrys was the first Pen Dragon. Emrys's lieutenant and successor, Gwenddolau son of Ceidio (Merlin's friend), was the second. The third was not, as might be supposed, Arthur, but, perhaps, Maelgwn, who fought at the Battle of Arderydd and who ended up a pensioner living with Merlin. I say 'perhaps' because the evidence for this is circumstantial at best. Maelgwn was at Arderydd. He was important enough to be included along with Taliesin as part of Merlin's household in the early seventh century. If I am correct and Taliesin was representative of the Druids, then it follows that Maelgwn was representative of the warrior class, in effect their leader. I believe it may reasonably be inferred that Maelgwn was the third and last Pen Dragon.

There is one other source of evidence, and in this Maelgwn is called dragon. The conventional wisdom, as we know, has Gildas writing in the early sixth century, although Professor Alcock has him 'in the middle of the sixth century'.[5] He dates Gildas with reference to a Maelgwn, but, in my opinion, in Maelgwn of Gwynedd he has the wrong Maelgwn. By my reckoning, Gildas wrote or at least compiled his most famous work, *De Excidio et Conquestu Britanniae*, in the late 590s. In the third section of *De Excidio*, Gildas excoriates five Celtic leaders. The first of these is Constantine, Languoreth's son (by my account); the second is Maelgwn, a man Gildas called (in chapter 23 of the *Excidio*) 'Dragon of the island'. The conventional wisdom does not accept that Gildas's Maelgwn was the same as the Maelgwn I have identified as Merlin's friend, although there is no consensus as regards Maelgwn's identity. The most favoured candidate, Maelgwn of Gwynedd in Wales, is said to have died *c*.547. He was a grandson of a chief called Cunedda who emigrated to North Wales from the Manau region of Scotland in the early fifth century, but there are other candidates. Not one of these contenders has more than a vague coincidence of names to recommend him.

Gildas's Maelgwn fought and killed kings and was castigated by the writer for his trouble. Merlin's Maelgwn fought for Emrys, a man of low social rank, against King Vortigern and his son Pascent, and against the allied kings at Arderydd. Gildas's Maelgwn is chastised because, although he had power and strength, he did not use it in favour of the Church. After Arderydd, Merlin's Maelgwn, as one of Emrys's and later Gwenddolau's lieutenants, would have held great power: power he had won fighting Christians. Gildas says that Maelgwn's major faults (omitting, as he says, his domestic and light offences) included rebellion. By my account, this would be against Vortigern and his family (although Maelgwn was himself of that family). Emrys had risen to lead the resistance to the Angles, but he had had to surround himself with sub-commanders who were men of high social station, just as he had to enlist learned men such as Merlin to help him run his country. Gildas's Maelgwn purported to come over to the Christian side and became a monk, but that did not last. Gildas had had great hopes for Maelgwn, but they were not to be fulfilled:

> Oh how great a joy should it have been to our mother church, if the enemy of all mankind had not lamentably pulled thee, as it were, out of her bosom! . . . Oh what great rewards in the kingdom of Christ would have been laid up for thy soul against the day of judgment, if that crafty wolf had not caught thee . . . and made of thee a lamb, a wolf like unto himself, again?[6]

Merlin's Maelgwn had every reason to pretend to be a Christian after the Battle of Arderydd. The alternative was to take to the woods or be killed. Clearly, Maelgwn's conversion was not sincere, and, given his later actions, it is easy to believe that the 'enemy of all mankind', 'that crafty wolf' (probably Merlin or Taliesin) would have had little trouble persuading Maelgwn to go back to his old ways. Maelgwn, as Gildas depicts him, was not cut out to be a churchman:

> Yet neither is thy sensual mind (which is overcome by the excess of thy follies) at all checked in its course with committing so many sins, but hot and prone (like a young colt that coveteth every pleasant pasture) runneth headlong forward, with irrecoverable fury, through the intended fields of crime, continually increasing the number of its transgressions.[7]

These transgressions included, according to Gildas, putting aside his wife for his nephew's widow and later killing his wife and his nephew and marrying his nephew's widow.

There is too little evidence to reach a firm conclusion as regards the name Maelgwn. It is a common name among Welsh princes, and, it is said, may be connected with the name Malcolm, which is said to mean 'disciple of Columba' or to be perhaps derived from the Latin *maglocunus*, great hound. It is all rather confusing. Gildas's version describes Maelgwn not only as non-Christian but as something worse, a man who professed to be a Christian and then went back on his word. Such a man would be considered deceptive and treacherous. In Scots Gaelic, *meabhal* means treachery and *meall* to deceive or cheat. *Gwn*, in Welsh, means robe or gown. It may be that, as so often, Maelgwn was not a personal name but a nickname, that he was called something that rang of treachery and, later, as the language changed and the original meaning was lost, and because the nickname sounded like the Welsh name Maelgwn, it became the name Maelgwn. If Welsh speakers added the robe/gown element, it may suggest the name originally meant he who was wrapped in treachery. There is too little evidence to say anything more with any certainty.

According to Geoffrey's *Vita*, Taliesin accepts that it is also time for him to retire from active involvement with the world and says:

'I too shall stay with you and make the third . . . turning away from the traffic of the world. I have spent long enough in empty living; now the time has come to recover myself, and you shall lead me.'[8]

This need not be taken literally; Taliesin did not necessarily live with Merlin, although Merlin's home would have been an ideal place for him, and many of the old way must have gravitated there. Even if there was no organised school, even if Merlin only passed on knowledge to individuals, his very existence would have encouraged those of the old way and constituted a dagger pointed at the heart of the establishment, the regime of the Mungo Christians.

After Rhydderch died and Languoreth's son, Constantine, took the throne, there was no place for Languoreth at court. Languoreth must have known the kind of man her son was and been glad to distance herself from him, and the Christians must have been glad to see her go; the last thing they wanted was Languoreth influencing the new king as she had influenced his father. She left the court and joined Merlin in the house she had given him:

> She had been leading a retired life since the death of the king. She who till now had been the queen of a large nation under the appointed law, now found nothing pleasanter than living in the woods with her brother.[9]

In 612, after his father's death, Constantine made a deal with the followers of the recently deceased Mungo. In exchange for their support in taking the throne, Constantine agreed to allow the Mungo Christians power in Strathclyde. This close Christian alliance meant that Constantine got a 'good press' from the Christians who kept the records after his death. Jocelyn gives the following account:

> And so the boy flourished with a distinguished character in age and in grace, being loved by God and men. And after his father had submitted to fate and he succeeded him to the kingdom by hereditary right, Constantine was always subject to the bishop, even as his father had been. And because the Lord was with him, he suppressed all the barbarian nations near to his people without the shedding of blood. And all of the kings who had ruled in the kingdom of Cambria before him he surpassed in riches and glory and honour and holiness, which is more excellent. Wherefore being famous for his merits and completing in triumph to the end of his days in goodness, he deserved to be crowned with glory and honour in heaven, and he is accustomed to be called Saint Constantine by many up to the present.[10]

In reality, Constantine caved in and became the tool of the Mungo Christians. In the twelfth century, when Jocelyn was writing, the

Church in Glasgow was asserting its temporal power, and the reference to an historical precedent that put the Church above the state would have been very useful to the bishop of Glasgow, Jocelyn's patron.

Constantine's reign was short and inglorious. He did not excel in war, a fact Jocelyn covers up by claiming he did what he did without blood. It is unlikely in the extreme that nearby barbarians were bloodlessly suppressed and more likely there were no major wars during his reign. Constantine's canonisation can be explained as his reward for being a tool of the Christians.

Unlike Jocelyn, who wrote more than half a millennium after Constantine's death, Gildas was his contemporary. He has a very different and, almost certainly, more accurate story to tell.

The first of the five Celtic leaders excoriated by Gildas in *De Excidio* is a man called Constantine, sometimes supposed to have been Arthur's successor, although, as is now generally accepted, Arthur was not a king and so did not have a successor. Professor Alcock says that Constantine is 'probably to be placed in Dumnonia [Cornwall]', but, perhaps worried that someone might correct him with reference to a possible northern location, he covers himself by saying, 'It should not be overlooked that in Ptolemy's *Geography* the Damnonii inhabited the Forth–Clyde isthmus . . . the Kingdom of Strathclyde.'[11]

No Welsh candidate fits the bill like Constantine of Strathclyde. Gildas describes Constantine as the 'Tyrannical whelp of the unclean Damnonian lioness', which, in my view, can only mean Languoreth. Who else, in the eyes of the fundamentalist fanatic Gildas, was the whelp of the Lioness of Damnonia, Languoreth? It is frustrating when scholars conclude that Constantine was probably of Dumnonia, as opposed to Damnonia, when the text says Damnonia.

When Gildas homes in on Constantine, he says he is one of those who, 'Hav[ing] stood before the altar, swearing by the name of God, they go away and think no more of the holy altar than if it were a mere heap of dirty stones.'[12]

The *Annals of Ulster* say that Constantine converted to Christianity about 589, just after the Great Angle War, when he was, by my reckoning, 29 years old. It is doubtful that he took up Church orders voluntarily – his career in the Church proves that. More likely, he was pressured into it after proving himself unsuitable to be king in the year that followed Arthur's victory at the Battle of Badon. If he was a churchman, he could not succeed to the throne. Constantine's crimes involved 'deceit against his countrymen' (treason) and adultery. It was probably only his princely rank that prevented his being executed. His punishment suggests that his actions were concerned with the succession, as do the events that followed:

> In the habit of a holy abbot amid the sacred altars, [he] did
> with sword and javelin, as if with teeth, wound and tear
> . . . two royal youths . . . And not one worthy act could he
> boast of previous to this cruel deed.[13]

Constantine was pretending to be a Christian, and he couldn't even do that properly. No wonder Gildas was angry. Gildas probably wrote his diatribe against Constantine in the immediate aftermath of Constantine's assassinations – by my account, in the early 590s. When Mungo returned to Strathclyde in the mid-590s, Constantine would have seen him as offering him a way back. Gildas would have been surprised that, in less than two decades, Constantine would be the Christian candidate for the throne of Strathclyde. It took a cynical man such as Constantine to seek the favour of one Christian sect having been properly excluded from another. It took another cynical man, Mungo, to accept such a prince as an ally.

Mungo and Constantine used each other for their separate but complementary purposes.

Merlin, Languoreth and the Telleyr Christians, whose Church Constantine most probably defiled back in the 590s, must have been appalled by the alliance between Constantine and the Mungo Christians that developed in the first decade of the seventh century. Constantine would allow the Mungo Roman Christians power in Strathclyde in return for their support of his candidacy, or perhaps he was simply their cat's paw. Constantine duly succeeded to the throne, but his reign was not a happy one. His character was too unstable, and he was soon deposed.

Constantine's reign was doubtless dreadful, given his nature, although, because he was lauded as a saint in later years, detrimental details are scant. I suspect he was a burnt-out husk by the time he came to the throne, because, when he was forced to resign his throne in c.618–20, in favour of Neithon ap Guithno, a distant cousin, it was not thought necessary to have him killed. He was allowed to retire into the Church, some say initially in Ireland, but this is unlikely. He may have been a derelict man by this time, but he could still have been made a figurehead in a coup. It is more likely he was kept close by. In any event, some short time later he was in a church in Govan just across the Clyde from Partick, where he remained a watched man until he died.

The story is told that he lived quietly in Govan and could be heard talking to himself as he hand-ground corn with a stone. People passing would say: is this Constantine the King, who wore a helmet and bore a shield, drudging at a hand mill?[14] This connection with Govan, his usefulness to the Church (for a short time) and the fact he had been a king all made him memorable in local lore, and, in time, as memories blurred, he became useful again when he was made a saint. He died and was buried in Govan, where his shrine can still be seen.

Languoreth must have left the court with sadness. She had lost a husband she loved, and her ferocious son was about to take control of the land she and Rhydderch had protected for more than 30 years. A way of life that was dear to her was obviously in the descendent, and she was old. Doubtless, she found the company in Merlin's house more congenial than that of the court, but there was no escaping the fact that all she had worked for was now in danger. This is how Geoffrey describes it in his *Vita*: 'So, one day when she stood in her brother's hall and gazed at the house and at its windows glittering in the sun, she uttered . . . dark sayings out of a dark heart . . .'[15] Languoreth was clever. She knew that the failure of the old way presaged a dark age. She could not have known it would last 1,000 years.

CHAPTER TWENTY-SEVEN

Dumpelder

Taneu, Mungo's mother, was tried at Dunipace. The evidence provided earlier in this connection does not include the most clear-cut clue: the name of the place. Jocelyn's *Life of Kentigern* says that Taneu 'was led on the command of the king to the brow of the highest mountain, which is named Dumpelder, so that she could be cast headlong downward from there and be broken bit by bit into pieces and torn limb from limb'.[1] The name Dumpelder is vital to understanding what happened to Merlin in the last few years of his long life.

I rejected the magical elements in Taneu's story because people do not float to the ground when thrown from high hills, and little boats without oars or sails do not float upstream against river flow and tides, but I saw no reason to doubt the evidential value of the name Dumpelder. Jocelyn had reason to enhance Mungo's status by surrounding his prenatal life with paranormal happenings, but he had no reason to invent the name Dumpelder, or, indeed, any other name. What did Dumpelder mean, and where was it? One suggested solution has it derived from the P Gaelic *Dun-Paladyr*, meaning the fort of the palisade, but every fort has a palisade or some protective surround, so this makes no more sense than, say, fort of the walls or fort of the battlements. It is a possible interpretation, but it is, I think, unlikely. It has also been suggested that the word 'Dun-pelder' is formed from two Gaelic words and means 'steep hill'. *Dun*, hill fort, almost works in this connection, in that the hill element is present, but I can find no authority that suggests *pelder*, or anything that sounds like it, meaning steep. Again, giving a hill the name 'steep hill' seems to me to be pointless, bland and unhelpful, particularly in an area where there are hills of innumerable shapes and sizes everywhere. This, too, is a possible interpretation, but again I think it unlikely.

Dun means hill fort. *Dum* is a corrupt variant of *dun*, and so we find *Dun*bartonshire and a town *Dum*barton. *Dum* is also a corrupt form of the Gaelic *Druim*, meaning a back of land, a ridge of land, a large rise of land or a hump of land. In Irish and Old Irish Gaelic, it would be *Druimm*. (The Latin word *dorsum* comes from the same root, and from this we get dorsal, and other 'back'-related words.) Drumalban, in the west-central Scottish Highlands, is an example of a *drum* name. Drumalban is not one mountain but a mound of mountains. *Drum* plus *Alban* (Scotland) describes this massive rise of land perfectly.

I took it that the first part of the name *Dumpelder* was probably best understood as *Drum* and so looked for other Drum place names that might be relevant. I had the advantage of local knowledge. I knew a place which not only started with the Drum element but which also sounded a little like Dumpelder, and even more like Drumpeleder. In my mid-20s, I lived for a short time in the west of Coatbridge, a town in central Scotland, in the district of Drumpellier. Peter Drummond in his *Placenames of the Monklands* reached the same conclusion. He wrote, '*Dunpelder*, which we can recognise as Drumpellier'.[2] Drumpellier in Coatbridge, however, did not make sense as the place where Taneu was tried; it was too far from Dunipace.

The evidence in Jocelyn's *Life of Kentigern* suggested that Dumpelder lay south of Culross, across the Firth of Forth, and while Drumpellier fitted that criterion, the evidence also suggested that Dumpelder was close enough to the shore opposite Culross to allow officers of the court to make the journey there and back in one day. With Drumpellier in Coatbridge as a starting point, it would perhaps have been possible for the king's servants to make it there and back in one day, while the king waited, but this would have involved a round trip of forty-four miles and this does not seem practical or likely.

Drumpellier in Coatbridge is almost certainly too far from the shore opposite Culross to be Dumpelder, and, if I was right about Dunipace being the area where Taneu was tried, too far from Dunipace to make sense. The place of execution was almost certainly nearer the place of trial. Why would anyone try Taneu at Dunipace and then send her south to Drumpellier in Coatbridge to be thrown from a hill, thus denying the crowd a chance to see 'justice' done? There are many hills in the Dunipace area, and many are higher than the hills of Drumpellier in Coatbridge.

What also weighed against this location was that, unlike the Dunipace area, there is no history of Coatbridge's Drumpellier ever having been a place of parley, far less of trial or execution.

I backtracked and looked at the names Dumpelder and Drumpellier again. As usual with sixth-century names, there were innumerable versions. I broke these down into two categories: DP and DM. The DP versions include: Dumpelder; Dunpelder; Dunpeleder; Dunpender; Dunpaledyr; Dumpender; and Drumpellier. The DM versions include: Dunmeller; Drimallier; Drumaillier; Drummailler; Drumelzier; and Drumalzier.

I looked for the meaning of the second part of the name using the DP versions, but this proved fruitless. I began to sympathise with the people who had (I suspect desperately) plumped for the meanings 'fort of the palisade' and 'steep hill'. Then, in the DM versions, I found a meaning that made sense. The Drumaillier, Drummaillier versions were the key. In Scottish Gaelic, *maille ri* means 'with' (in the sense of alongside). In Irish Gaelic, *maille ri* is *maille re*. In Old Irish Gaelic, this would be *immalle* or *malle*. *Immalle* is derived from *imb-an-leth*. According to MacBain's *Etymological Dictionary*, *imb-an-leth* means 'by the side'. This would be a sensible part of any place name. Allowing for the fluidity of names in the first millennium CE, and working forwards from the oldest name, *imb-an-leth*, to the Old Irish *immalle* and from there to the more recent Irish and Scottish Gaelic, *maille re* and *maille ri*, it is easy to see, when the prefix *drum* is added, how the name Drumaillier came to be. Drum-imb-an-leth became Drum-immalle, and Drum-immalle became Drummailler or Drumaillier. In time, P Gaelic speakers gave currency to the DP versions, so Drumaillier became Drumpellier.

There were no definitive or universally accepted spellings in the sixth century; people wrote what they heard, so many variations of the same descriptive place name would appear. Drumpellier, by my reckoning, means 'the land by the side of the *drum*', that is, the land by the side of a rise of land.

Once I understood the 'name' part of Dumpelder, the 'place' part was easy. There is a distinct *drum* between Glasgow and Edinburgh, to the east of both Drumpellier in Coatbridge and Dunipace. This is a wide range of hills, a back or ridge of land, dividing south central Scotland. The down slope heading west affords an uninterrupted view across the fertile triangle of land bounded by the River Clyde, the Campsie Hills and the *drum* itself.

Millennia ago, this fertile triangle of land to the west of this rise of land would have been called just that, the land to the side of the *drum*. That is, Drum-imb-an-leth.

Taneu was tried at Dunipace and taken to be executed at Dumpelder, which suggested that Dunipace and Dumpelder lay close to each other. I was sure of the Dumpelder–Drumpellier connection, but modern Drumpellier in Coatbridge did not make sense. Why? I was looking at the name Drumpellier when I should have been looking at the word 'modern'. The problem, and so the answer to the problem, lay not in the name but in the time. I had been looking at the right place name but in the wrong time. The question I should have asked was: where was Drumpellier in the sixth century?

In 1140, David, king of Scots, and his infant son Malcolm, granted the lands of 'Dunpelder' to the Cistercian monks of Newbattle Abbey near Edinburgh, and, for a time, Drumpellier was, literally, the land of the monks. The clause in the grant vesting this land to the monks reads, 'Dunpelder by its right marches with Metherauch and Mayneuth and Glarnephyn as far as Dunduffel in the east.' Peter Drummond's *Placenames of the Monklands* says, 'apart from Dunpelder which we recognise as Drumpellier'[3], the other names that define the extent of Drumpellier are unclear. Drummond suggests that Metherauch became Matherucks, which today is Medrox, between Glenboig and Mollinsburn. Mayneuth is, according to him, now North and South Mynot, which lie, one on each side of the railway line, south of Cumbernauld.[4] 'Glarnephyn as far as Dunduffel in the east'[5] is, says Drummond, less easily explained. Glarnephyn, he suggests, may be Torphichen, near Linlithgow, but Torphichen is on the wrong side of the high ground of the *drum*. In any event, Torphichen does not sound like Glarnephyn. Glen Avon, another Drummond suggestion, sounds more likely, in that at least it has a hint of the Glarnephyn 'GN' element in it, but 'glen of the river' is such a basic common name that it is unlikely it would have been corrupted sufficiently to become as obscure as it is today.

Again, I had local knowledge from the time I had lived in both Coatbridge and Airdrie. My first school was Gartsherrie Academy, and I was baptised in Gartsherrie Parish Church. In my opinion, *glar*, which otherwise has no known meaning, is a corrupt form of *gart*, meaning enclosure (Gartsherrie means 'enclosure of the foals'). Gartnephyn would, therefore, mean Nephyn's Enclosure. In the early sixth century, Brychan II, king of Manau, married Ingenach, a princess of Strathclyde. Their daughters included Lluan (who married the Scot Gabhran, the grandfather of Arthur) and Nefyn, who married Cynvarch son of Meirchon. Gartnephyn could well have belonged to this Nefyn, Arthur's aunt, or to some other woman of the same name. We cannot be sure. Neither do we know where it is.

Drummond suggests that Dunduffel may be Dun Daugh Farm, situated in the rise of hills between Glasgow and Edinburgh, and that this name was derived from Dun Davach, meaning the hill fort in the hollow, but this seems to me to be contradictory. If a hill fort was in a hollow, it would not be a hill fort. According to Drummond, the most likely location for Dunduffel is the Blackhill that stands 285 m high on the high point of the *drum*. I say 'the' Blackhill because there are several Blackhills in central Scotland. *Dun*, meaning hill fort, added to *dubh*, Gaelic for black, often Anglicised to Duff, gives names like Dunduff and Dunduffel.[6] Blackhill is east of the other names in the descriptive clause of the deed of 1140, so Drummond's explanation makes sense.

The exact boundaries may be unclear, but plainly, and this is the important point, Drumpellier was larger in the twelfth century than in the twenty-first century.

In the two centuries following the grant of 1140, the name Monklands became attached to the lands granted to Cistercian monks. It was first recorded with reference to these lands in a charter attested in 1323, during the reign of the hero king Robert Bruce, by which time the Monklands were smaller than those originally granted in the twelfth century.

In the sixteenth century, a reformation of the Christian Church ended the power of the monks, and Drumpellier became the Monklands in name only, as the lands of the Monks were broken up. Not all of the resultant parcels of land could be called Drumpellier, so the name Drumpellier denoted smaller and smaller areas, until it was reduced to being the name of one district in the west of the town of Coatbridge.

In the late twentieth century, following local-government reorganisation, Monklands District Council was created. This Monklands, a creature of statute, was smaller than the Monklands of the Reformation, which was smaller than the Monklands in the reign of Robert Bruce, which was smaller than the original grant of Dunpelder (Drumpellier) in the twelfth century.

Drumpellier was originally a large area, and the record shows that its boundaries increase the further back we go in time. It would, therefore, be reasonable to suppose that if we were to go back further still, these lands would be larger still. There is evidence to back this up. If, in the sixth century, Mayneuth referred not just, as Drummond suggests, to the area about the Mynot farms, but to Myot Hill, further north, near the River Carron, then the boundary would no longer run east and then east again. By my reckoning, the boundary stretched north, and there was a Greater Drumpellier in the sixth century, one that covered the whole lands to the side of the *drum* and stretched south from Dunipace near Myot Hill.

I believe the name Drumpellier was originally used to identify the triangle of land west of the *drum*, south of the Campsie Hills, and north-east of the River Clyde. The land in this area is relatively flat and low lying. In the sixth century, it would have been fertile farmland. Being the land to the side of the *drum*, it would be called just that, *Drum-maille-ri*, and then one or other of the many various developments and corruptions of this name.

Why, then, was the name Drumpellier preserved particularly in the westerly part of Coatbridge? In the sixth century, the land of Drumpellier extended from modern Drumpellier, Coatbridge, to Blackhill. Over succeeding centuries, the population grew as the ground was cleared for farms and settlements, and naturally the number of farm and village names increased. Eventually, there were several lands, all with new names, to cross before the Blackhill was reached. Drumpellier in Coatbridge is on the main road going west to east. It was at modern Drumpellier that the main road from Glasgow to Edinburgh first touched the land of Greater Drumpellier. The name Drumpellier came to describe only this first parcel of land. This evidence was to lead me to clues that would corroborate the location of Merlin's grave.

CHAPTER TWENTY-EIGHT

The Grave

There are innumerable places where Merlin is said to have died and been buried: Merlin's Mound in Marlborough College, Wiltshire, England (because of a mistranslation that Latinised Marlborough to Merleburgia); le Tombeau de Merlin near Paimpont, Brittany, France (actually a Neolithic galleried tumulus); Ynys Enlli, Bardsey Island, off the Lleyn Peninsula, Wales (following a late Welsh legend that had Merlin imprisoned there in an invisible glass house!); and Bryn Myrddin, Merlin's Hill, near Carmarthen, again in Wales (this time because Carmarthen was mistakenly or mischievously read as Caer Myrddin).

In Scotland, the prime candidate has always been Stobo, in the Scottish borders, because the *Silvestris* says that Merlin was killed near Drumelzier Castle and that this was near where the Pausayl Burn meets the River Tweed. This burn and river come together a few miles south of Stobo at a place now called Drumelzier and Merlindale.

Drumelzier is, of course, one of the many variants of the name given to the land by the side of the *drum*, although, applied to the Stobo area, this does not make geographical sense. The *Silvestris* is specific: 'That town [where Merlin is buried] is thirty miles distant from the city of Glasgow. In its territory Merlin lies buried.' The problem with this evidence is that Drumelzier near Stobo is, by the old roads, 50 miles from Glasgow.

Either Merlin was killed and buried where the Pausayl Burn meets the River Tweed or he was killed and buried 30 miles from Glasgow; it cannot be both. Does the *Silvestris* get the location or the distance from Glasgow wrong? Unless the writer of the *Silvestris* invented 30 miles, and there is no reason why he should, he must have had evidence to that effect. Why, then, would he say that Merlin was buried where the Pausayl Burn meets the Tweed? I believe the confusion arose because the writer of the *Silvestris* had not visited Stobo. He had, however, heard about Stobo in connection with Merlin because, in 580, at the end of Merlin's exile, Mungo and Merlin met there. There is no reason to believe that Merlin had occasion to return to this place to be killed, or that he should want to be buried there. On the contrary, for security reasons, Merlin would not have agreed to meet Mungo at his forest home, so their meeting place would have held no sentimental value for him.

The writer of the *Silvestris* probably had access to information that included references to the Pausayl Burn–River Tweed meeting place, a place called Drumelzier and a distance of thirty miles from Glasgow and mistakenly concluded that all three related to the same place, which they plainly do not, and that Merlin not only met Mungo at this one place but also died and was buried there. Unfortunately for this writer, Drumelzier, the real Drumelzier, was 30 miles from Glasgow, and his claimed location of Stobo remained a stubborn 50 miles by the old road routes from Glasgow. It was easier to apply the name Drumelzier to the area about the junction of Pausayl and Tweed than to move the meeting place of those two waters; the fact that this results in a location nowhere near thirty miles from Glasgow seems to have been ignored. To my knowledge, no one since then has ever suggested that Drumelzier was anywhere other than near Stobo.

I believe that the Pausayl Burn–River Tweed location relates to the Mungo–Merlin meeting only. If I am right, the question arises: is there a Drumelzier 30 miles from Glasgow? There is. Drumelzier is the name of an area of rolling hills lying contiguous with the western boundary of the modern town of Dunipace on the northern approach to the lands of Drumpellier, the lands by the side of the *drum*. It has an eponymous farm in the middle of it. Dunipace is, by the old roads, albeit in modern miles, 25 miles from Glasgow, but the discrepancy is easily understood when we consider the relatively indirect nature of sixth-century paths, which ran from settlement to settlement, and the inaccuracy of measuring sixth-century miles, which were not the same as modern miles. This Drumelzier fits the profile of the place where Taneu was said to have been executed. The Dunipace Drumelzier was Taneu's Dumpelder. It was an important meeting place. It was where the north–south road first touched the lands of Old Drumpellier. Seventy years after Taneu's trial, Merlin too had occasion to present himself before the people assembled at Dunipace and, like Taneu, to face death at Drumelzier (near to the 'castle' referred to in the *Silvestris*). Everything that happened to Merlin in the last few years of his life – why he was killed, where he was killed, who killed him and exactly where he was buried – makes sense when considered with reference to Dunipace.

Unlike the Stobo Drumelzier, there is no reason to suspect that the Dunipace Drumelzier has been given this name with a view to creating a Merlin connection. There is no local tradition to that effect. As far as I am aware, no one until now has made this connection. Merlin died and was buried at Drumelzier, but not Drumelzier near Stobo. Merlin died and was buried at the Dunipace Drumelzier.

From at least the reign of the Roman Emperor Severus, 193–211 CE, to at least the time of Edward I in the late thirteenth century, Dunipace was a busy central location where people met to negotiate alliances, settle disputes and conduct trials involving cross-border issues, but, by the nineteenth century, its importance was sadly reduced. In 1880, in his *The History of Stirlingshire*, William Nimmo wrote:

> It is a curious fact that forty years ago there was neither a medical man nor a clergyman, a smith nor a wright, nor even a resident beggar in [Dunipace] parish; and it was only in 1838 that there was either a baker or a tailor.[1]

The *Second Statistical Account of Scotland*, for the 1840s, says:

> This parish [Dunipace] takes its name from two beautiful earthen-mounts [*sic*] called 'the Hills of Dunipace' . . . situated in a small but beautiful plain, traversed by the river Carron, they are about sixty feet in height,[2] and both together cover about two Scots acres. . . . About two miles to the westward of these hills, there was a very beautiful one about forty feet in height and covering nearly three roods of ground . . . [3]

George Buchanan in the sixteenth century described the larger hill as round, resembling an oven, and about 60 ft in height; the smaller hill was, he said, triangular at the base, with an irregular superstructure.[4] Today, now surrounded by a graveyard, the east hill is still largely intact, although the west hill is reduced, depleted and somewhat sad. When I came across the above passage in the *Statistical Account*, I did not know where the Hills of Dunipace were. I had assumed they were or had been in Dunipace.

The other hill was an earthen mound like the Hills of Dunipace, only it was a 'very beautiful' instance of its kind. Something must have made this one special. In the late 1830s, the civil authorities in the Dunipace and Denny area sent men to quarry this very beautiful hill, despite its beauty: '[It was] mutilated, from time to time, for the purpose of repairing roads and other purposes. It was entirely removed about six years ago, to form an embankment on the turnpike road near Denny Bridge.'[5]

The *Second Statistical Account* was published between 1834 and 1845, so, if these dates are taken as base points, the demolition of the very beautiful hill must have occurred between 1835 and 1839.

Having assumed that Dunipace town was built on the Hills of Dunipace, when I found this reference to a very beautiful hill which had been located 'about two miles to the westward' of the Hills of Dunipace, I looked two miles west of the town. I was unable to find to find anything in the names or locations I found there. Frustrated in my search, I worked with the evidence in the *Statistical Account* and tried to make sense of it, or to find another clue, but without success. I then looked for other written records to help me in my search. This led me, in November 2004, to contact Jean Gallagher, the Church of Scotland minister charged with the care of Dunipace and Larbert Parish, to ask if she knew of any records or diaries that might have been left lying about in her manse since the 1840s. The chances were slim, but I was prepared to take any tack, no matter how hopeless it might seem. I told Jean Gallagher about the hill I was looking for and that, according to the information I had, it had been two miles west of the Hills of Dunipace, that is, two miles west of Dunipace town. She corrected me and told me that the Hills of Dunipace were not in the town of Dunipace, they were not even in her parish, but halfway between Dunipace and Larbert, a neighbouring town. I had the answer I was looking for.

Armed with Jean Gallagher's local knowledge, I took my new starting point to be the true Hills of Dunipace, two miles east of Dunipace town, and found what I was looking for: a site for

Merlin's burial that combined all the strands of evidence I had been working on.

There was no point in my trying to find the actual hill, because the *Statistical Account* made it clear that it had been excavated to extinction, but I wanted to see if I could find out where it had been. All there was on my modern Ordnance Survey map was Dunipace town with the M80 motorway running along its western edge, cutting it off from the area named Drumelzier. ('Drumalzier' on that particular map, but I use Drumelzier to avoid confusion.)

I visited Dunipace and Drumelzier farm with my three children, but we could see nothing to indicate where the hill might have been. Dunipace has little to offer tourists, far less children who can only see it from the back of a motorcar and who want to picnic. The following week, I told a friend, Michael Gallagher, of my lack of success and mused that if I was correct in what I supposed, 'I could double the number of tourists who visit Dunipace in a year.' To which Michael replied, 'You did that last week.'

One Saturday, early in 2005, I visited Dunipace alone for the first time and drove again to Drumelzier farm. I thought, even if the hill has been removed, there must still be some evidence left. There are hills all about the farm, but there was nothing to suggest one was missing.

Leaving the farmhouse, I drove north on the minor road that parallels the motorway and saw on my left, about 1,500 m north of the farmhouse, Northfield Quarry. I had driven up and down the M80 many times, but neither the quarry nor Dunipace is eye-catching from the motorway. Now, of course, every time I drive south, I see Northfield Quarry and am conscious of how close to Dunipace it is and surprised that I did not make the connection earlier. My only excuse is that I focused overmuch on the farm.

A road of watery, grey mud led into the quarry, where I saw the long wall of stone that edged the diggings and accepted that the very beautiful hill was gone. There could be little doubt but that the working which had started in the early nineteenth century had continued and that this quarry was the result. On the bright side, if the quarrymen had not demolished the beautiful hill, they would not have found a grave at its top:

> On the top of this hill, and about three feet below the surface, was found a coffin or tomb, composed of five large unwrought stones, in which were the bones of a human body, scull [sic] and teeth not much decayed. Along with these, was a vase of coarse unglazed earthenware, containing a small quantity of material resembling the lining of a wasp's nest, probably decayed paper or parchment, which in the lapse of ages had assumed that appearance. No conjecture could be formed about the individual here interred, tradition being entirely silent on the subject; but this circumstance corroborates the opinion of some writers, that the hills of Dunipace might have been used as burying-places for ancient chiefs.[6]

Five unwrought stones is explicable if the coffin is pictured as consisting of four sides, a base and a missing lid. It is probable the workmen broke the sixth stone that formed the lid of the coffin. It would have been obvious to them that they had stumbled on a grave and that it contained a body. A grave was not something these men would have tampered with lightly, given the social and religious taboos in play at the time. They would have reported their find to someone in authority. In the social world of the day, that meant a formally educated and generally respected person such as the local minister or schoolteacher.

The report in the *Second Statistical Account of Scotland* was written in the main by the Church of Scotland minister of the parish of Dunipace and Larbert, John Bonar, a man of high principle and great learning who came out against the establishment forces in his Church in the Great Disruption of the Church of Scotland in 1843. The grave passage appears to have been written by a local schoolteacher, Robert Watson. I believe Watson was an eyewitness to the find at an early stage; his report seems to me to have been written by someone who had first-hand knowledge. Bonar could have told him about it later, but this must be considered unlikely.

Watson's account of the scene on the top of the beautiful hill is stark. He does not engage in speculation. Whereas I have assumed that a sixth stone, the lid, was broken when the quarrymen came across the grave, Watson makes no such assumption. He saw five stones; he mentioned five stones. He said exactly where the coffin was found and what it was made of. He said what it contained and what it looked like. The grave was the only one found on the hill. He recognised the absence of any local tradition and reached the conclusion that the bones may have been those of an ancient chief.

This is a reasonable conclusion, given the name Dunipace means Hill of Death. If this name referred only to the fact that people were buried there, it would be reasonable to suppose that many more graves would have been found in the area and, given the number of graveyards there are in the country, that the name Dunipace would be more common than it is in Scotland today. It would also be reasonable to suppose that any other graves on that hill would have been found and the finds recorded. The site does not seem to have been part of a graveyard or charnel pit dug in the aftermath of a battle. It was obviously the burial place of someone important, because he or she was buried alone on top of a hill. The person in the grave was obviously someone of importance, almost certainly a chief – but what kind of chief?

In my view, Robert Watson was wrong when he said that tradition was silent on the identity of the individual interred in the grave.

There is direct evidence connecting Dunipace and its surrounds with Merlin. In an area of history where exact facts are scarce, the *Silvestris* says, 'Thirty miles distant from the city of Glasgow. In [this] territory, Merlin lies buried.' Dunipace, as we have seen, fits this description.

Drumelzier is some two miles from the Hills of Dunipace proper. In ancient times, 'previous to the erection of the bridges in this district [Dunipace], the ford in the vicinity of these Hills [of Dunipace] was the principal passage over the Carron'.[7] It was only when the bridges were built, at about the time the grave was discovered, that the population moved west and the modern town of Dunipace grew from the humble community Nimmo describes it as in 1840.

If the person in the grave (whom I take to be a man, as there was nothing there to suggest a woman) was a warrior, or even an important man in his community, he would have been buried with a weapon, perhaps a sword, or some other artefact signifying his place in the community. This is a well-known practice, common in innumerable ancient graves. The body in this grave was buried with 'a vase of coarse unglazed earthenware, containing a small quantity of material resembling the lining of a wasp's nest, probably decayed paper or parchment'. If warriors were buried with weapons and important people with status symbols, it would be reasonable to suppose that someone buried with paper or parchment was someone for whom reading and writing were significant, that is, a scholar, and not only a scholar but a scholar who lived at a time when writing was practised. Given the paucity of grave goods, it may be supposed the body was buried in haste.

My first thought, when I read the account of the grave, was that it was the grave of the Beaker people. According to the historian A.A.M. Duncan, the Beaker people became active in Scotland around 4,000 years ago, when a new type of burial ritual emerged:

> [T]he body was disposed of crouched within a stone cist too short to carry it elongated, and with it were placed a pot of a shape known as a Beaker and occasionally other simple grave goods such as an arrow, or stone battleaxe . . . The cist might then be covered by a mound of stones . . .[8]

Beaker-people graves have also been found to contain vessels containing food and drink for the afterlife, daggers, arrows, archer's arm bracers, cups and other artefacts. The evidence suggests that this was not a grave of the Beaker people. The vase did not contain the remnants of food or an empty space that had once held liquid. The Beaker people flourished more than 1,000 years before writing and longer still before parchment and paper were used in Scotland. If what Robert Watson found was decayed paper or parchment, this would suggest the grave dated from a time when paper or parchment might reasonably be expected to be about, that is, after the late first millennium BCE.

I put the evidence according to Robert Watson before an archaeologist and was told it sounded like an early Bronze Age burial. When I replied that the vase was found to contain what was probably decayed paper or parchment, I was told that it didn't make sense, and that what had been found must be the remnants of food. That is not what the only eyewitness who left a report thought. He thought what he saw most closely resembled paper or parchment.

No Christian iconography was found in the grave, which suggests the body did not belong to a Christian, which suggests that the grave dated back to before Christianity became prevalent, that is, to before the seventh century.

The evidence suggests that Merlin was killed and hastily buried in a lonely grave at a place called Drumelzier, 30 miles from Glasgow.

The grave found on the beautiful hill outside Dunipace was found at a place called Drumelzier 30 miles from Glasgow. It was the only grave found in that place. This grave contained a vase that contained material that suggested the body it held was a scholar. The fact that nothing else was found in the grave is consistent with a hasty burial. Geoffrey says that Merlin died in the 'fields near Drumelzier Castle'. The remnants of a sixth-century hill fort still remain on the top of the hill, one side of which is contiguous with Northfield Quarry.

The destruction of the gravesite does not necessarily mean that the stones, vase, parchment and bones were lost at the same time. There are several possibilities. The stones that made up the coffin may have been used to found the planned embankment, although, given the find was attended upon by educated people at an early stage, they may have been removed for preservation and later lost. The vase and parchment were more fragile, so, unless particular steps were taken to preserve them, it is likely they too are gone. The bones are a different matter. The best-case scenario would be that they were passed to a museum or university. I was told when I contacted the National Museum of Scotland that the 1830s were 'wild and woolly times', and that what happened to items found was very much up to the person finding them. It appears that landowners would put finds on display for a time and then throw them away. It may be that Robert Watson or John Bonar or another local antiquarian took the bones home in a box and left them to lie until they fell into the hands of someone who knew nothing of their provenance and who might have had them buried somewhere without keeping a record or simply lost them.

However, in the 1830s, no matter what attitude was taken as regards the stones, vase and parchment, human remains would have been treated with respect. There is, therefore, a strong possibility that the bones were given a Christian burial. If so, I thought, it is also possible that some record of this still exists. I visited Callendar House, Falkirk, where the local archives are kept, and checked the parish records of Dunipace and Larbert to see if there was some record, perhaps of expenditure incurred in having the bones re-interred, but I found nothing relevant.

When the paper record failed me, I did some groundwork to try to identify a possible burial place. I reconnoitred the graveyards in the Dunipace area to see which ones were in use in the early nineteenth century and by which Christian denomination. My plan was to identify a potential graveyard and then see if there was any sign of a reburial of the bones found on the beautiful hill in the church's grounds or records. I found nothing in local graveyards or in the records. On the morning of 20 March 2007, I sent the manuscript of this book to my publishers. That afternoon I found another place to look.

As the years passed, the location of Merlin's grave was largely forgotten, although some memory of it must have remained to provide evidence, albeit in a garbled form, to prompt the writer of the *Silvestris* to accurately record the name Drumelzier as the name of the place where Merlin died and was buried, along with the distance from Glasgow. Of course, this same writer simultaneously concluded erroneously that the Drumelzier in question was close to Stobo.

It would have been dangerous for Dunipace people to lay claim to the site of Merlin's grave. The town lay at the centre of events over centuries, and the Christians would not have allowed anything that challenged their establishment's view to have been aired in public and broadcast. Even as late as the fourteenth century, when Edward I, it will be remembered, was concluding treaties there, the authorities' view of Merlin was, at best, ambivalent. This left the field free for the good people of Stobo. They lived off the beaten track, so were less heavily oppressed than their fellows further north. They were, literally, country dwellers (the name Pagan is, of course, derived from the Latin for country dweller). People who did not live under the eye of the authorities were better able to keep old traditions alive and vital. This freedom allowed the people of Stobo to retain the folk memory of Merlin's meeting with Mungo in their oral tradition. They would have known through this lively tradition that Merlin died at Drumelzier. It would have been easy for the people of Stobo, who already had a Merlin connection, to attach another legend to their locale. When, eventually, the true site of Merlin's grave, Drumelzier near Dunipace, was forgotten and the memory of the location of the actual grave was lost, the name Drumelzier stuck to the Stobo site, and the legend that Merlin died and was buried there was allowed to prosper untrammelled by truth and history.

CHAPTER TWENTY-NINE

Mordred's Queen

D ramatic reasons demand that Merlin is written out of the picture at an early stage in most of the works in the Arthurian canon. A mentor has a place when the hero is young, but later he becomes a distraction or, worse still, makes the hero look stupid by comparison. It is also awkward having a wise man about the place when the hero is being cuckolded; and so, as the romantic fiction of Guinevere and Lancelot gained in popularity, it made sense to have Merlin absent.

Geoffrey, in his *Vita*, does not say how Merlin died but ends his story with Merlin, old and worn out, retiring from the struggle. In his earlier *Historia Regum Brittaniae* and in Wace's *Roman de Brut*, Merlin simply disappears early in the story.

Other accounts tell of Merlin being swallowed up by the earth because he sat in the seat at the Round Table reserved for the purest knight of all, but most accounts of Merlin's death involve a woman as prime mover, usually the Lady of the Lake in one of her many guises. These stories vary in detail, particularly in the names given to the villain,[1] but Merlin is usually said to have fallen in love with a woman who wanted to learn his secrets, only to find his love unrequited. Besotted and hoping to gain her favour, he teaches this woman his magic, even though he knows this will lead to his death. As he has anticipated, she uses the knowledge she has obtained from him to seal his doom; specifically, to seal him in a rock, a cave, an enchanted wood, a tower, a thorn tree, a thorn bush or a castle of air – the versions vary.

Malory's *Le Morte d'Arthur* contains a typical example: 'Merlin fell in a dotage on the damosel . . . of the lake . . . Nimue.'[2] She played him along: 'Ever she made Merlin of good cheer till she learned of him all manner [of] thing[s] that she desired . . .' When she tired of him, she buried him under a stone from which he 'came never out for all the craft he could do'.

Much of these romantic stories, written more than 500 years after Merlin died, steeped as they are in magic, is obvious fanciful nonsense. All I have been able to gain from them is a sense that a woman had a hand in Merlin's death (and that he liked women). Merlin may well have had a young mistress – he probably did; the tenor of his reputation is of a man who liked women. He may also have made a fool of himself over a woman, but there is nothing to suggest a realistic scenario in Merlin's death that involved his love life.

Medieval writers, enamoured of the popularity of romantic endings, contrived plots that allowed Merlin to be laid low by love rather than the more mundane politics that actually brought about his end. When the early sources are considered, it can be seen that two women were involved in Merlin's death and that passions ran high in both of them. The first woman learnt all Merlin knew, just as Nimue did in the story, but she was not romantically involved with him. She was his sister, Languoreth. The second woman was a queen who had Merlin incarcerated, just as Nimue did in the story, but she was not romantically involved with Merlin either. She harboured a passionate hatred of him. More than this, she was the wife of Mordred, the man who traditionally, and, indeed, historically, played a major part in the death of Arthur.

It is likely that the earliest sources referred to Languoreth and that those who used them deleted her identity, for their own purposes, and inserted a mysterious romantic figure in her stead. It is also likely that these same or similar sources referred to a queen who hated Merlin and who was instrumental in bringing about his death, and that she too was deleted from the later stories – at least, in any form that could have led to her being identified as a specific woman in a specific time and place. This queen is clearly rooted in Scotland, which would not have suited those who wanted a southern Arthur–Merlin scenario. Medieval writers conflated the characters of Languoreth and this 'other woman' and made the resultant composite character a romantic figure to slake the demands of their audience. For writers in the Middle Ages, this had the added advantage of avoiding any explication of history that might have fixed the story in a real time and place, thus detracting from its entertainment value.

Merlin taught both women and men. The old way was neither afraid of, nor antagonistic towards, women, so Merlin would have seen no reason to teach one gender and not the other. This teaching did not include the use of magic to seal people in rocks, trees or any other thing. These elements are obvious fiction.

The surviving evidence concerning Merlin's death has been arranged by storytellers to appeal to their audiences and written within the confines imposed by the censors employed by whatever religious leaders were in power at the time. The *Silvestris* contains evidence of places and names that can be tested on the ground. I concluded in Chapter 28 that Merlin died and was buried at the Dunipace Drumelzier.

Evidence such as the distance of Merlin's grave from Glasgow lends considerable weight to the credibility of the *Silvestris*. Of course, it is a still a much-warped source and an obvious piece of anachronistic Anglo-Christian propaganda, but, when the magic is excised and the romantic nonsense recognised for what it is, it is still possible to glean in its pages something of the real events that surrounded the death of Merlin, despite its author's best efforts.

The *Silvestris* begins with the meeting between Mungo and Merlin in the woods that led to Merlin's return to court seven years after the Battle of Arderydd (c.580, by my reckoning). Ludicrously, the *Silvestris* also says that Merlin is a Christian and has him anxious to confess that the loss of life at the battle of Arderydd was all his fault. He is described as a naked and hairy madman, prone to disrupting Mungo's church services with horrifying shrieks. Mungo, on the other hand, is described as the chosen champion of the highest king.

The *Silvestris* also says that Merlin knows he is about to die and so asks Mungo for absolution. In Evelyn Waugh's *Brideshead Revisited*, Lord Marchmain, a man who rejected the Church when he was in good health, is given the last rites of the Church and said to have accepted Christianity on his death bed (when he was too weak to disagree). In effect, Merlin was 'Marchmained'.

Section one of the *Silvestris* concludes with Merlin predicting that he would soon endure a threefold death:

> It happened on that same day [as he was absolved by Mungo] he was stoned and beaten to death by certain shepherds of king Meldred [Mordred] and while he was in the throes of death he fell down the steep side of the river Tweed near the town of Drumelzier on to a sharp stake . . . and was impaled . . . his head fell forward into the water and so, just as he had prophesied, he gave up his soul to the Lord.

It is possible, I suppose, that Merlin could have predicted he would be stoned, fall onto a stake and drown, and that this might have happened as he had predicted, but the chances of it are so slight that to suggest it actually happened is as preposterous as the claim that Merlin converted to Christianity.[3]

If a man who had been a lifelong Christian converted to the old way and then, a few days later, was beaten up, fell onto a sharp stake and drowned in a river, his erstwhile fellow Christians would have attributed this awful death to his renouncing Christianity. However, the writer of the *Silvestris* asks us to believe that Merlin's conversion to Christianity immediately preceded his threefold death and yet sees no connection between the two.

Once preposterous passages such as Merlin's Christianity and the threefold death are disregarded, there remains some core evidence that is given nowhere else. If the events concerning Merlin's death did not happen, there would have been no reason for a Christian writer to invent them; on the contrary, a Christian writer would have a motive for removing them. There is reason to suspect that much that made events clearer, and which was damning from a Christian point of view, was deleted, and that all that remains in the *Silvestris* is a slight part of a lost record.

In the *Silvestris*, Merlin travels to Drumelzier twice. There is no dramatic reason for this. The story would make just as much sense – indeed, its drive would be more dramatic – if Merlin was killed immediately after his first visit. Small details like this lend weight to the *Silvestris* as a source of evidence.

Merlin is dead at the end of the first section of the *Silvestris* but still alive at the start of the second. The first section is the most fantastic. The second can stand alone. On any reading, the second section is more historically substantial than the first. While the first section can be accounted for by reference to legends that are found elsewhere, such as that of the triple death, the second section is unique.

Section two wastes no time in getting into the story; it begins with Merlin a prisoner in Drumelzier, but we are not told why. There is much that the writer does not say, and much that he does say is obviously garbled. Before putting the events surrounding the death of Merlin in their historical context and making sense of them, it will be instructive to look at the bare bones of the story in the second section of the *Silvestris*:

> It is said that [Merlin] was kept prisoner for a long time by the underking Meldred [Mordred] and he was held bound in thongs in his town of Drumelzier in order that the king might be privileged to hear some new prophecy from him. [Merlin] remained for three days without food and gave absolutely no answer at all to anyone, although he was approached by many people. On the third day, while the underking was sitting on a lofty throne, his wife came in, conspicuously carrying on her head a leaf from a tree that had caught in her wimple . . .

In the following passage, there is a recognisable version of the story of Languoreth's adultery, but with Mordred's queen as the adulterer. After this come several tortuous riddles. Mordred is unable to solve the riddles, so offers Merlin a reward if he will disclose the solutions. As a reward, Merlin asks for his freedom and to be buried where the Pausayl Burn meets the River Tweed because, 'it will come to pass in a few days that I shall die a threefold death . . .' The *Silvestris* continues:

> While he was spinning out this narrative and putting off for feigned reasons what they wanted to hear, [Mordred] and [his] queen and their court granted his request for burial and affirmed an oath that they would allow him to go free and unharmed wherever he wished.

Merlin is to be freed, even though he has not revealed the solution to the riddles. Clearly, the writer is making a sloppy job of adapting his sources.

When freed and 'standing ready to flee', Merlin turns on Mordred's queen, rails at her and accuses her of adultery. This was, if it had happened, at best, a foolhardy move. Even though he has already been told he is free to go, Merlin chooses this time to provide answers to the riddles he has been set, although these answers are obscure in the extreme.

> With these words Lailoken [Merlin] made for the trackless wastes of the wilderness. No one pursued him but all alike began to nod significantly. The adulteress in tears and devising guile began to try to win over [Mordred] with speeches as sweet as she could make them saying: 'Do not, my lord and revered king, believe the words of this madman . . . if you cease to pursue him, you will seem to be cherishing the insult to me . . .'

Mordred is not swayed by his wife's blandishments or arguments and, calling her the 'Most stupid of women', he lets Merlin leave Drumelzier in peace: 'At these words, the woman burst more copiously into tears, because she was not able to get what she wanted and she secretly prepared snares to bring about the death of [Merlin].'

Some years later, Merlin returns:

> After some years, it happened that [Merlin] was passing though the fields near Drumelzier Castle at sunset. . . . When certain shepherds, who had been stirred up against him by the wicked woman, discovered this . . . so we have heard, an end was made of him. The king, as it is said, handed over his dead body for burial in the place he himself had previously chosen for himself, while he was

335

still alive. That town is thirty miles distant from the city of
Glasgow. In its territory, [Merlin] lies buried.

The *Silvestris* ends at this point.

There was a Mordred active in Scotland in the land of the north
Gododdin at the time of Merlin's death: the late sixth and early
seventh centuries. He had a record of villainy that presaged the part
he played in Merlin's death.

There are innumerable possible genealogies for Mordred. I believe
that what follows is the most likely. Anna, Mordred's mother, is
said to have had five children: four sons (including Mordred) and
a daughter. Malory says that Mordred's half-brothers were Gawain,
Gaheris, Gareth and Agravain. If Mordred had half-brothers, then
Anna must have had children by someone other than Lot, unless
it was Lot who had children by a previous marriage. Lot, however,
was from the land of the Gododdin, Lothian in the east, and at
least one of Mordred's four half-brothers is from the west. Gawain
is closely connected with the Glasgow area. (Govan, the district of
Glasgow that contains Ibrox Park, the home of Glasgow Rangers
Football Club, is named after him.) This suggests that Anna had
children by a first husband. I believe that Gawain, because of his
western connections, was the son of Anna's first marriage (as were
Gaheris and Gareth).

By my reckoning, Anna was initially married to a man of Strathclyde
by whom she had three children, Gawain, Gaheris and Gareth. Lot
too was married before he married Anna. He had Agravain by his
first wife. After Anna married Lot, they had two children, Mordred
and a daughter, Clarisant. This would allow Anna her four sons and
a daughter. Agravain was Mordred's fourth half-brother.

The whole tenor of Arthuriana, as it involves these brothers,
has Gawain and his brothers Gareth and Gaheris allies of Arthur.
As they were the children of Arthur's sister Anna and her first

husband, and men of the west, this makes sense. Mordred and Agravain, the children of Anna's second marriage, were men of the east and Arthur's enemies. This antipathy can be attributed to political and family rivalry.

Evidence such as this, derived as it is from various uncertain sources, cannot be relied upon alone, but my construction lends weight to the suggestion that Mordred was active in the lands of the Gododdin and an enemy of Arthur and Merlin. In the 580s, when Mordred was very young, he was the titular leader of the Gododdin army that formed part of a coalition that forced the Angles back to the sea. Nennius tells us that, following this victory, Mordred, moved by jealousy, was a prime protagonist in the conspiracy that led to the assassination of Taliesin's patron, Urien, king of Rheged:

> Four kings fought against them [the Angles], Urien and Rhydderch Hen and Gwallawg and Morcant [Mordred]. Theodoric fought vigorously against Urien and his sons. During that time, sometimes the enemy, sometimes the Cymry [British] were victorious, and Urien blockaded them for three days and three nights in the island of Lindisfarne. But during this campaign, Urien was assassinated on the instigation of [Mordred], from jealousy, because his military skill and generalship surpassed that of all the other kings.[4]

Although Mordred was part of an allied army, it is clear that the brunt of the fighting was borne by Urien and his contingent. It is also clear that Mordred was the man behind Urien's murder. The traditional wisdom accepts that this Mordred was a prince of the Gododdin.

There is also evidence that places Mordred in the west lands of the Gododdin and so corroborates the *Silvestris* when it says he was the lord of Drumelzier. The first and most famous reference to Mordred is an entry in the *Annales Cambriae*: 'The battle of

Camlann in which Arthur and Medraut [Mordred] fell, and there was death in Britain and in Ireland.'[5]

Mordred betrayed and brought about the death of Arthur at the Battle of Camlann in 596. Camlann was fought at Camelon, Falkirk, five miles from Dunipace. Twenty years later, this same Mordred is the lord of Dunipace. Either Camlann was fought on his land, or, and this is more likely, he took the land in the Dunipace area as his share of the spoils following Arthur's defeat.[6] (It would be perfect if, as the romantic stories say, Mordred and Arthur died in the same battle, going to their deaths together like the fictional Holmes and Moriarty, but life is not like that.)

Mordred had a treacherous nature and reason to be antagonistic towards Arthur. Consequently, he had cause to be averse to Arthur's ally, Merlin. Mordred betrayed and brought both Urien and Arthur to their deaths.

Mordred also had reason to be in the right place at the right time to host an assembly at the Dunipace Drumelzier in 615, when the chiefs and kings of the British and their allies gathered there.

While it was Mordred who put Merlin in prison, it was his wife who was Merlin's most fervent enemy (after Mungo's death). In the oral tradition, later recorded in writing in Wales, Mordred married Cywyllog daughter of Caw and had two sons by her. Caw was a chief from the Cambuslang area, on the south side of the Clyde, almost four miles downriver from Glasgow. He was the father of Gildas and Hueil. Gildas, whom we have already met, was a fanatical Christian and scholar. Hueil was a warrior and, given he was a brother of Gildas, probably a Christian too. Arthur killed Hueil and earned the undying enmity of Gildas. It would be reasonable to suppose that Cywyllog, Gildas's sister, was also a Christian and hated Arthur, Hueil's killer, as much as her surviving brother.

As Arthur and Merlin were allies, Mordred's queen would have every reason to hate Merlin too. It would have been enough simply if Cywyllog was a Christian, particularly a Mungo Christian, even if Merlin was not party to her brother's death or an ally and friend of Arthur.

Mordred and Cywyllog are the two main antagonists in the *Silvestris*, but in history, the events played out at Drumelzier were not so simple. The writer of the *Silvestris* has made an accessible story out of more lengthy and informative source material. He took from his sources only what suited him.

Following the Great Angle War in the 580s, the Britons and their allies, the Scots and Men of Manau, were in the ascendant and the Angles subdued. In 596, a Gododdin British army defeated Aedan and Arthur's Scots and the Men of Manau at Camlann. The Gododdin Britons, buoyed by unjustified confidence, then turned south against the Angles, but their army was annihilated at Catterick (in Northumbria) two years later, in 598. In 603, Aedan, Arthur's father, had recovered sufficiently to wage war against the Angles in the south, but not enough to win a victory. At the Battle of Degaston, his army was comprehensively defeated.

In the next ten years, the Angles consolidated their power in Bernicia and gathered reinforcements from their homeland, across the North Sea. When they were ready, the Angles of Bernicia and their cousins from what is now the north of England struck south and west against the vulnerable British kingdoms that lay between them and the western sea. They won a battle at Chester (or Carlisle) in 615, effectively cutting off the Britons of the south from the northern Britons in the Lothians. In the following century, the northern Britons would seek refuge in the south. These refugees took their stories south with them and planted them there; these included the tales of Arthur and Merlin and the Great Angle War. The stories did not flourish in the south *despite* being distanced from their original roots; on the contrary, they survived because they were less trammelled by the baggage of history and so more susceptible to amendment.

It must have been clear to the Celts in the south of Scotland in 615 that the resurgent Angles would soon turn on them. They were right. Sporadic warfare ensued and pressure continually increased until, eventually, in 638, the Angles captured Edinburgh. Edinburgh became an Anglo-Scottish city for the first time.

I am not concerned with the warfare that occurred in the years between the Battle of Chester in 615 and the fall of Edinburgh in 638. My interest is in the fact that, after Chester, the Britons of the south of Scotland had cause to be afraid of a massive Angle invasion and reason to meet to discuss their common danger. There was to be no great attack similar to the Great Angle War of the 580s immediately after 615, but at that time no one could have known that. It was not war but rumours of war that brought the main political players in Scotland together and set in motion the events that would lead to Merlin's death. Rumours of war and, just as the legends say, a woman's hatred, brought about Merlin's assassination.

If the legends have no basis in fact, then why, given they were written in the south of Britain hundreds of years after the times they purport to describe, with the determined intention of bolstering Welsh and later English national pride and whatever establishment faction happened to be in charge at the time, do they contain so many specific references to Scotland? 'That town is thirty miles distant from the city of Glasgow. In its territory, [Merlin] lies buried' is but one pointed example. There are numerous references to Scotland in the southern sources because the events reflected in the English and Welsh legends happened in Scottish history. In the light of Scottish history, it is possible to see where, when, how and why Merlin died.

CHAPTER THIRTY

Le Morte de Merlin

Although the Christians were in power in Strathclyde in 615, they were not all powerful, and, although the old way was in retreat, it was by no means a spent force; indeed, the majority of the people were still of the old way. Their numbers alone would have dictated that steps be taken to encourage the Druids to encourage their people to support an alliance. If the Druids stood apart and the war against the Angles went badly, Christian leadership might be blamed, and those who benefited from it might lose ground. There was also the recognised danger that, as at the time of the Arderydd campaign, social dislocation would loosen Christian control and allow people to revert to the old way. It followed, therefore, that if the status quo of British Christian rule was to be maintained, the Christians had to ensure that the anti-Angle forces included the people of the old way. Suddenly, Merlin was useful again, albeit as a means to an end.

Merlin was not the only Druid leader, but he was the most respected and well connected, and so it was to him that the Christian kings and chiefs applied their immediate attention. He was the first among equals of the Druids, so he was invited, or, more probably, summoned to Drumelzier (Dunipace).

Mordred (Meldred in the text) had, since the Battle of Camlann in 596, been the lord of Drumelzier. As there was more than one king present, difficult questions of precedence were avoided by allowing Mordred, as host-lord, to chair the meetings, so he was in the chair when Merlin appeared before the assembled kings and chiefs to discuss the possibility of an alliance.

It may be fairly inferred from Mordred's history that he was an unscrupulous and ambitious man who would not have hesitated to attach himself to the waxing power of Christianity. This would have given him no greater reason to hate Merlin than any other Gododdin Christian – unlike his wife, Cywyllog.

The *Silvestris* does not detail the political events that brought Merlin to the door of Mordred and his wife, or list the other parties present. The demands of drama dictated that the political background be expunged and the cast of characters restricted. Only Merlin, Mordred and Cywyllog are given leading roles, but it is clear from any reading of the whole text that many more people were involved and that their concerns were not restricted to the affairs of one old man in his mid-70s. If, as the *Silvestris* suggests, the only matter in issue was the antipathy that lay between Merlin and Mordred's wife, why would Merlin have been there at all? There is no suggestion that he was captured and brought there, and he is hardly likely, in his old age, to have travelled 30 miles from home to be abused by the man who assassinated Urien and betrayed Arthur, as well as that man's vicious wife. It is more likely he attended this assembly of his own volition. (He was, however, abused and imprisoned when he got there.)

Merlin was but one party among many assembled at Dunipace at that time of danger. Present were kings, sub-kings, chiefs, sub-chiefs, priests, monks, clerks, Druids, all with their respective retinues of warriors and servants and the usual hangers-on, all assembled at and about the Hills of Dunipace and camped in the surrounding lands of Drumelzier. The matters that stood to be discussed affected not only Strathclyde and the Gododdin but the Scots of Dalriada, the Picts of the north and the people of Manau too. They would all have been represented.

The second section of the *Silvestris*, the part that deals with Merlin's time at Drumelzier and with his death, begins with Merlin as Mordred's prisoner. The traditional stories that have Merlin encased in a rock may be a romantic echo of this incarceration created for popular consumption. It does not make sense to suppose that Merlin was immediately thrown into jail for no reason as soon as he arrived in Drumelzier. When he was in prison, steps were taken to persuade him to reach an accommodation with his gaolers. It therefore makes sense to suppose that imprisonment was not Merlin's enemies' first resort. It is more likely that the Christian kings, chiefs, monks and priests tried to persuade him to join them and bring the people of the old way with him into the alliance they were forming and that he was imprisoned when he refused. The people of the old way were as opposed to Angle conquest as the Christians, so the Merlin who drove a hard bargain in 580, when Rhydderch wanted him to cooperate with Mungo before the Great Angle War, and who negotiated an advantageous retirement package in the 590s, is unlikely to have been averse to doing a deal on this occasion. The question was, of course, what kind of deal? The parties were doubtless agreed in relation to the need for a military alliance, so the breakdown of negotiations was probably a result of their failure to settle their religious differences. Whatever reason there may have been, Merlin ended up in prison.

There are innumerable precedents whereby a person is imprisoned to encourage him to change his mind, one of the most famous being the imprisonment of Galileo by the Church in the seventeenth century because he espoused rational views based on observation and experimentation that ran counter to the revealed 'truth' of the Church that the Sun went round the Earth. Merlin's imprisonment suggests the parties were so far apart that Mordred and the Christians gave up hope of reaching an amicable settlement and decided to use force. Merlin was 'bound in thongs' and imprisoned 'for a long time'.

The *Silvestris* says that Mordred imprisoned Merlin 'in order that the king might be privileged to hear some new prophecy from him'. This does not make sense. If Merlin was a prophet, why would he refuse to prophesy? If he did refuse to prophesy, what made Mordred think that locking him up would make him change his mind? It just does not make sense to suppose that, even if Merlin had the gift of prophecy, which he did not, Mordred would imprison him to encourage him to use it. I suspect the prophecy 'reason' was inserted simply because the writer needed some explanation for Merlin's captivity. The truth, that Merlin was a Druid who was locked up for political reasons, was not an option.

Just as censors and self-censoring writers avoided references to Druids by calling them bards, they concealed the scholarship in which the Druids engaged by referring to fictitious gifts of prophecy. This is often simply code for the works of the Druids. When it is said that Merlin was imprisoned because he refused to prophesy, this may be taken to mean that Merlin would not bring his fellow Druids and the people of the old way into the proposed alliance.

Imprisonment had no effect, so Merlin's jailers stepped up the pressure. Merlin was imprisoned for a 'long time' and was denied food for 'three days'. Again, small details such as this, that the author does not expand upon or explain, lend weight to the *Silvestris* as a source and give rise to the suspicion that there was much more going on than we are openly told in its pages: '[Merlin] remained for three days without food and gave absolutely no answer at all to anyone, although he was approached by many people.'

Even when starved, Merlin remained resolute, although many people tried to persuade him to cooperate. The reference to 'many people' approaching him in his prison reinforces my belief that the events being played out at Dunipace did not involve Merlin, Mordred and Cywyllog alone. No doubt, the people who approached Merlin in prison included friends worried about his well-being and enemies anxious that he should agree to their demands. The many people who had come to see him in his prison, both those who were for him and those who were against him, must have had a say in his fate. What was to happen to Merlin was a matter of moment for kings and chiefs, not a matter to be determined by personal animosity, not even the vehement antipathy of Cywyllog, the Lady of Drumelzier, at least, not this time. For the great majority of those concerned, what to do with Merlin was strictly business, not personal.

Neither a long time locked up, nor a period of starvation, nor all the persuasive powers of supporters and opponents induced Merlin to sacrifice the interests of the people of the old way, so, after three days without food, he was taken from his prison cell and arraigned before the kings and lords and chiefs and other people assembled in the great hall at Dunipace.

Here, just when we might expect something politically substantial, the *Silvestris* deliberately veers off into riddles and a garbled version of the story of the fish and the ring to avoid revealing too much about what was going on.

No doubt, Merlin asked why the people of the old way should band together with the Christians to fight the Angles if, after the war, they were to be oppressed again. Guarantees of religious freedom could always be ignored once the danger had passed, so the real hurdle standing in the way of agreement was probably a demand on the part of the people of the old way for immediate and open religious freedom. That is, if they were to fight, they were to be allowed to fight under the aegis of the old way. The Christians could not cross this hurdle. They would have known that if the people were free to choose for themselves, many, if not most, would rally beneath the old banners. Whatever the cause of dissension, there would have been those, like Cywyllog, who were determined that there be no agreement with Merlin, not at any price.

Our view of events is necessarily limited by the paucity of the extant sources of evidence, but we can still use our intuition to glean something of what happened from the slight facts available. The many parties present represented various interests, some collective and some individual. Some of the people sympathised with Merlin, and some were his inveterate enemies. No one party was in absolute authority.

Those present the day Merlin was released from prison were engaged in real and vital negotiations because they envisaged real danger, so, no doubt, Merlin was again put under pressure to comply with the wishes of the Christian kings and chiefs. It may even be that the chiefs of the old way also saw sense in reaching a compromise and that they too urged Merlin to reach agreement. Merlin was wily on this occasion (at least for a short time). If he agreed to the demands made of him, he would have been acting contrary to his conscience and betrayed the interests of the people of the old way. If he refused, definitely and obviously for the last time, he would have been placing himself in danger. He would have ceased to be potentially useful and become a fixed obstacle. Such was the hatred of him in some quarters, it is likely that in this event an attempt would have been made on his life. (When it later became clear to his enemies that he would not fit in with their plans, steps were in fact taken to have him assassinated.)

According to the *Silvestris*, this quandary led Merlin to prevaricate and put off 'for feigned reasons what they wanted to hear'. He may have hinted that he was tending toward agreement but that he could not come out and say so there and then. Perhaps he suggested that, if he could be given some time, he would return to Partick and see what he could do to bring others to agree to the compromise suggested. Merlin must have given his enemies some hope that he would bend. If he had not, I suspect he would not have got out of Dunipace alive.

The assembly remained divided and became resigned to Merlin's intransigence. Unwilling to take drastic steps against him at that time because he could still command a significant number of supporters, the parties assembled agreed to let him go 'and affirmed an oath that they would allow him to go free and unharmed wherever he wished'.

Merlin, according to the *Silvestris*, then turned on Mordred's queen, railed against her and accused her of adultery, even though he was 'standing ready to flee'. In isolation, this does not make sense. The accusation of adultery is fiction, cobbled together with the ring and the fish story that related to Languoreth and events more than 30 years earlier. It was a device used to make the story simple and accessible to the audience. The real enmity between Merlin and those represented by Mordred and his queen was inspired by complex political differences. There was, however, a history of bad blood between Merlin and Cywyllog, and it is possible that, in among the political exchanges, prompted by personal animosity, Merlin fired a Parthian shot at Cywyllog.

Even so, Merlin had just escaped imprisonment and perhaps execution, so it is hard to believe that, on the point of escaping, he would taunt his most fervent enemy. Of course, it could be that the old hot-headed Merlin, lacking all judgement and driven by emotion, indulged himself. The alternative, and this is more likely, is that when Cywyllog saw that Merlin was about to escape with his life and that the party of the old way was not to be subjugated, she turned on him and verbally attacked him before the whole assembly, and Merlin responded in kind. Whatever happened, Merlin left Dunipace free to return to Languoreth and his home at Ardery-land, Partick, 30 miles away. He was now a marked man, and everyone knew it: 'Lailoken [Merlin] made for the trackless wastes of the wilderness. No one pursued him but all alike began to nod significantly.'

Cywyllog, incensed that Merlin had been allowed to leave, tried to persuade Mordred to pursue Merlin, bring him back and kill him, but Mordred, conscious of the support that Merlin had and bound by the decision of the assembly to set him free, refused and chastised his wife. For the next two or three years, Cywyllog nursed her wrath and plotted Merlin's destruction.

In the far south of Scotland and the north of England, the Angles enjoyed the spoils of their victory at Chester (or Carlisle) and stamped out remaining resistance. When they had secured their rear, they were free to turn their attention to the Celtic British kingdoms in the south of Scotland. The danger that had been anticipated before the Angles began their campaign in the south became an immediate threat for Strathclyde, the Gododdin and their neighbours. Another summit meeting was arranged to be held at Dunipace, prompting the second of Merlin's visits.

In the years that followed his escape from the first summit, we may be sure that Merlin did not appear amenable to the Christian cause and that this was noticed by his enemies, especially Cywyllog. At the urging of Cywyllog and Merlin's other inveterate enemies, even the more moderate Christian kings and chiefs must have given up hope of obtaining his cooperation and realised there was nothing to gain and everything to lose if he were again allowed to present his case to the assembled notables. There were other, younger, more malleable Druids, with more time left to lose than Merlin, and less time invested in the struggle to keep the old way alive, who could be used to bring the people of the old way into the coalition. Merlin had now become a lost cause and a dangerous liability. It was decided that he had to be killed.

Cywyllog would not have dared arrange the death of Merlin by herself, but she was probably party to the planning, as her husband, Mordred, was surely involved in the plot. Mordred had experience of assassination and would have been a key member of the conspiracy of kings, chiefs, monks and priests who stood to gain most from Merlin's death.

When summoned for the second time, Merlin set out on the 30-mile journey from Glasgow to Dunipace. As we know, he was not to complete it. He was murdered while 'passing through the fields near Drumelzier Castle at sunset'. The circumstantial evidence (some known, that Merlin died at sunset, and some unknown until now, that Merlin died at the Dunipace Drumelzier) fits together exactly. It is unlikely a man of Merlin's age would have trekked from Partick, thirty miles, to Drumelzier in one day; it is more likely he divided his journey into two days, and, taking his time, making the most of the daylight, timed his arrival for the end of the second day. The *Silvestris* does not tell us in which direction he was travelling, but if he was heading west from the Hills of Dunipace back towards his home in Partick, he would have covered only one or two miles before he got to Drumelzier Castle at sunset, which would mean that he set out just before nightfall – something that must be considered unlikely. He must have been travelling from his home to this second summit. This is important because it suggests that Merlin was killed before he could attend the assembly at the Hills of Dunipace, which suggests he died a man of moment who was still dangerous to his enemies; alternatively, that Cywyllog could not wait for her revenge. Perhaps both of these alternatives applied.

Not only does the time of day of Merlin's death suggest a journey from the west, but, unlike the first visit, we are told nothing of any events that occurred on any second occasion when Merlin was at Dunipace. This is because he did not get there the second time.

The end that was made of Merlin was not, in my opinion, the much-touted triple death. No assassin, outside the pages of a serial-killer thriller, is likely to go to the trouble of staging a triple death. It is much too complicated, and it would have no purpose. Dead is dead.

Merlin, in the company of friends and supporters, approached Dunipace as the sun set. As he neared the fort at Drumelzier, assassins fell on him and stabbed, strangled or stoned him to death. He was buried in a simple grave near where he was killed.

His murderers had reason to prevent his body being taken back to Partick, where there was the danger that his funeral might prove a focus of unrest. Those who remembered Mungo burying the body of Fergus on the Necropolis hill and all the trouble that had caused would have wanted to avoid a funeral where the circumstances of Merlin's death might be rehearsed to a sympathetic crowd. With Merlin dead, it was easier to bury him where he fell and claim that was what he wanted. The simplicity of the grave found in the 1830s fits a scene in which Merlin is hastily buried. Merlin's people, cowed and hurried, would only have had time to gather stones for his coffin.

Those who conspired to have Merlin killed remained in charge in the years that followed. There was no one to bring them to account. Downplaying Merlin's funeral would have meant that only a decreasing few would know where his grave lay, and it would have been dangerous for people of the old way to visit it to pay their respects, although no doubt many did. There was no prospect of its becoming a place of pilgrimage. This was not a custom of the people of the old way, and, in any event, this would not have been tolerated.

As the years passed, the location of Merlin's grave was largely forgotten, although some memory of it must have remained to allow the *Silvestris* to accurately record the name and the distance from Glasgow of the place where he died and was buried.

After Merlin's death, Languoreth, 'She who . . . had been the queen of a large nation',[1] lived on in his house on Partickhill. She was not alone. The circle that had formed about Merlin and Languoreth remained, frequently replenished by those who came to Merlin's house to learn about the way that had been the way of the Celts for thousands of years.

Morken's daughter, Rhydderch's wife and queen, Constantine's mother, Merlin's sister: Languoreth was all these things and more. Above all, she was an individual who stood to be included among the great ones of her long lifetime: Emrys, Gwenddolau, Rhydderch, Arthur, Taliesin and Merlin. So it was, when Merlin left her for the last time, to go to Dunipace and his death, he left all he valued in Languoreth's charge.

Later references to her wisdom and learning were carefully couched to disguise the truth, because she was of the old way and, 'worse', a woman, but some suggestions of her merits remain: 'She . . . was from time to time exalted in spirit to sing often of the future of the kingdom.'[2] Languoreth's singing is a coded reference to the old way. The specifics of the prophecies Geoffrey attributes to Languoreth are, of course, anachronistic nonsense,[3] but their importance lies in the fact that they are attributed to her at all. Languoreth, like Merlin, was a scholar. Merlin refers to her as a 'refuge of songs',[4] a clear reference to her intellectual capacity and her adherence to the old way.

When Languoreth 'prophesised':

> Her friends listened in amazement. So also did her brother, who after a while went up to her and congratulated her in kindly words, saying, 'Sister, is it you the spirit has willed to tell the future? He has curbed my tongue and closed my book. Then this task is given to you. Be glad of it, and under my authority declare everything faithfully.'[5]

Neither Merlin nor Languoreth had the gift of prophecy, because no such gift exists, but they could predict that when Merlin left for Dunipace that last time, he would not be coming back. They were, after all, clever people with experience of the ways of the world who knew the intentions of Merlin's enemies.

Languoreth succeeded Merlin when his book was closed. No one knows how long she lived; no record of her death has survived. Everyone has heard of Merlin, while Gwyneth, the Lioness of Damnonia, the swan-necked woman, Languoreth, is all but unknown, except as an adulteress queen. Yet she played a great part, centre stage, for 50 years, in the last great fight before the darkness fell. They should be remembered together, Lailoken and Languoreth, the chief of the Druids and the Golden One.

kentigern myrddin

Timeline

410	Romans leave Britain
475–548	Arthur usually said to have flourished between these dates – Emrys, Gwenddolau and Vortigern usually placed in this same period
528	Taneu's trial – Mungo born
540	Merlin and Languoreth born at Cadzow (Hamilton)
544	Ida, the Angle, lands on east coast
547	Ida's coup – overthrows Vortigern
c.548–50	Vortimer son of Vortigern's resistance
c.550	Vortigern takes to the hills
c.550–2	Angle advance to the western sea at Solway (not Severn)
c.552	British resistance in south of Scotland – guerrilla war – Merlin and Languoreth taught by Cathen – Mungo murders Telleyr
c.553	Rise of Emrys – victory – Mungo becomes bishop in Glasgow
c.554	Vortigern in hiding in Caer Vortigern/Caer Gwenddolau
c.555	Emrys burns Caer Vortigern and kills Vortigern – Mungo arrives in Glasgow, desecrates the Druidic grove – Merlin's father leads the opposition
c.556	Hengist battles with Emrys – Emrys's victory – Languoreth marries Rhydderch son of king of Strathclyde – Merlin joins Emrys and the resistance
c.557	Emrys becomes Pen Dragon

c.558	Emrys's settlement of the Britons – exiles return – Pascent given Caer Vortigern and Isle of Man
c.559	Pascent's alliance with the Angles
559	Birth of Arthur – Merlin's resistance to Mungo
c.560	Emrys's victory over the Pascent aristocratic Britons and Angles
c.561	Pascent goes over to the Scots and Gillomanius
c.562	Gillomanius and Pascent attack from Isle of Man
c.563	Assassination of Emrys – Gwenddolau takes command and becomes the Uther Pendragon – Merlin with the army – Pascent and Gillemanius battle Gwenddolau – Gwenddolau victorious
c.564	Octa son of Hengist meets Gwenddolau in battle – Gwenddolau victorious
c.565	Gwenddolau's diplomacy with Strathclyde and Dalriada – Merlin's diplomatic work
566–8	The aristocrat Gododdin Britons wage war on Gwenddolau
c.567	Mungo steals Morken's grain – Morken attacks Mungo – Merlin active in opposition to Mungo
c.568	Gwenddolau's health fails
c.568	Lot and Urien fight the Angles
c.569	Cathen assassinated
c.570	Mordred assassinates Urien of Rheged
c.570	Alliance of all Britons against Gwenddolau
572	Mungo exiled from Strathclyde – goes to Wales
573	Battle of Arderydd – Merlin goes into exile
574	Aedan, Arthur's father, becomes king of Scots – Arthur becomes Scots' war chief
575+	Languoreth meets with Merlin in the woods
c.578	Mungo leaves Asaph in Wales and sets up in Hoddam

580	Tutgual dies – Rhydderch becomes king and Languoreth queen – Mungo returns – Mungo and Merlin meet near Stobo
581	Mungo accuses Languoreth of adultery – she is saved by Merlin – Mungo goes into exile again, to Rome – Merlin becomes chief counsellor in Strathclyde – forms alliance to fight the Angles – appoints Arthur supreme commander
582–8	Great Angle War – ends with Battle of Badon, 588
588+	Restoration of peace – beginning of ten years of plenty
594	Mungo returns
595	Columba visits Glasgow
596	Arthur betrayed and killed in battle – Mordred takes Dunipace area
598	Merlin castigates Mungo from the Necropolis of Glasgow – civil unrest
598	The harrowing of Galloway and the Catterick campaign – Merlin lends financial support
598	Gildas completes *De Excidio*
c.600	Merlin leaves Partick and sets up home at Ardery-land outside Partick
603	Aedan, Arthur's father, defeated at Degaston
604	Mungo retires to the seaside
612	Mungo dies – Rhydderch visits Merlin at Partick/Ardery-land – Taliesin comes to stay with Merlin – Rhydderch dies – Languoreth comes to stay with Merlin – the chiefs offer Merlin charge of the kingdom – he refuses – Constantine becomes king
615	The Angles cut Britain in two at Chester/Carlisle
615	Merlin summoned to Dunipace – refuses to cooperate and returns to Partick
c.618	Merlin again summoned to Dunipace – assassinated on the way there – Languoreth takes over

Notes and References

INTRODUCTION

1   Barber, p. 20.
2   Version A, Harleian Collection No. 3859 (British Library). Version B, folio MS in flyleaves of an abridged copy of the *Domesday Book* (Public Records Office). Version C, Cottonian Collection, Domitian A, i. (British Library). The 'dd' ending of Arderydd is not clearly legible in the original text.
3   Alcock, 22.

CHAPTER ONE: THE LEGEND

1   Phillips and Keatman, p. 36.
2   Malory, I:3.
3   Ibid., III, 1.
4   John Lawlor, Introduction to *Le Morte d'Arthur*, p. viii.

CHAPTER TWO: MORKEN'S CHILDREN

1   The *Silvestris* is a short, anonymous work, less than 4,000 words long and dating from the twelfth century (see Bibliography).
2   Geoffrey of Monmouth, Clarke (trans.), *Vita*.
3   'Dialogue Between Myrddin and His Sister', in the *Red Book of Hergest*.
4   Gruffudd, 'The Story of Myrddin Wyllt', in *The Chronicle of Elis Gruffudd*, National Library of Wales, MS 5276D.
5   'Thenew' in the text.
6   The *Aberdeen Breviary* says Caidzow, but there are innumerable versions of the name. I use the modern version.
7   'The Legends and Celebrations of St Kentigern, his friends and disciples', translated from the *Aberdeen Breviary*, p. 7.

CHAPTER THREE: THE ANGLES

1   Tacitus, para. 29.
2   Ibid., para. 30.
3   Ibid., para. 31.
4   Ibid.
5   Mitchison, p. 2.
6   Gildas, chap. 14.
7   Ibid., chap. 19.
8   Ibid.
9   Ibid.
10   Ibid., chap. 20.
11   Ibid., chap. 21.
12   Ibid., chap. 22.
13   The umbrella term 'Saxons' is used in the extant manuscript (eleventh century).
14   Gildas, chap. 23.
15   MS Bern Bürgerbibliothek Codex 178, f. 116.
16   Gildas, chap. 23.
17   Nennius, chap. 50.
18   In 843, Kenneth MacAlpin, a descendant of Fergus, united the Picts and Scots and founded the modern Scottish nation.

CHAPTER FOUR: SIGNS AND PORTENTS

1   Jocelyn, Prologue.
2   Ibid.
3   Jocelyn never did find a source that suited him. Although only a few parts of it survive, a more detailed biography of Mungo, known as the *Fragmentary Life*, was written by an anonymous writer no later than 1164, some 25 years before Jocelyn wrote his *Life of Kentigern*.
4   Jocelyn, Prologue.
5   Ibid., chap. 1.
6   Ibid.
7   Ibid., chap. 2.
8   Ibid., chap. 3. (No doubt she was pleased she was not sentenced by the Christians.)
9   Ibid.
10   Ibid.
11   This was a natural crossing point. The modern Kincardine Bridge is only 15 miles upstream.

12   Forbes, p. 247.

13   See *Aberdeen Breviary*, p. 66, where Eugenius is described as the son of Erwegende.

14   Smout, p. 167.

15   Both the *Aberdeen Breviary* and the *Fragmentary Life* say that Ewen dressed as a woman and tricked Taneu into having sex with him. See also Forbes, p. 247.

CHAPTER FIVE: THE OLD WAY OF THE DRUIDS

1   Dr Samuel Johnson, quoted in *Prehistoric and Early Wales*, p. 13.

2   Laertius, Introduction, I:5.

3   Ellis, p. 48; Renfrew, p. 83. (Although, in Greek, the word for oak is cognate with the English word for beech.)

4   Ellis, p. 48.

5   Pliny the Elder, *Historia Naturalis*.

6   Strabo, II:4, p. 247.

7   Holland, p. 243.

8   Ibid., p. 245.

9   Ibid., p. 340.

10   Julius Caesar, 6:13, p. 140.

11   Strabo, II:4, p. 246.

12   Julius Caesar, 6:14, p. 127.

13   The poet Hugh MacDiarmid used to say that a Scot could hold two competing views at the same time.

14   Julius Caesar, 6:14, p. 140.

15   Ogham writing at first, and later, it is thought, in Greek, using Greek letters. Ogham is also called 'Tree Alphabet', because each letter corresponds to a tree and an associated meaning. The letters were, in fact, engraved onto sticks as well as larger standing stones.

16   Julius Caesar, 6:14, p. 127.

17   In Catal Huyuk, Turkey, the number of figures of female gods found vastly outnumber the number of male god figures. Seals found in the Indus Valley show male and female gods, and innumerable mother goddess terracotta statues have been found.

18   Priests were allowed to marry in Scotland in the sixth century. It was not until the twelfth century that this practice was eradicated. Married or not, they lived with guilt because they were sexual people.

19   As late as 1567, every few months, homosexuals were burnt on the Castle Hill of Edinburgh. Smout, p. 77.

20   Quoted in Nick Griffin, 'The Celts, Part II: Celtic Folkways and the Clash with Romans and Germans', *National Vanguard Magazine*, No. 116, August–September 1996.

21   Julius Caesar, 6:14, p. 127.

CHAPTER SIX: MERLIN AND LANGUORETH

1   Jocelyn, chap. 4.

2   Ibid., chap. 5.

3   Ibid.

4   Ibid.

5   Ibid., chap. 8.

6   Macleod, p. 42.

CHAPTER SEVEN: THE MAGI AND THE BARDS

1   When the Celts sacked Delphi, they laughed at the Greek idea that gods could have human form. There is limited evidence of god figures in Celtic graves, which suggests that idols were not a significant feature of the old way. See Ellis, p. 175.

2   Ellis, p. 160.

3   Caesar, 6:14, p. 127.

4   Ellis, p. 174, quoting Prof. Myles Dillon, *Celts and Aryans: Survivals of Indo-European Speech and Society*, 1975.

5   Ellis, p. 174.

6   I believe, contrary to accepted wisdom, that this tells of events in the early sixth century.

7   It is no coincidence that the stories of the Arthurian canon became popular with the rise of these wandering minstrels.

8   Smout, p. 185.

9   Both of these peoples were Scots at this time. The modern nation of Scotland did not exist until 843.

10   Skene, *Celtic Scotland*, II:25.

11   Bede, III.25, p. 187.

12   Ibid., pp. 189–91.

13   'Wise men' in the King James version of the Bible.

14   Simon Magus was a wise man and competitor of Peter. He is said to have tried to purchase the power of laying on of hands from Peter. From this, we get the sin of 'simony', purchasing of the favours of the Church.

15   *Catholic Encyclopaedia*, III.

NOTES AND REFERENCES

CHAPTER EIGHT: ANGLE LAND

1   Gildas, chap. 23.
2   Nennius, chap. 36, re. Thanet. Re. Lindisfarne, see too chap. 35.
3   Gildas, chap. 23.
4   Nennius, chap. 43.
5   Ibid., chap. 45.
6   Ibid., chap. 40.
7   Bede, 5:24.
8   Gildas, chap. 24.
9   Ibid.
10   Ibid.
11   Ibid., chap. 25.
12   Ibid. This is the only time that Gildas mentions Emrys.
13   Ibid.
14   See, for example, Gardner, p. 171.
15   Nennius, chap. 40.
16   Ibid., chap. 42.
17   See, for example, William of Malmesbury, *Gesta Regum Anglorum*.
18   Nennius, chap. 43.
19   Although N. Tolstoy thinks that Lugubalia was not Carlisle but Arderydd itself.
20   Geoffrey of Monmouth, *Historia*, VIII:2, p. 188.
21   Ibid., VIII:4, p. 189.
22   Ibid., VIII:5, p. 191.
23   Ibid.
24   Nennius, chap. 48.
25   Geoffrey of Monmouth, *Historia*, VIII:9, p. 194.
26   Ibid., VIII:13, p. 199.
27   Ibid.
28   The conventional wisdom would have this as Cambria, Wales. Cymry, Cambria and Cumbria all spring from the same etymological root.
29   Skene, *Four Ancient Books of Wales*, chap. 6, 'Manau Gododdin and the Picts'.
30   Paulus Orosius, quoted in *Monumenta de Insula Manniae (A Collection of National Documents Relating to the Isle of Man)*, IV, pp. 6–7.
31   Skene, *Four Ancient Books of Wales*, p. 84.

CHAPTER NINE: THE HILL OF DEATH

1   Jocelyn, chap. 3.

2   Buchanan, in an entry in the *Second Statistical Account of Scotland*, 'Parish of Dunipace: Topography and Natural History'. The *Second Statistical Account* was published in three formats. The first edition was published between March 1834 and October 1845. A reissue in 33 county volumes was published between 1841 and 1845. A second reissue, in 1845, took the form of 15 collected county volumes.

3   The *Fragmentary Life* says the name of the hill was Kepduf, that is, *Caer-dubh*: Black Fort.

CHAPTER TEN: THE MURDER OF TELLEYR

1   Jocelyn, chap. 9.

2   Ibid., chap. 10.

3   Ibid.

4   Ibid.

CHAPTER ELEVEN: MORKEN THE CHIEF

1   Jocelyn, chap. 19.

2   Ibid.

3   Ibid., chap. 20.

4   Ibid.

5   The name Damnonia has been confused with Dumnonia, an area in the south-west of England. This was a convenient coincidence used to confuse the facts by some who were minded to move the Arthurian canon south.

CHAPTER TWELVE: CATHEN THE DRUID

1   Jocelyn, chap. 21.

2   Geoffrey of Monmouth, Parry (trans.), *Vita*.

3   Jocelyn, chap. 21.

4   Ibid.

5   Ibid.

6   Ibid.

7   Ibid., chap. 22.

8   Ibid.

9   Ibid. The ruler was Tutgual. The next sentence suggests it was Morken, but this cannot be correct or Mungo would have died that day. This, I believe, reflects some clumsy editing on Jocelyn's part.

10 Ibid.
11 Ibid.
12 Ibid.
13 Malory, I:17, p. 41.
14 Goodrich, p. 52.
15 Ashley, p. 333.
16 Jocelyn, chap. 22.
17 See, for example, Pliny, *Naturalis Historia* XVI, p. 249 and Bates, p. 119.
18 Pliny, *Naturalis Historia* XVI, p. 95.
19 I know nothing about foot tumours. This may be a gory way to go.
20 Jocelyn, chap. 22.
21 Ibid., chap. 23.
22 Ibid.
23 The *Catholic Encyclopaedia* says that Mungo went to Wales c.553. I believe this is too early; by my reckoning, he would have been only 25 at this time. I would contend that he left for Wales c.570+, when he was about 42 years old.

CHAPTER THIRTEEN: UTHER PENDRAGON, SON OF THE SKY GOD

1 John Jay Parry, 'Vita Merlini', *Studies in Language and Literature*, University of Illinois, August 1925, No. 3.
2 Geoffrey of Monmouth, *Historia*, VI:5, p. 151.
3 Ibid., VIII:17, p. 202.
4 See, for example, Ashe, p. 123.
5 'Pa Gur' is contained in the *Black Book of Carmarthen*, National Library of Wales, Peniarth, MS 1, dating to the middle of the thirteenth century, believed to have been the work of a scribe at the Priory of St John, Carmarthen.
6 The name Mabon is also the name of a deity. The loch could be named after this god or a person of that name. All I can say is that there is a coincidence in names.
7 Geoffrey of Monmouth, *Historia*, VIII:14, p. 200.
8 Ibid.
9 Geoffrey has Merlin interpret the meaning of a comet that portends Emrys's assassination and Merlin and Gwenddolau only finding out that he is correct after the battle.
10 Geoffrey of Monmouth, *Historia*, VIII:15, p. 201.
11 Ibid.

12   Ibid., VIII:19, p. 206.
13   Morcant in the text (of Strathclyde, according to a genealogy
      attached to Nennius, probably through his wife, the daughter
      of Caw of Cambuslang, near Glasgow). He was a chief of the
      Gododdin in his own right.
14   A settlement of monks near Berwick. Berwyn, it has been
      supposed, means Bear Friend in Anglo-Saxon.
15   Geoffrey of Monmouth, *Historia*, VIII:21.

CHAPTER FOURTEEN: THE BATTLE OF ARDERYDD

1   Jocelyn, chap. 29.
2   Blake, p. 189.
3   Geoffrey of Monmouth, Clarke (trans.), *Vita*.
4   Ibid.
5   Ibid.
6   Ibid.
7   Ibid.
8   Ibid.
9   'Dialogue Between Merlin and Taliesin', in the *Black Book of
      Carmarthen*.
10   The text says 'Scots', but this is an obvious anachronism.
11   Geoffrey of Monmouth, Parry (trans.), *Vita*. Geoffrey says the
      Britons were fighting the Scots, but this is obvious nonsense.
      He also says that Merlin was on the same side as Rhydderch,
      which is also patently inaccurate.
12   Ibid.
13   'Dialogue Between Merlin and Taliesin', in the *Black Book of
      Carmarthen*.
14   Geoffrey of Monmouth, *Historia*, VIII:24, p. 211.
15   Geoffrey of Monmouth, Parry (trans.), *Vita*.
16   Ibid.
17   'Dialogue Between Merlin and Taliesin', in the *Black Book of
      Carmarthen*.
18   Skene, *Four Ancient Books of Wales*, p. 10.

CHAPTER FIFTEEN: THE WILDERNESS YEARS

1   Sometimes this poem is called 'The Little Pig', because the
      literary device of having Merlin address a little pig is used.
2   'The Greetings', in the *Black Book of Carmarthen*.
3   In the text, this is Gwendyyd, which is generally accepted as
      another name for Languoreth.

4   'The Greetings', in the *Black Book of Carmarthen*.

5   Seven hundred years later, these same woods hid William Wallace and his men when they were waging a guerrilla war against the occupying English. They were big woods.

6   Geoffrey of Monmouth, Parry (trans.), *Vita*.

7   See Tolstoy, p. 53.

8   Jocelyn, chap. 33. (In chap. 31, Mungo's god 'imposed' upon him to return to Glasgow; instead he goes to Hoddam. In chap. 33, he is 'admonished by a divine revelation' to go to Glasgow.)

9   'Dialogue Between Myrddin and His Sister', in the *Red Book of Hergest*. I will continue to use the name Languoreth to avoid confusion, although she is called Gwendydd in the text. The primary source of what follows is a poem written in Wales in the middle of the Middle Ages that purports to be a dialogue between Merlin and his sister.

10   Ibid., v. 15 (for convenience of reference, I have numbered these verses myself).

11   Ibid., v. 1.

12   Ibid., v. 2.

13   Ibid., v. 34.

14   Morken is simply a spelling I have chosen and stuck with for simplicity's sake. There are innumerable variants, including Merfyn.

15   'Dialogue', v. 80.

16   Ibid., v. 4.

17   Ibid., v. 7.

18   Ibid., vs 107–8.

19   Ibid., v. 109.

20   Ibid., v. 115.

21   Ibid., v. 118.

22   Ibid., v. 119.

23   Ibid., vs 119–20.

CHAPTER SIXTEEN: BATTLE REJOINED

1   Jocelyn, chap. 31.

2   Ibid., chap. 32.

3   Under the alternative name Lailoken.

4   Geoffrey of Monmouth, Clarke (trans.), *Vita*.

5   Ibid.

6   Ibid.

7   Geoffrey of Monmouth, Parry (trans.), *Vita*.
8   Ibid.
9   Ibid.

CHAPTER SEVENTEEN: THE RING
1   Jocelyn, chap. 36.
2   Ibid. (The fish and ring part of the story is taken from the biblical story in which Peter takes a fish from the sea and finds a coin in it. (Matthew 17:27.))
3   Ibid., chap. 22.
4   Ibid., chap. 36.
5   Ibid., chap. 28.
6   Adamnan, I:15, p. 123.
7   Alternatively, the sources he was using presented him with versions of these stories that were already doctored.

CHAPTER EIGHTEEN: THE ARMY OF STAGS
1   Geoffrey of Monmouth, Clarke (trans.), *Vita*.
2   Ibid.
3   Ibid.
4   MacLennan, *A Pronouncing and Etymological Dictionary of the Gaelic Language*.
5   MacBain, *Etymological Dictionary of Gaelic*. The word *damh* also connotes champion or hero.
6   Geoffrey of Monmouth, Clarke (trans.), *Vita*.

CHAPTER NINETEEN: ROME
1   Geoffrey of Monmouth, Clarke (trans.), *Vita*.
2   'Saxons' in the text.
3   Nennius, chap. 50.
4   Jocelyn, chap. 27.
5   Ibid., chap. 28.
6   Russell, p. 377.
7   Ibid., p. 378.
8   Jocelyn, chap. 27.

CHAPTER TWENTY: TWILIGHT OF THE DRUIDS
1   Jocelyn, chap. 27.
2   Ibid., chap. 28.
3   Ibid.
4   Ibid.
5   Ibid.

CHAPTER TWENTY-ONE: THE HARROWING OF GALLOWAY

1   Jocelyn, chap. 34.
2   Ibid., chap. 33.
3   Ibid., chap. 34.
4   Y Gododdin, v. 32.
5   Ibid., v. 58.

CHAPTER TWENTY-TWO: MADMAN

1   Geoffrey of Monmouth, Parry (trans.), Vita.
2   Quoted in Graham, The Great Infidel.

CHAPTER TWENTY-THREE: ARDERY STREET

1   The Ardrey name has Masonic connections, but I believe the
     location of this hall is only a coincidence. Sometimes a cigar
     is just a cigar. The hall there is known as the Ardrey or Ardery
     Street Masonic Hall, Galen No. 1285, St John, Whiteinch.
2   The Triads refer to reciprocal raiding by Aedan and Rhydderch.
3   Groome, Ordanance Gazetteer of Scotland, entry on 'Govan'.
4   Geoffrey of Monmouth, Clarke (trans.), Vita.
5   Ibid.
6   Paul, p. 67.
7   Jocelyn, chap. 45.

CHAPTER TWENTY-FOUR: STONEHENGE

1   Wace, Roman de Brut.
2   Speaking on BBC News, 31 August 1999.
3   Alternatively, 'where stones of wonderful size have been erected
     after the manner of a doorway'. See David Hinton, British
     Archaeological Review, vol. 34, May 1998.

CHAPTER TWENTY-FIVE: 'RHYDDERCH IS DYING'

1   'Another cross . . . he built solely of the sand of the sea at
     Lothwerverd.' (Jocelyn, chap. 41.) W.J. Watson, in his History
     of Celtic Placenames of Scotland, p. 151, says this is
     Lochquhariot, Lothian, but I cannot see that Mungo would
     retire to the east. Mungo travelled about erecting crosses. In
     1534, there was mention of a Kentigern's Well at
     Lochquhariot.
2   Jocelyn, chap. 42.
3   Ibid., chap. 43.
4   Ibid.
5   Ibid., chap. 44.

6   Ibid., chap. 45.
7   Rodarch in the text.
8   Geoffrey of Monmouth, Clarke (trans.), *Vita*.
9   Ibid.

CHAPTER TWENTY-SIX: THE DARK HEART

1   Geoffrey of Monmouth, Clarke (trans.), *Vita*.
2   Maeldin in the text. This may also have been the Maelgwn attacked by Gildas in *De Excidio*.
3   Geoffrey of Monmouth, Clarke (trans.), *Vita*.
4   'Dialogue Between Merlin and Taliesin', in the *Black Book of Carmarthen*.
5   Alcock, p. 121.
6   Gildas, chap. 34.
7   Ibid., chap. 35.
8   Geoffrey of Monmouth, Clarke (trans.), *Vita*.
9   Ibid.
10   Jocelyn, chap. 33.
11   Alcock, p. 122.
12   Gildas, chap. 28.
13   Ibid.
14   It is said he lived anonymously at first but when his identity was revealed he was promoted, became an abbot and founded churches. This is too good to be true. I suspect that Constantine burnt out, lost much of his reason and lived out his days a shattered man at Govan.
15   Geoffrey of Monmouth, Clarke (trans.), *Vita*.

CHAPTER TWENTY-SEVEN: DUMPELDER

1   Jocelyn, chap. 2.
2   Drummond, p. 3.
3   Ibid.
4   Ibid., pp. 3, 4.
5   Ibid., p. 4.
6   Ibid.

CHAPTER TWENTY-EIGHT: THE GRAVE

1   Nimmo, chap. 23.
2   Dunipace is more than 40 m above sea level, so this passage must mean 60 ft above the surrounding land.

3 *Second Statistical Account of Scotland*, 'Parish of Dunipace: Topography and Natural History'.

4 Buchanan, chap. 4, 'Ancient Monuments'.

5 *Second Statistical Account*, 'Parish of Dunipace: Topography and Natural History'.

6 Ibid.

7 Ibid.

8 Duncan, I.

CHAPTER TWENTY-NINE: MORDRED'S QUEEN

1 Nimue, Niniane, Nymenche, Uiuiane, Vivian and other versions.

2 Malory, IV:1.

3 In the *Silvestris*, Merlin's alleged conversion is told at the same time as he predicts the death of a king, a bishop and a lord, just as in Jocelyn he predicts the death of a king and a lord. If Merlin had converted to Christianity, there can be no doubt that Jocelyn would have said so. This piece of propaganda could be tried (unsuccessfully) in the south but not in the north, where Merlin lived and where the oral tradition preserved the truth.

4 Nennius, chap. 63.

5 This dates Camlann in accordance with the conventional wisdom of the south at 537 or 540. The entries were not compiled until the tenth century, almost 400 years after the date of the actual events they purport to describe. They are not to be relied upon without corroboration.

6 No evidence, known to me, connects Mordred and Stobo.

CHAPTER THIRTY: *LE MORTE DE MERLIN*

1 Geoffrey of Monmouth, Clarke (trans.), *Vita*.

2 Ibid.

3 These include references to Oxford, where Geoffrey was active for decades, and Lincoln, where his patron was bishop. These also include an intriguing reference to the protective powers of an 'antique oak' that echoes the sacred groves of oaks of the people of the old religion.

4 'Dialogue Between Myrddin and His Sister', in the *Red Book of Hergest*.

5 Geoffrey of Monmouth, Clarke (trans.), *Vita*.

Select Bibliography

Aberdeen Breviary, The Legends & Communications & Celebrations of St Kentigern his friends and disciples translated from the Aberdeen Breviary & the Anglo-Saxon Chronicle, trans. by James Ingram, London, Everyman Press, 1912

Adamnan of Iona, *Life of Columba*, trans. by Richard Sharpe, London, Penguin, 1995

Alcock, Leslie, *Arthur's Britain*, Penguin Books, London, 1971

Aneirin, *Y Gododdin*, trans. by Joseph P. Clancy, *Earliest Welsh Poetry*, Macmillan, London & New York, 1970

Anglo-Saxon Chronicle, edited from the translation in *Monumenta Historica Britannica* by J.A. Giles, Bohn's Antiquarian Library, London, 1912

Annales Cambriae (447–954), A Text: MS Harleian Collection, No. 3859; B Text: MS E. 164/1, Public Record Office, Kew, London; C text: MS Cotton Domitian A i, British Library, London

Arbuthnott Manuscript (1509), Edinburgh, private printing, 1872

Ashe, Geoffrey, *The Discovery of King Arthur*, Stroud, Sutton, 2003

Ashley, Michael, *King Arthur*, London, Constable & Robinson, 2005

Barber, Richard, *The Figure of Arthur*, London, Longman, 1972

Bartrum, P.C., *A Welsh Classical Dictionary*, National Library of Wales, Cardiff, 1993

Bede, *Ecclesiastical History of the English People*, London, Penguin, 1995

Black Book of Carmarthen, Aberystwyth, National Library of Wales, Peniarth MS 1 (c.1250)

Blake, Steve and Scott Lloyd, *The Keys of Avalon*, London, Rider Books, 2003

Bonar, John, 'Parish of Dunipace I, Topography and History', *Second Statistical Account of Scotland*, Vol. VIII, Edinburgh, 1845

Caesar, Julius, *The Gallic War*, trans. by Carolyn Hammond, Oxford, Oxford University Press, 1996

Camden, William, *Britannia*, trans. by Philimon Holland, Bristol, Thoemmes, 2003

Catholic Encyclopaedia, New York, Robert Appleton Company, 1910

Cunliffe, Barry, *The Extraordinary Voyage of Pytheas the Greek: The Man who Discovered Britain*, London, Penguin Books, 2001

Dictionary of National Biography, London, Oxford University Press, 1975

Drummond, Peter, *Placenames of the Monklands*, Airdrie, Monklands Library Services, 1987

Duncan, A.A.M., *Scotland: The Making of the Kingdom*, Edinburgh, Oliver and Boyd, 1978

Ellis, Peter Beresford, *The Celts*, London, Constable and Robinson, 1998

Finlay, Ian, *Columba*, Richard Drew Publishing, Glasgow, 1990

Forbes, A.P., *The Lives of Saint Ninian and Saint Kentigern*, The Historians of Scotland Series, Vol. 5, Edinburgh, Edmonston and Douglas, 1874

Foster, I.L. and Glyn Daniel (eds), *Prehistoric and Early Wales*, London, Routledge and Kegan Paul, 1965

Fragmentary Life (twelfth century), British Library, MS Cotton Titus.xix.f.76–80

Gardner, Laurence, *Genesis of the Grail Kings*, London, Bantam, 2005

Geoffrey of Monmouth, *Historia Regum Brittaniae*, trans. by Lewis Thorpe, London, Penguin Books, 1966

Geoffrey of Monmouth, *Vita Merlini*, trans. by Basil Clarke, Cardiff, University of Wales Press, 1973

Geoffrey of Monmouth, *Vita Merlini*, trans. by John J. Parry, Urbana, University of Illinois Studies in Language and Literature, Vol. 10. no. 3, 1925

Gilbert, Adrian, *The Holy Kingdom*, London, Corgi, 1999

Gildas, *De Excidio et Conquestu Britanniae*, trans. by J.A. Giles, London, 1841

Gododdin, The: The Oldest Scottish Poem, trans. by Kenneth Jackson, Edinburgh, Edinburgh University Press, 1969

Goodrich, Professor Norma Lorre, *Merlin*, New York, Harper & Row, 1988

Graham, Roderick, *The Great Infidel: A Life of David Hume*, Edinburgh, Birlinn, 2004

Green, Miranda, *The Gods of the Celts*, Stroud, Sutton Publishing, 1986

Grimble, Ian, *Clans and Chiefs*, Blond & Briggs, Oxford, 1980

Groome, Francis Hinde, *Ordnance Gazetteer of Scotland*, Edinburgh, T.C. Jack, 1882–5.

Gruffudd, Elis, 'The Story of Myrddin Wyllt', in *The Chronicle of Elis Gruffudd*, ed. and trans. by Thomas Jones, Aberystwyth, National Library of Wales, MS 5276D, 1947

Henry, Archdeacon of Huntingdon, *Historia Anglorum: The History of the English People*, trans. by Diana Greenway, Oxford, Oxford University Press, 2002

Highland Society of Scotland, *A Dictionary of the Gaelic Language*, William Blackwood Publishers, Edinburgh, 1828

Holland, Tom, *Rubicon*, London, Abacus, 2003

Jocelyn, *The Life of Kentigern*, trans. by Cynthia Whiddon Green, from a Masters Thesis presented to the Faculty of the Department of English, University of Houston, Texas, USA, 1998

Johnston, James Brown, *Placenames of Scotland*, John Murray Publishing, London, 1934

Key to the Parochial Registers of Scotland, Murray & Gibb, Pub., compiled by V.B. Bloxham in consultation with D.F. Metcalfe, Provo, Utah, Stevenson Genealogy Center, 1979

Laertius, Diogenes, *The Lives and Opinions of Eminent Philosophers*, trans. by C.D. Yonge, London, George Bell and Sons, 1895

Lynch, Michael, *Scotland: A New History*, London, Pimlico, 1992

MacAlpine, Neil, *Pronouncing Gaelic-English Dictionary*, Gairm Publications, Glasgow, 1971

MacBain, Alexander, *An Etymological Dictionary of the Gaelic Language*, Glasgow, Gairm Publications, 1982

MacKillop, James, *Oxford Dictionary of Celtic Mythology*, Oxford, Oxford University Press, 2004

MacLennan, Malcolm, *A Pronouncing and Etymological Dictionary of the Gaelic Language*, Edinburgh, Acair and Mercat Press, 1925

Macleod, John, *Highlanders: A History of the Gaels*, London, Sceptre, 1997

Mabinogion, The, trans. by Jeffrey Gantz, London, Penguin Books, 1976

Malory, Thomas, *Le Morte d'Arthur*, London, Penguin Books, 1969

Mitchison, R.M., *A History of Scotland*, London, Methuen, 1970

Moffat, Alistair, *Arthur and the Lost Kingdoms*, London, Phoenix, 2000

Monumenta de Insula Manniae or *A Collection of National Documents Relating to the Isle of Man*, ed. and trans. by J.R. Oliver, Manx Soc., iv, vii, ix, 1860–2

Morris, John, *Nennius: British History and The Welsh Annals*, London, Phillimore, 1980

Nennius, *Historia Brittonum, The History of the Britons*, trans. by J.A. Giles, London, H.G. Bohn, 1841

Nimmo, William, *The History of Stirlingshire*, London, Hamilton Adams & Co., 1880

Parry, John Jay and Robert Caldwell, 'Geoffrey of Monmouth', in *Arthurian Literature in the Middle Ages*, Roger S. Loomis (ed.), Oxford, Clarendon Press, 1959

Paul, Robert M., *Partick Anecdotes*, Helensburgh, J. Paul and E. Greer, 1998

SELECT BIBLIOGRAPHY

Phillips, Graham and Martin Keatman, *King Arthur: The True Story*, London, Century, 1992

Pliny the Elder, *Naturalis Historia*, Loeb Classical Library, London, Heinemann, 1938–62

Randall, John, *Stobo Kirk: A Guide to its Building and its History*, Walter Thomson, Selkirk, 1997

Red Book of Hergest: The Dialogue Between Myrddin and His Sister Gwenddydd, Vol. I, Jesus College, Oxford, MS.111

Renfrew, Colin, *Archaeology and Language: The Puzzle of Indo-European Origins*, London, Penguin, 1987

Ross, David, *Scottish Place-names*, Birlinn, Edinburgh, 2001

Russell, Bertrand, *History of Western Philosophy*, London, Routledge, 2000

Skene, William F., *Celtic Scotland: A History of the Scottish Nation*, Edinburgh, David Douglas, 1886

Skene, William F. (ed.), *Chronicles of the Picts and Scots and Other Early Memorials of Scottish History* (1867), HM Gen. Reg. House, Edinburgh

Skene, William F., *The Four Ancient Books of Wales, containing the Cymric Poems attributed to the Bards of the Sixth Century*, Edinburgh, Edmonston & Douglas, 1868

Smart, Ninian, *The Religious Experience of Mankind*, London, Fontana, 1971

Smout, T.C., *A Century of the Scottish People*, London, Fontana Press, 1986

Sprouston Breviary, c. 1300, NLS MS 18.2.13b, fos. 35v-38v.

Strabo, *The Geography*, Loeb Classical Edition, Cambridge Mass., Heinemann, 1923

Tacitus, *Life of Cnaeus Julius Agricola*, trans. by Alfred John Church and William Jackson Brodribb, London, MacMillan, 1869

Tolstoy, Nikolai, *The Quest for Merlin*, London, Little, Brown, 1985

Vita Merlini Silvestris, trans. by Professor John MacQueen and Winifred MacQueen, *Scottish Studies* 29:77, Edinburgh, 1989

Wace, *Roman de Brut*, trans. by Judith Weiss, Exeter, University of Exeter Press, 1999

Watson, W.J., *History of Celtic Placenames of Scotland*, London, Blackwood & Sons, 1926

Whitaker, John, *The History of Manchester*, London, 1771–75

White, T.H., *Once and Future King*, London, Voyager, 2001

William of Malmesbury, *Gesta Regum Anglorum*, Oxford, Clarendon Press, 1998

Index

377

INDEX